FAITH ODYSSEY

FAITH ODYSSEY

A Journey through Life

Richard A. Burridge

William B. Eerdmans Publishing Company
Grand Rapids, Michigan / Cambridge, U.K.

First published 2000 by
The Bible Reading Fellowship
Peter's Way, Sandy Lane West
Oxford OX4 6HG

This edition published 2003 by
Wm. B. Eerdmans Publishing Co.
255 Jefferson Ave. S.E., Grand Rapids, Michigan 49503 /
P.O. Box 163, Cambridge CB3 9PU U.K.

Printed in the United States of America

08 07 06 05 04 03   7 6 5 4 3 2 1

Library of Congress Cataloging-in-Publication Data

Burridge, Richard A., 1955-
Faith odyssey: a journey through life.
p. cm.
Originally published: Oxford: Bible Reading Fellowship, 2000.
Includes bibliographical references and index.
ISBN 0-8028-0974-X (pbk.: alk. paper)
1. Lent — Prayer-books and devotions — English. I. Title.
BV85.B87 2003
242'.34 — dc21
2003048061

www.eerdmans.com

In memory of

ALAN BURRIDGE

3rd September 1927–6th February 2000

At rest at the journey's end

ACKNOWLEDGMENTS

Scripture quotations taken from The New Revised Standard Version of the Bible, Anglicized Edition, copyright © 1989, 1995 by the Division of Christian Education of the National Council of the Churches of Christ in the USA, are used by permission. All rights reserved.

Scripture quotations taken from The Revised Standard Version of the Bible, copyright © 1946, 1952, 1971 by the Division of Christian Education of the National Council of the Churches of Christ in the United States of America, are used by permission. All rights reserved.

The Post-Communion Prayer from *The Alternative Service Book 1980* is copyright © The Central Board of Finance, 1980; The Archbishops' Council, 1999, and is reproduced by permission.

The Collect for the 8th Sunday Before Easter from *The Alternative Service Book 1980* is copyright © Provincial Trustees of the Church of the Province of Southern Africa and is reproduced by permission.

The prayer over a newly baptized person from *Common Worship: Services and Prayers for the Church of England* is copyright © The Archbishops' Council, 2000, and is reproduced by permission.

The prayer over the water taken from the Baptism service from *Common Worship: Services and Prayers for the Church of England* (Church House Publishing, 2000) is copyright © 1985 by the General Synod of the Anglican Church of Canada and is reproduced by permission of the publishers.

The Collects for Trinity 5 and Bible Sunday from *Common Worship: Services and Prayers for the Church of England* (Church House Publishing, 2000) is adapted from *The Book of Common Prayer,* the rights in which are vested in the Crown and reproduced by permission of the Crown's Patentee, Cambridge University Press. The Collects in this form are reproduced by permission of the publishers.

p. 155: Prayer used by kind permission of Jim Cotter.

The following words/phrases are proprietary names or are registered in the United Kingdom or as Community trade marks: Anakin Skywalker; Artoo-Detoo (R2-D2); Chewbacca; Ewok; Gryffindor; Harry Potter; Hermione Granger; Hogwarts; Luke Skywalker; Obi-Wan Kenobi; Princess Leia Organa; Ron Weasley; See-Threepio (C-3PO); Star Trek; Star Trek: Enterprise; Star Trek: The Next Generation; Star Trek: Deep Space Nine; Star Trek: Voyager; Star Wars; Yoda, the Jedi Master.

Contents

	Preface to the Revised Edition	x
	Acknowledgments	xi
	Introduction	xiii
PART 1:	**THE MESS**	**1**
1.	Stardust and Ashes	3
2.	East of Eden	6
3.	Under the Thumb	10
4.	Stranger in a Strange Land	14
PART 2:	**THE WAY IN**	**19**
5.	Splashdown	21
6.	The Gateway	25
7.	Pursuit and Escape	29
8.	New Life through the Water	33
9.	Setting Out into the Darkness	37
10.	Reluctant Heroes	41
11.	Turning Around	45

PART 3: THE COMPANY **49**
12. The Company 51
13. Travelling Together 55
14. Life in Common 59
15. Breaking Down Barriers 63
16. Turning Away 67
17. Many Gifts, One Crew 71
18. Expansion and Growth 75

PART 4: THE CONFLICT **79**
19. Cosmic Conflict 81
20. Falling to the Dark Side 85
21. Worship Me! 89
22. The Good Spirit 93
23. Shields Up! 97
24. Resistance Is Not Futile 101
25. The Spirit of Adoption 105

PART 5: FINDING THE WAY **109**
26. Ups and Downs 111
27. The Master 115
28. Page the Oracle 119
29. Phone Home 123
30. Strength in Silence 127
31. The Guidebook 131
32. Dreams and Visions 135

PART 6: HEALING AND FEEDING **139**
33. Oases 141
34. The Healer 145
35. Regeneration Cycles 149

36. The Exorcist 153
37. Desert Springs 157
38. Food for the Journey 161
39. Soul Food 165

PART 7: GREATER LOVE 169
40. The Return of the King 171
41. A Good Clear-Out 175
42. Betrayal 179
43. Greater Love 183
44. The Agony 187
45. Death or Victory? 191
46. Good Grief! 195

PART 8: TO INFINITY AND BEYOND! 199
47. He's Alive! 201
48. All Good Things 205
49. Lift-Off 209
50. The Celestial City 213

Appendix 1: Material for Group Study 218
Appendix 2: Books, TV, Films and Resources 222
Appendix 3: Index of Bible Passages 226

Preface to the Revised Edition

The keeping of the season of Lent began as a period of preparation for those hoping to be baptized at Easter — but has become a time for study and reflection for all Christians. Similarly, this book began as a set of Bible studies for Lent — but many readers have found it useful for study throughout the year. I am grateful for the encouragement of Richard Fisher (at BRF) and Sam Eerdmans (at Eerdmans) to enable it to be revised for wider use. I am also grateful to the many individuals and groups who gave me helpful reactions and responses to using the book. It can be followed for the fifty days from Ash Wednesday to Easter Wednesday, or over any eight-week period as a general introduction to the basic beliefs and themes of the Christian faith. Further suggestions for its use are provided in the Appendix on group study, and at the Faith Odyssey website, www.faithodyssey.net.

Acknowledgments

I am grateful for the inspiration and enjoyment of all the books, TV shows and films mentioned in this book, especially for *2001: A Space Odyssey* and its sequels. It was an honour to meet Sir Arthur C. Clarke when he visited King's College, London, as one of our distinguished former students. I enjoyed discussing his work and our different ideas about theology, and I am grateful for his continuing interest and our e-mail conversations. I am also grateful to all the writers and producers who have entertained me over the years and whose works have elicited this response. Wherever possible, I have given brief references or page numbers in the text. The full details of all the various books and resources which I have used or quoted are listed at the back of this book — and I hope that it will encourage others to read or watch them.

I would particularly like to thank Naomi Starkey, my editor, for her personal interest in the material for this book and her constant encouragement — and for her patience and that of other staff at the Bible Reading Fellowship as deadlines became pressing, especially Lisa Cherrett, with thanks for her careful copy-editing. The Bible passages and quotations tend to be from the Revised Standard Version or New RSV, or are my own version of the original.

This book was produced over a period of considerable personal and professional pressure which affected all those around me. I am very appreciative of colleagues at King's College, London, who had to cope with the Dean being busy writing, especially Claire Waddell, my secretary, and Tim Ditchfield, the Chaplain. Many students, colleagues and friends were deluged with e-mails of chapter outlines and drafts, and contributed ideas from their own reading and recreation, especially Elizabeth Wilkinson, Fernando Gros, Will Ingle-Gillis, Anna Pascall, Tony and Jane Collins, Rich Cline, Anji Waring and Gloria Chandra. To all of you, a big thank you.

The biggest impact fell once again upon my wife, Sue, and our daughters, Rebecca and Sarah. Sue read (and corrected!) each piece as soon as it appeared, and the girls had to cope with endless repeats of *Star Trek* on the video recorder. Without their love and understanding, this book would never have been finished.

My father died just as I was preparing to write this through Lent 2000. I am grateful to my sister, Carole, for all her help and support through the months which followed. Dad may not have been a fan of science fiction, but his own journey through life, his struggle with illness and his sacrificial way of life have been a constant inspiration to me. I gladly dedicate this book to his memory. May he finally find healing and rest in the Celestial City!

Introduction

It's Bible Study, Jim, but not as we know it!

I am not sure what was my introduction to space or science fiction, though I do remember my first *Fireball XL5* jigsaw puzzle and collecting *Thunderbirds* photocards. As I grew up (or got older anyway) TV series like Dr Who gave way to Star Trek, and my reading graduated through C. S. Lewis' stories about Narnia to J. R. R. Tolkien, Isaac Asimov or Olaf Stapledon. I was stunned by Kubrick's film *2001: A Space Odyssey,* and its opening fanfares from Strauss' *Thus Spake Zarathustra* imprinted themselves in my memory as they repeatedly introduced TV coverage of the moon landings. Along the way, I inherited my grandmother's love for *The Pilgrim's Progress,* and eventually her illustrated copy when she died, while an initial fascination with the travels of Odysseus led to academic study of Homer's original hexameters and early Greek archaeology in my degree.

Through it all, I was captivated by the question of our place in the cosmos and whether there was anyone else out there. While I found some answers to those questions through my growing Christian faith, and my professional research and writing about Jesus of Nazareth, my imagination continued to be entertained by an ever growing deluge of *Star Trek* and *Star Wars* shows and films, and their many successors and parodies. Sometimes people laughed or objected about the combination, but other Christians seemed to share my interest.

Then I noticed that there was something familiar about the narrative which so many of these stories have in common. Often they begin with a hero or two in a mess, being oppressed or threatened. As the heroes seek to escape, they find a portal or gateway, some kind of amazing experience which sends them out on a journey. Along the way they find fellow travellers, fight against enemies, discover places to rest, and have to find their way to a great climax, which often involves great self-sacrifice. And then, of course, we all like a happy ending of homecoming and rejoicing.

But wait! I know this adventure! It is oddly like the story of salvation, of the journey from the old ways of sin through Christian initiation in baptism and conversion to sharing in the pilgrimage of the church towards the kingdom of God. And where shall we find a greater hero or self-sacrifice than in Jesus of Nazareth?

And so the ideas for this book were born. At one level, it is a very traditional series of Bible studies, which will take you through sin, baptism and the call of God, the church, spiritual warfare, prayer, guidance, silence, the Eucharist and so forth, until we come to the passion, death and resurrection of Jesus. On the other hand, it is an idiosyncratic collection of stories and excerpts from the science fiction films and other stories I have loved in my life. Each day, a chosen Bible passage is set alongside an extract or description taken from two or three other books and films. Hopefully, if you do not know one of them, you will recognize the others, and I try to explain them as we go along. The choices are not arbitrary or just for fun, but to inspire your imagination, which is one of God's gracious gifts to us. To misquote Mr Spock to Captain Kirk, 'It's Bible Study, Jim, but not as we know it'!

My hope and prayer is that those who know these Bible passages and traditional themes of basic Christianity so well may find a new light cast on them by letting their imagination play with these other stories. Meanwhile, those who are fans of this kind of literature may be amazed to discover that the Bible has been telling them a similar story all these years, one which all our deepest human longings have pointed towards and which is actually the true story. If you want a technical term for it, call it 'inter-textual hermeneutics' — interpreting one text in the light of another. In other words, read the Bible passage and my comments, think and pray about the links and let God inspire your imagination. Perhaps you could find one or two others who have similar interests and discuss it together (there are some suggestions for groups at the back) — and don't forget to enjoy it. This is a journey into life after all!

May the Spirit be with you!

Richard A. Burridge
King's College, London

PART 1

THE MESS

We begin with stardust and ashes and have to face the basic human problem — our anger and hatred, oppression of others and the sense of alienation and being lost. Can we find a new way on our journey?

1

Stardust and Ashes

Have mercy on me, O God, according to your steadfast love; according to your abundant mercy blot out my transgressions. Wash me thoroughly from my iniquity, and cleanse me from my sin. For I know my transgressions, and my sin is ever before me. . . .

Hide your face from my sins, and blot out all my iniquities. Create in me a clean heart, O God, and put a new and right spirit within me. Do not cast me away from your presence, and do not take your holy spirit from me.

PSALM 51:1-3, 9-11

Therefore I despise myself, and repent in dust and ashes.

JOB 42:6

It was a clear, starry night. I lay on my back in the grass on the top of a hill and looked up into the infinite universe above. We were out on an all-night hike with the Scouts, and someone had brought a transistor radio. The peace of the 'wee hours' was broken. 'Ground Control to Major Tom; Ground Control to Major Tom' — David Bowie's song, 'Space Oddity', drifted out towards those stars. Even if Major Tom had 'something wrong' with his spaceship, we knew then that soon our turn would come to travel out into space, on our own 'space odyssey'. Even as we watched the sky that night in the late 1960s, somewhere above us Apollo astronauts were on their way to the moon. Within a few decades, we thought we would all be able to do it, as 'scientific man' came of age and set off on the journey to the stars. We were amazed by the scientific discovery that our bodies actually contained molecules of heavy elements which had been formed within the gravity of stars. In America, hippies were celebrating at the Woodstock pop festival. Its theme song contained the chorus, 'We are stardust, we are golden, and we've got to get ourselves back to the garden'.

Yet within a few years, it was a different story. The 'love-children' at Woodstock found that they could not get themselves 'back to the garden'. The hippie dream ended bogged down in the mud of Woodstock. Love turned to violence as people were murdered while the Rolling Stones played at a subsequent concert in Altamont. Stardust had turned to ashes, the heavy molecules of long-dead stars. David Bowie changed his tune and sang 'Ashes to ashes', in which Major Tom is a junkie, 'strung out in heaven's high, hitting an all-time low'. The Apollo lunar modules and rover buggies still sit on the moon, undisturbed. We are stuck on this planet, going nowhere.

The biblical writers too reflected upon our place in the cosmos. 'In the beginning, when God created the heavens and the earth', he 'formed the man from the dust of the ground' (Gen. 1:1; 2:7). We really are created from dust and ashes, from these molecules which were formed in stars' gravities. The molecules were spread through space when the stars exploded, to end up as part of everything around us. So God warns Adam, 'You are dust and to dust you shall return' (Gen. 3:19). So when we die, we return our molecules to the universe, dust to dust, ashes to ashes. This is the paradox of human existence: we live because God has given us 'the breath of life', but this life is lived in frail bodies, earthen vessels of a few chemicals and water. We should never forget our origins. Even Abraham, the 'friend of God', when he was so bold as to plead with God not to destroy Sodom, knew his human weakness: 'Let me take it upon myself to speak to the Lord, I who am but dust and ashes' (Gen. 18:27).

No wonder that ash became a symbol of repentance, for both individuals and communities. When Job suffered his misfortunes, he 'took a potsherd with which to scrape himself, and sat among the ashes'. He blamed God, for 'he has cast me into the mire, and I have become like dust and ashes'. But when Job has finished his argument with God and heard the Lord's answer out of the whirlwind, he says, 'Therefore I despise myself, and repent in dust and ashes' (Job 2:8; 30:19; 42:6).

Fasting and being clothed in sackcloth and ashes was a way for whole communities to show their repentance. After the preaching of Jonah, 'When the news reached the king of Nineveh, he rose from his throne, removed his robe, covered himself with sackcloth, and sat in ashes' (Jonah 3:6). Jesus upbraided the towns which did not believe in him: 'Woe to you, Chorazin! Woe to you, Bethsaida! For if the deeds of power done in you had been done in Tyre and Sidon, they would have repented long ago in sackcloth and ashes' (Matt. 11:21). Peter recalls the story of Abraham and God's judgment, 'turning the cities of Sodom and Gomorrah to ashes', and warns his readers to repent (2 Peter 2:6). And for all our scientific progress, we now have the capacity with our nuclear weapons to turn all our world's cities to dust and ash.

So here we are at the beginning of our journey. We recall that, despite all our great achievements, we are stardust, the ashes of dead stars, formed from the dust of the ground and the molecules of the universe. People have ash put upon their foreheads in many churches as a reminder of human frailty and a sign of repentance for sin, especially on 'Ash Wednesday' at the beginning of Lent. Yet it is also a sign of hope, for God is also the one who 'raises the poor from the dust, and lifts the needy from the ash heap' (Ps. 113:7; 1 Sam. 2:8). The God who created us knows that 'we are but dust' and sent his Son to live among us and to raise us up, back to himself. For the ash used in Ash Wednesday services is traditionally made by burning the old palm crosses from last year. Our Faith Odyssey is always a journey towards the events of Holy Week and Easter, when we receive new palm crosses as we commemorate Jesus' death for our sin and receive new life through his resurrection. Then our ashes shall be transformed to stardust, not just 'back to the garden' but also beyond the stars 'in heaven's high'.

For Prayer and Meditation

Remember you are dust, and to dust you shall return.
Turn away from sin and be faithful to Christ.

Words used in the Ash Wednesday liturgy
when ash is put onto people's foreheads

2

East of Eden

Now the man knew his wife Eve, and she conceived and bore Cain, saying, 'I have produced a man with the help of the Lord.' Next she bore his brother Abel. Now Abel was a keeper of sheep, and Cain a tiller of the ground. In the course of time Cain brought to the Lord an offering of the fruit of the ground, and Abel for his part brought of the firstlings of his flock, their fat portions. And the Lord had regard for Abel and his offering, but for Cain and his offering he had no regard. So Cain was very angry, and his countenance fell. The Lord said to Cain, 'Why are you angry, and why has your countenance fallen? If you do well, will you not be accepted? And if you do not do well, sin is lurking at the door; its desire is for you, but you must master it.' Cain said to his brother Abel, 'Let us go out to the field.' And when they were in the field, Cain rose up against his brother Abel, and killed him. Then the Lord said to Cain, 'Where is your brother Abel?' He said, 'I do not know; am I my brother's keeper?' And the Lord said, 'What have you done? Listen; your brother's blood is crying out to me from the ground! And now you are cursed from the ground, which has opened its mouth to receive your brother's blood from your hand. When you till the ground, it will no longer yield to you its strength; you will be a fugitive and a wanderer on the earth.'

GENESIS 4:1-12

2001: A Space Odyssey begins not in the future, but in the 'primeval night' of one hundred thousand years ago in the valleys and plains of East Africa. A group of early man-apes led by 'Moon-Watcher' (the name is significant) eke out their existence by a small stream, which divides their territory from 'the Others', a similar group next door. Their existence, and the whole future of the yet-to-be human race, is changed for ever by the arrival of the 'monolith', a machine or computer sent by an alien spacefaring race. As Moon-Watcher and his tribe poke and prod it, it begins to enhance their intelligence and teach them various skills. As a result, Moon-Watcher uses his new-found brainpower to fashion bone knives and clubs, with which they kill and eat animals for the first time: 'he need never be hungry again'. But this 'Utopia' is shattered by the inevitable daily confrontation at the water with the Others. One-Ear, their leader, jumps and shrieks in the water as usual, but this time he is suddenly felled by a fearsome blow from Moon-Watcher's new weapon — and he is quickly beaten to death by all the bone clubs of the tribe. In the novel, this section ends with the pregnant statement: 'For a few seconds, Moon-Watcher stood uncertainly above his victim. . . . Now he was master of the world, and he was not quite sure what to do next. But he would think of something' (*2001*, pp. 11-37). In Stanley Kubrick's film version, Moon-Watcher hurls his bone club into the air where it turns end on end in slow motion and then transforms into an orbiting space-gun platform of the year 2001.

The Bible also begins with the dawn of the human race and a similar story moving from paradise to murder. Here too the names are significant: 'Adam' refers to the ground or soil from which he was created, while 'Eve' means 'life'. After they are expelled from the garden of Eden, Eve 'produces' a son, whom she calls Cain, from the Hebrew for 'produce', followed by his brother, Abel, whose name is connected with 'breath'. They develop different ways of life, as Abel is a 'keeper of sheep' and Cain 'a tiller of the ground' (v. 2). Thus we see straight away the early division of human beings between the cultures of the nomadic herder and the farmer. They even have different religious practices, as Cain offers his fruit to God, while Abel sacrifices a first-born animal for its fat. How quickly we turn our brothers and sisters into 'the Others', with their different way of life and their different beliefs and practices. It is usually thought by Old Testament scholars that Cain represents an ancestor of the Kenites, a tribe who lived on the borders of Israel with whom there was always an uneasy relationship. And so the human story rolls on from border disputes to bloody territorial wars, from earliest days to our own time, still around the land of Israel and Palestine, or from tribal disputes in Africa to Northern Ireland and the former Yugoslavia.

The story does not tell us why God accepts Abel's offering but not his brother's, any more than *2001* explains why the monolith chooses to teach one tribe and not the 'Others'. Yet God still cares for Cain, and warns him about the danger of his resentment, the sin 'lurking at the door' (v. 7). But Cain goes ahead, taking his brother into the field to kill him. As in *2001*, the first human action after leaving paradise is to murder a brother. After Adam and Eve sinned, God came and asked, 'Where are you?'; now he questions their son, 'Where is your brother?' (Gen. 3:9; 4:9). Cain's response to the Almighty is a flippant pun: 'Am I my brother's keeper?' sneering at his brother's pastoral life as a 'keeper of animals'. But God is not to be joked with and spilled blood cannot be hidden. Adam was named after the ground from which he came, and Cain was the 'tiller of the ground' — but he has sown the wrong crop, putting his brother's blood in the soil which can only cry out its agony to God (vv. 10-11).

From Cain's murder of his brother to Moon-Watcher's killing the 'Other', such rivalry and death is at the heart of much of human history and story. Every border in the world has been soaked with the blood of those who live on one side or the other — or usually of both! Gruesome though it is, the murder of close family or friends is central to so many stories, even or especially those for children. Just think of all the fairy tales or pantomimes where the little hero's parents are supplanted by an evil uncle or stepmother. In C. S. Lewis' stories about Narnia, King Caspian is murdered by his brother Miraz, who usurps the throne from his nephew, Prince Caspian. Harry Potter, the teenage wizard phenomenon who has so captured the imagination of children and adults alike, grew up an orphan after his parents were betrayed by Peter Pettigrew, who had been their classmate at school, to the evil Voldemort who murdered them. In the greatest cycle of murder and revenge in human literature, Aeschylus' *Oresteia* trilogy, the Greek king Agamemnon sacrifices his daughter to get a fair wind for Troy, only to be slaughtered by his wife upon his return, who is then killed by their son, Orestes — and the blood goes on crying out to the heavens, until it is all finally stopped by the intervention of the 'kindly gods'.

And us? We are so clever, so advanced, our brains enhanced by our computers and our hands extended by our technology. We live in a world where we need 'never be hungry again', yet millions are malnourished and starve to death. We talk of peace and international cooperation, yet spend billions making and developing Moon-Watcher's clubs into weapons of mass destruction to sell to Others to kill our brothers and sisters. As in the film of 2001, now we even want to put weapons into space. But God still loves us and warns us of sin, 'lurking at the door', which will destroy us unless we change. Cain's punishment is to become a fugitive, losing his connection with the ground, and wandering 'in the land of Nod, east of Eden' (Gen. 4:12-16). Thus sin leads to alienation, and our journey through life is a search to find the way back home. But we do not walk alone. God continues to protect Cain in his wandering with a 'mark' to stop Others killing him (v. 15). In our world today, we too have the blood of brothers and sisters on our hands, but the mark of Cain on our forehead. Moon-Watcher's bone club, hurled into the sky, goes into earth orbit at the start of the *Space Odyssey,* and begins a journey to the stars. With Cain we may be east of Eden, but we are still 'stardust', trying to get 'back to the garden' as we set out on this Faith Odyssey.

For Prayer and Meditation

For this is the message you have heard from the beginning, that we should love one another. We must not be like Cain who was from the evil one and murdered his brother.

1 John 3:11-12

Lord, forgive us for our greed and sin,
for what we have done to our brothers and sisters;
give us your love that we may love one another.

3

Under the Thumb

Now a new king arose over Egypt. . . . He said to his people, 'Look, the Israelite people are more numerous and more powerful than we. Come, let us deal shrewdly with them, or they will increase and, in the event of war, join our enemies and fight against us and escape from the land.' Therefore they set taskmasters over them to oppress them with forced labour. They built supply cities, Pithom and Rameses, for Pharaoh. But the more they were oppressed, the more they multiplied and spread, so that the Egyptians came to dread the Israelites. The Egyptians became ruthless in imposing tasks on the Israelites, and made their lives bitter with hard service in mortar and brick and in every kind of field labour. They were ruthless in all the tasks that they imposed on them.

EXODUS 1:8-14

The smoke from an open fire drifts across the encampment. Children clad in rags play outside the makeshift dwellings, while their parents, hollow-eyed and fearful, watch from the shadows as two uniformed officers walk into the camp. One of them, an attractive but bitter young woman, stops and removes her Starfleet jacket, draping it around the shoulders of a little girl. 'That was me,' explains Ensign Ro, remembering her time as a refugee after she had been forced to watch her father tortured to death by the Cardassians who have occupied her planet, Bajor, for the last forty years. Her superior, Captain Picard of the famous starship USS *Enterprise,* is visibly shocked by the hunger and deprivation he sees — not quite the terrorist base he had been expecting to find.

When that single TV episode of *Star Trek: The Next Generation* was first aired in October 1991, no one knew what lay ahead. The writer, Rick Berman, explained that the Bajorans were not modelled on any particular group: 'The Kurds, the Palestinians, the Jews in the 1940s, the boat people from Haiti — unfortunately, the homeless and terrorism are problems in every age' (*TNG Companion,* p. 178). The story turns on oppression and slavery and how what some authorities see as terrorism may be for others their struggle for freedom.

A few months later, Berman and his colleague, Michael Piller, drew on this episode for the basic idea of what became the highly successful third *Star Trek* series — *Deep Space Nine.* Here the parallels with the Israelites under the ancient Egyptians, and so many other oppressed and enslaved peoples, are clear. The Cardassians mine the rich mineral deposits in Bajor's planetary crust, which are then taken up to an orbiting space station, called *Terok Nor,* which is a refining plant to extract the valuable uridium ore from the rocks. It is hard work, undertaken by Bajoran slave labourers, who are given little food and no resources and are beaten to get the work done. The TV series tells the story of the first few years after the Cardassians have left, when the station has become *Deep Space Nine,* shared by the Bajorans and the United Federation of Planets — with the occasional attempt by its old taskmaster, the Prefect Gul Dukat, to take it back.

This theme of the journey out of slavery and oppression is central to many other classic science fiction stories. Frank Herbert's influential *Dune* novels (and the 1984 film, starring Sting) begin with the oppression of the planet Arrakis, or 'Dune', where the indigenous people are forced to produce the all-important melange spice (which is essential for space travel) for the occupying forces of the Harkonnen, who have killed its rightful ruler, the Duke Atreides. Similarly the 1999 film, *The Matrix,* has as its premise that this world is a computer-generated illusion, planted in the minds of human beings who are actually being kept unconscious in cylinders by artificially intelligent machines which are harvesting our bodies' biochemical electricity.

All of these have echoes of the oppression of the children of Israel in ancient Egypt and can also be seen as images of the human condition without God. C. S. Lewis makes this link in his science fiction trilogy *Out of the Silent Planet, Voyage to Venus* and *That Hideous Strength,* where earth is under the command of a rogue *eldil,* a kind of angelic figure in rebellion, thus akin to the devil. Similarly, in his better-known children's stories, the White Witch has the land of Narnia 'under her thumb' and she makes it 'always winter and never Christmas' (*The Lion, the Witch and the Wardrobe,* p. 23).

It is as though there is something deep in the human psyche which sees our world in which human beings oppress and kill each other as itself under oppression and slavery. Whether it is the ancient Israelites under Pharaoh, the Jews under Hitler or the Palestinians in modern Israel, the same pattern gets repeated. Most often it is driven by fear — fear that what *2001: A Space Odyssey* called the 'Others' will become 'more numerous and powerful than we' as Pharaoh says in today's passage (Ex. 1:9). The only option seems to be to oppress and enslave them. So they are forced into slave labour, working under hard task-masters to build cities for their Egyptian masters (1:11). But what such masters never seem to learn is that oppressed people appear to go on growing, and so their fear increases all the more — and the only option is to respond with ever more oppression, making 'their lives bitter with hard service' (1:12-14). Eventually, the Israelites are not even given the means of production, but have to make 'bricks without straw', being savagely beaten to deliver the same number as before (Ex. 5:5-19). And so this sad tale has been repeated down through history and around our planet, from ancient Egypt through the negro slaves in the cotton fields to the diamond mines of South Africa under apartheid, and on into the imagined futures like Bajor.

Yet, we do not have to be under physical oppression to know the experience of making 'bricks without straw'. For many people, life does feel like that — a struggle from day to day simply to survive. According to Christian belief, this is because, without God, we are prey to meaningless vanity and the oppression of sin. Paul describes the original state of his readers as 'enslaved to sin' (Rom. 6:6, 16-17), or 'captive through philosophy and empty deceit, according to human tradition, according to the elemental spirits of the universe' (Col. 2:8). Thus, in his classic story of the spiritual pilgrimage, *The Pilgrim's Progress,* John Bunyan describes this world as 'the City of Destruction'. His hero, called 'Christian', is 'a man clothed with rags' who carries 'a great burden on his back' — and who is desperately searching for a way to become free.

And this is the focus of all of these stories. Despite the context of the oppression and slavery, their main concern is this longing for freedom and the hope of a liberator to come. Thus the Bajorans are waiting for their 'Emissary' and Arrakis for its 'Dune Messiah'. Those who fight the Matrix argue whether the computer-hacker Neo is the 'One' (rearranging the letters of his name), while the hero of C. S. Lewis' science fiction trilogy, who will free the 'Silent Planet' earth, is called 'Ransom', and his stories of Narnia are filled with rumours of the coming of Aslan, the great Lion and son of the Emperor-beyond-the-sea. So too for our journey of faith. Like Moon-Watcher and Cain, we are out of paradise, where brothers and sisters are killed and people are enslaved. But we too long to be free — and these stories tell us to look for the coming of the Liberator.

For Prayer and Meditation

O God and Father of all humankind,
who heard the cry of your ancient people under Pharaoh's yoke,
look with mercy on all who suffer oppression and slavery
and those whose lives feel like making bricks without straw;
hear our prayer and bring us
into the glorious freedom of the children of God
through your Son our Saviour Jesus Christ.

4

Stranger in a Strange Land

By the rivers of Babylon —
there we sat down and there we wept
when we remembered Zion.
On the willows there we hung up our harps.
For there our captors asked us for songs,
and our tormentors asked for mirth, saying,
'Sing us one of the songs of Zion!'
How could we sing the LORD*'s song in a foreign land?*
If I forget you, O Jerusalem, let my right hand wither!
Let my tongue cling to the roof of my mouth,
if I do not remember you,
if I do not set Jerusalem above my highest joy.

PSALM 137:1-6

2001: A Space Odyssey is all about the journey of exploration, going out into the solar system where human beings have never been before. After the initial sections about the monolith enhancing Moon-Watcher and his companions, and the uncovering in the year 2001 of another monolith which had been buried on the moon, the bulk of the story concerns the voyage of the ship, *Discovery.* It was originally being built for the first manned trip to Jupiter — but now its task is to investigate what is waiting for Moon-Watcher's descendants out there in the cold expanse of space.

The original series of *Star Trek* had the same aim, as its famously ungrammatical (and sexist!) opening announcement proclaimed the mission of its aptly named USS *Enterprise* — 'to boldly go where no man has gone before'. Gene Roddenberry, its creator, often described it as '*Wagon Train* to the stars', picking up that sense of pioneering into the unknown from the old days of exploration of the Wild West. Like *2001,* it had that supreme confidence in the ability of science to find all the answers on the trek into outer space, so typical of the 1960s. Roddenberry's vision of the future was an optimistic secular harmony where technology had rendered poverty and disease obsolete. By the mid-1980s, things had changed, both in our world and in Roddenberry's imagined future. In *Star Trek: The Next Generation,* while the new USS *Enterprise* continued to zip around the galaxy as its setting, the focus of interest moved from the trek into outer space to the journey into 'inner space' through its individual human stories and the high profile given to the Counsellor on board. In turn, its successor *Deep Space Nine* seemed to have given up journeys altogether with the action taking place on a space station where nothing really works properly and everything is centred around the Promenade — a set of shops and Quark's bar!

But as the end of the millennium approached, the fourth series once again picked up the original journey theme, being named after its ship, *Voyager.* However, there is a major reversal from the 1960s. Early in the feature-length pilot episode, the USS *Voyager* is suddenly taken right across the galaxy, together with a smaller ship full of Maquis, freedom fighters against the Cardassians. Then both are stranded there, some 70,000 light years from home, a journey which even *Voyager*'s top-of-the-range new engines will take some seventy years to accomplish. The sense of exploration may be back, but it is as though the writers are saying 'never mind about going out where none have gone before; we are lost — does anyone know the way back home?' This constant yearning to get home, to rejoin family and friends, develops in the pilot episode and runs throughout the years of the series until they eventually get home in the final episode. Captain Janeway's last words then are the same as her closing speech in the pilot episode: 'Set a course — for home!' It is all very reminiscent of Homer's original *Odyssey,* where Odysseus is trying to get back home to his wife and family in Ithaca after the Trojan War, and all the trials he has to go through over ten years before arriving there at last.

Interestingly, Arthur C. Clarke also has a similar reversal in his last volume. Like *Voyager,* it is the fourth in the series and it is entitled *3001: The Final Odyssey.* This is also about a journey back home, as the thousand-year-old body of Frank Poole, one of the original crew of *Discovery* in *2001,* is discovered frozen in outer space and brought back to a very different earth. He searches to make contact with his former colleagues from a thousand years previously and the book ends with human beings once again alone in the universe: 'Whatever godlike principalities and powers lurked beyond the stars, Poole reminded himself, for ordinary humans only two things were important — Love and Death' (*3001*, pp. 247-248). Furthermore, the latest Star Trek series, called simply *Enterprise*, has stepped back from the glamour of previous shows. It is set in 2151, more than a century before the time of Kirk and Spock. There is much less technology or optimistic confidence — but more uncertainty and distrust of others like the Vulcans.

It is as though we are going into the new millennium not looking forward with the 1960s' confidence, but rather with a nostalgic glance over the shoulder and a sense of not belonging here. Some are disillusioned, and others are angry. We are indeed 'strangers in a strange land', lost and a long way from home. The search for an 'alien nation' has just uncovered our own sense of alienation.

This is the feeling of the ancient Jews 'by the rivers of Babylon'. Over half a millennium after Moses brought them out of slavery in Egypt, they suffered the conquest and destruction of Jerusalem and its temple in 587 BC. Once again they were put into slavery and this time taken far away into exile by their captors. The 'rivers of Babylon' were the famous Tigris and Euphrates, a long way away from Jerusalem and Mount Zion — so all they could do was to sit and weep with the painful memory (Ps. 137:1). Even worse, their captors tormented them by asking them to sing songs of God's praise for their entertainment; no wonder they hung up their instruments on the riverside willows (137:2-3). As strangers 'in a strange land' they cannot sing 'the Lord's song' here. The memory of Jerusalem, back home, has to be the most important thing. If that is given up, the Psalmist prays that his hand may never again be able to play his harp, nor his tongue sing praises any more: Jerusalem must be above his highest joy (137:4-6).

Christians, too, have used this psalm and the name of Babylon to describe our situation here on earth. Paul, a Roman citizen, counts that for nothing, saying that we do not really belong here: 'Our citizenship is in heaven, and it is from there that we are expecting a Saviour, the Lord Jesus Christ' (Phil. 3:20). Similarly, Peter describes this life as a 'time of your exile' or a 'sojourning' on earth, as we prepare for the 'revelation of Jesus Christ' (1 Peter 1:13, 17). No wonder the black slaves used to sing, 'I've got a home in glory land that outshines the sun, look away beyond the sky'!

Yet we do not just have to sit here by the waters of Babylon, for the

Christian story is that God has come looking for us, as a good shepherd goes looking for his lost sheep (Lk. 15:3-6). The journey of faith offers us the opportunity of a way back home to God. These themes of our first week do indeed paint a sorry portrait of the Mess we're in — where the hopes of stardust turn to ashes, where people sin and murder Others, oppress and enslave them. No wonder we feel alienated and lost. Both the Bible and our contemporary films and novels tell the same sad story of the context in which we start our journey. But there is hope, so 'set the course for home'!

For Prayer and Meditation

'We are alone in an uncharted part of the galaxy. We've already made some friends and some enemies. We have no idea of the dangers we are going to face. . . . Somewhere along this journey we'll find a way back. Set a course for home.'

Captain Janeway's final speech to the crew of *Voyager*
at the end of the first episode, 'Caretaker'

Father of all, we give you thanks and praise, that when we were still far off, you met us in your Son and brought us home. Dying and living, he declared your love, gave us grace and opened the gate of glory. . . . Keep us firm in the hope you have set before us, so we and all your children shall be free, and the whole earth live to praise your name, through Christ our Lord, Amen.

The Post-Communion Prayer, *Alternative Service Book 1980*, p. 144

PART 2

THE WAY IN

After the Mess, our journey really gets under way in the first full week. It begins as Jesus enters our world and we respond to God's call in our many and different ways.

5

Splashdown

Then Jesus came from Galilee to John at the Jordan, to be baptized by him. John would have prevented him, saying, 'I need to be baptized by you, and do you come to me?' But Jesus answered him, 'Let it be so now; for it is proper for us in this way to fulfil all righteousness.' Then he consented. And when Jesus had been baptized, just as he came up from the water, suddenly the heavens were opened to him and he saw the Spirit of God descending like a dove and alighting on him. And a voice from heaven said, 'This is my Son, the Beloved, with whom I am well pleased.'

MATTHEW 3:13-17

It is not a pretty picture. Despite all the great advances of science and technology, the world seems still a Mess. Indeed, those very scientific advances even contribute to it: the awesome power from splitting the atom led to the destruction unleashed upon Hiroshima and Nagasaki and the shadow of the Bomb over the second half of the twentieth century. The discovery of the structure of DNA has brought us to the point of mapping the whole human genetic make-up with all its potential for healing and preventing some diseases — or for cloning and warping future generations. The knowledge of being made from star-dust turns to ashes in our mouths while the cry of millions suffering from poverty and oppression brings home the brutality of our world. This is why so many today feel alienated and lost.

Thus it is not surprising that a large part of science fiction stories and contemporary fantasy is about getting away from earth. Some people accuse those who read or watch these stories of escapism, while devotees see it more as exploration. The problem is that wherever human beings go in the universe, they take themselves — and with them go greed, murder, sin and oppression. Something needs to be done about it here and now.

The Apollo astronauts were the first men to escape this planet and walk upon the surface of another heavenly body, the moon. Their journeys ended with a fiery re-entry through the upper atmosphere, lighting up the skies, followed by a splashdown landing in the ocean's cold water.

The paradox is that the real entry is not about us leaving or escaping from this world, but God entering into it. Apollo may have ended in the sea, but the Christian journey *starts* with a splash as Jesus comes from Galilee to the waters of the Jordan river. Why would God want to enter our world at all? And, once he was here, why not come in power and majesty, lighting up the sky, rather than starting with a muddy bath?

Most of us as children have goldfish or other little creatures as pets. I did — and so have my own children. And although we are so much greater than these helpless creatures, we love them and care for them. The problem is — how can the goldfish know this? We may create a wonderful environment for them, with water at the right temperature, interesting sunken galleons to frolic around and lots of tasty fish food and ants' eggs — but the goldfish take it all for granted, going round in circles opening and closing their mouths. Perhaps we could put electrodes into their brains and pass them messages of love — but they would only think that something odd which they had eaten had given them hallucinations. If we were to strip off and dive in to join them, we would only terrify them — and destroy their world. At the end of the day, goldfish only understand other goldfish.

So too for God. He can create this amazing universe, in which stars have formed and earth has cooled to just the right temperature to support life in so much abundance, to produce human beings and our food — and we go round in circles opening and closing our mouths and taking it all for granted. He can send us messages of love through prophets and mystics, and we humour them, or put them away in padded cells — so much kinder than the old habits of stoning them, don't you think? But if he were to enter our little world in his power and glory, his presence would turn us back to stardust and ashes with hardly the time to be terrified. In the end, human beings only understand other human beings.

And so we have a very human coming, as Jesus leaves his daily life in Galilee for the Jordan river. Mark begins his Gospel here, for this is the start of the real action, the entry point for the rest of Jesus' ministry among us. Matthew and Luke use this for the start of their main narrative, but preface it with brief stories about his birth and childhood. It is John who puts it into the cosmic scale in his prologue: 'In the beginning was the Word, and the Word was with God and the Word was God' (Jn. 1:1). Jesus was there, right before the start of anything, and he was involved in the creation of everything, the source of all life and light. Yet that very same divine Word, life and light 'was coming into the world' and 'became flesh and dwelt among us' (Jn. 1:9, 14). In its Latin roots, 'in-carnation' means 'en-fleshment', as God is embodied in Jesus to reveal himself to us.

While some science fiction stories may begin with escaping from this world, it is true that others, especially about computer worlds, pick up these ideas of incarnation. In the 1999 blockbuster, *The Matrix,* the central character, a computer programmer called Neo, is disturbed by others who have broken into his world from outside. Nor is it just into his world — for the whole world as we know it is actually an elaborate computer-generated illusion run by artificially intelligent machines. When Neo joins these cyber-rebels, he too has to re-enter this world, to take the same form as the other humans there, in order to save his friends — and eventually the whole world. A similar motif was used in the 1982 Disney film, *Tron.* Here another computer programmer, Kevin Flynn (played by Jeff Bridges), designs some early computer games, little realizing that this creates a virtual world in his computer where the various characters live and fight and die — while having discussions about whether they 'believe in the User'. When the programmer, 'the User', is shot by a laser and assimilated into his own program, he has the same form as his characters as he battles to save them and their world, as well as to prevent the computer taking over the real world.

This is what happens at the baptism of Jesus. He is the visitor from another realm, he is the Maker and the User — and yet he comes also as the carpenter of Nazareth, just another ordinary person from Galilee coming to be immersed in the waters of the Jordan. He goes down into the water like everyone else — but when he comes up from the water, the heavens are torn open and the veil between our little world and the vast universe is momentarily torn aside. In the coming of Jesus, the gulf between earth and heaven is bridged and the power of God's Spirit comes down upon him. However, it is not a frightening rending of the sky, nor a terrifying descent — but something as gentle as a dove landing on his shoulder (Matt. 3:16).

And yet, this immediately causes a problem for later theological understanding. If Jesus is God entering our world, the perfect and sinless one coming among us, how can he stoop so low to go under the river's water and why did he need to be baptized at all? St Jerome quotes a fragment from a later apocryphal book, the Gospel according to the Hebrews, in which Mary suggests to Jesus and his brothers that they should all go to be baptized by John; Jesus responds by asking in what way he has sinned that he should need this (St Jerome, *Against Pelagius,* III.2). Matthew's version also seems to be trying to answer this question, when John the Baptist at first wants to prevent Jesus, saying, 'I need to be baptized by you' (3:14). Jesus' reply that John should let this happen 'to fulfil all righteousness' is another way of stressing Jesus' total identification with human beings in their plight, sin and alienation. No wonder the voice from heaven declares that Jesus is 'my Beloved Son', the one in whom God is well pleased (Matt. 3:17).

We begin our faith journey not by leaving our world, but with Jesus' 'splashdown' in our waters. It is not that we are trying to escape; instead he has come looking for us. Finite, puny human beings cannot launch out into the infinite spaces of the cosmos. But the maker of the universe has bridged the gap from infinity into our existence. Because he has come to our world, we can eventually travel to his far country. The real miracle is that, as we enter upon this journey, so Christ enters not just our world, but into each and every one of us.

For Prayer and Meditation

May God, who has received you by baptism into his Church,
pour upon you the riches of his grace,
that within the company of Christ's pilgrim people
you may daily be renewed by his anointing Spirit,
and come to the inheritance of the saints in glory.

The prayer over a newly baptized person, *Common Worship*

Think about your own baptism, whether as a child or adult; look at any photos, certificates or records you may have. Bring that experience into the present in your prayers now and recommit yourself to the Christian journey.

6

The Gateway

'Very truly, I tell you, anyone who does not enter the sheepfold by the gate but climbs in by another way is a thief and a bandit. The one who enters by the gate is the shepherd of the sheep. The gatekeeper opens the gate for him, and the sheep hear his voice. He calls his own sheep by name and leads them out. . . . Very truly, I tell you, I am the gate for the sheep. All who came before me are thieves and bandits; but the sheep did not listen to them. I am the gate. Whoever enters by me will be saved, and will come in and go out and find pasture. The thief comes only to steal and kill and destroy. I came that they may have life, and have it abundantly.'

JOHN 10:1-3, 7-10

The huge satellite dishes sweep the sky and their monitors produce a random mixture of interstellar static and radioactive beeping. All over the world, scientists analyse the huge piles of data in the hope of finding something which is neither random nor natural — evidence of broadcasts or transmissions from alien beings. The Search for Extra-Terrestrial Intelligence (SETI) programme continues its tedious and frustrating quest through the vast reaches of outer space. Suddenly, a young astronomer, Dr Ellie Arroway (are both 'arrow' and 'way' significant?), realizes that there is a pattern in one signal. Mathematical formulae and prime numbers reveal the first evidence of non-human intelligence, while more detailed later analysis discovers the instructions to build some kind of machine or device, a portal through which the first person can travel to meet alien life. There is great debate about who should be this ambassador for the human race and Dr Arroway is rejected because she does not believe in God. Eventually, after sabotage by religious fanatics destroys the initial attempt, she gets to travel through this portal, a roller-coaster ride of images, colours and lights across the universe.

The SETI programme is real and happening at the moment, although it has not yet produced any evidence. Carl Sagan's novel, *Contact,* explores what might happen if — or is it when? — they do. It is full of the scientific basis and understanding to be expected from this leading scientist. Sagan himself worked for NASA, and was a regular commentator and expert on TV during the Apollo missions and moon landings. The film version of his novel, in which Dr Arroway is played by Jodie Foster, allows great scope for special effects as she travels through the 'portal'. Interestingly, Nicholas Sagan, Carl Sagan's son, has gone to become a regular scriptwriter first for the final season of *Star Trek: The Next Generation,* and then through the more recent series of *Deep Space Nine* and *Voyager.*

Many science fiction stories use this idea of a 'gateway' or 'door' through which humans might travel across the universe. A similar device appears in the film *Stargate* and the subsequent TV episodes, where an ancient Egyptian set of concentric circles is excavated and eventually decoded. Their proper alignment and use opens a 'stargate' through space to another world where aliens dressed like ancient Egyptian gods oppress humans in just the way Pharaoh did the Israelites.

Of course, it is not easy to find or use these openings into another world. In the first of the hugely successful novels about a teenage wizard, Harry Potter has to find Platform Nine and Three-Quarters at King's Cross Station to get the train to Hogwarts School for Wizards. His disbelieving Uncle Vernon and Aunt Petunia mockingly leave him between Platforms 9 and 10, where nothing is to be seen except an ordinary ticket barrier. It is only when he meets other wizard children that he learns that you have to walk straight into the barrier, without stopping or being scared, and then he finds himself magically on Platform Nine and Three-Quarters (*Harry Potter and the Philosopher's Stone,* pp. 68-71). In the film version, it is even more dramatic, as Harry has to charge full speed into — and through — a brick wall, only to find himself by the magnificent Hogwarts Express.

In C. S. Lewis' stories, Lucy enters into Narnia through the wardrobe, has tea with Mr Tumnus the faun and returns to our world without any time having elapsed here. When she brings her sister and brothers to the wardrobe, it is perfectly normal with a wooden back. When Edmund also goes through it into Narnia, and then later all the children, it is as a result of nothing they can do or know — and the subsequent trips all involve other magic ways through.

In John Bunyan's *The Pilgrim's Progress,* Christian is directed by Evangelist towards the 'Wicket-gate'. He only reaches it after falling into the Slough of Despond, nearly succumbing to the advice of Mr Worldly-Wiseman and despairing beneath the legalism of Mount Sinai — but eventually he knocks, and it is opened by Goodwill.

So it is also for our journey from the oppression and alienation of this world. Jesus has made his 'splashdown' among us, entering this world as a human being to identify with us. But he is also the Gateway through which we can enter upon the journey to God. Much of ancient Israel-Palestine was rough, stony pasture, better suited to herding flocks than for agriculture and crops. Thus the wandering shepherd with sheep or goats was a very common sight. They were kept more for their wool or milk than for meat, and so the shepherd would travel with them for many years. There were dangers aplenty to threaten the animals, especially at night, both from wild beasts and from other humans, thieves and bandits. To protect the flocks, courtyard-type sheepfolds were built, with only one door in and out. Large ones would have a doorkeeper, allowing shepherds to leave their animals there for the night, perhaps with sheep from other flocks. Smaller folds might just have one gap in the wall, across which the shepherd could sleep to prevent his sheep leaving, or others entering. In both cases, the only way in or out was through the door — and those who tried to scale the walls for other ways in were thieves and bandits.

In John's Gospel, Jesus uses this image of the sheepfold, the shepherd and the sheep as a 'figure of speech' (Jn. 10:6), which is the nearest John gets to the parables found in the other Gospels. What is interesting here is the stress on the door or Gateway. Throughout the Gospel, Jesus is depicted as being the fulfilment of all of Israel's hopes and images: 'I am the bread of life' or 'I am the light of the world' (Jn. 6:35; 8:12). Sheep and shepherds were common images in the Hebrew Scriptures for God and his people, so it is no surprise when later in this chapter, Jesus says, 'I am the good shepherd' (Jn. 10:11, 14). But he can only be the good shepherd of those who choose to become his sheep — and so first we have this claim, 'I am the door' (Jn. 10:7, 9). He is the entrance itself, the portal or the Gateway, through which we have to enter if we are to find safety and protection. In his incarnation, he has entered our world and shared our human nature. In his baptism, he has identified with us in our sin and lostness. Because of all this, he is also the one who can offer us a way out — the door not just across the universe but to eternal life itself.

The paradox is that Jesus is both the door and the way, the beginning and the journey itself. So a few chapters later, we come to the last supper where Thomas says to Jesus, 'Lord, we do not know where you are going. How can we know the way?' Jesus replies, 'I am the way, and the truth, and the life. No one comes to the Father except through me' (Jn. 14:5-6). He is not just the gate or entry point, but he is the very way to the Father. This is a stupendous and unique idea. Many religious teachers and philosophers have tried to be signposts or even doors, opening up new ways to truth and life for others. But only Christianity says that Jesus is 'the way, the truth and the life'. Just as we cannot reach across interstellar distances unless some alien radio signal breaks into our world with instructions, so too we cannot bridge the gulf to the infinity of God. We can point to it, strive and struggle after it — but only one who has come from the infinite, from God himself, can be both the door and the way to the Father.

For Prayer and Meditation

'Ask, and it will be given you; seek, and you shall find; knock and the door will be opened to you.'

Matthew 7:7

Take some time in prayer to ask, seek and knock; go through the Gateway and begin the exciting journey to real life.

7

Pursuit and Escape

As Pharaoh drew near, the Israelites looked back, and there were the Egyptians advancing on them. In great fear the Israelites cried out to the Lord*. . . . Then Moses stretched out his hand over the sea. The* Lord *drove the sea back by a strong east wind all night, and turned the sea into dry land; and the waters were divided. The Israelites went into the sea on dry ground, the waters forming a wall for them on their right and on their left. The Egyptians pursued, and went into the sea after them, all of Pharaoh's horses, chariots, and chariot drivers. At the morning watch the* Lord *in the pillar of fire and cloud looked down upon the Egyptian army, and threw the Egyptian army into panic. He clogged their chariot wheels so that they turned with difficulty. The Egyptians said, 'Let us flee from the Israelites, for the Lord is fighting for them against Egypt.' Then the* Lord *said to Moses, 'Stretch out your hand over the sea, so that the water may come back upon the Egyptians, upon their chariots and chariot drivers.' So Moses stretched out his hand over the sea, and at dawn the sea returned to its normal depth. As the Egyptians fled before it, the Lord tossed the Egyptians into the sea. The waters returned and covered the chariots and the chariot drivers, the entire army of Pharaoh that had followed them into the sea; not one of them remained. But the Israelites walked on dry ground through the sea, the waters forming a wall for them on their right and on their left.*

EXODUS 14:10, 21-29

After its introductory words, 'A long time ago in a galaxy far, far away . . .' have crawled up the screen, the movie *Star Wars* begins with the memorable scene of a small spacecraft trying to escape shots being fired from a pursuing battleship. As the camera moves back, the sheer size of the pursuers becomes apparent. On the little ship, Princess Leia hastily records her plea for help — 'Obi-Wan Kenobi, you're my only hope' — into one of her android servants. Just before the princess and her people are recaptured by the evil Darth Vader, the droids are sent off in an escape pod, which lands on the desert planet of Tatooine. Any hope of escape from the clutches of evil now depends upon them.

The sequel film, *The Empire Strikes Back,* has similar themes, as it begins with the escape of the rebels from their planet, Hoth, through the midst of the attackers; later, our heroes' ship, the *Millennium Falcon,* has to weave its way through dangerous asteroids which destroy its pursuers. In both films, the theme of pursuit and escape from evil is the impetus to get things underway. We have seen already how so many stories start with the Mess, the sin, murder, oppression and alienation, in which we live. No wonder our heroes want to get away from the evil.

As we have already noted, the problem is that wherever we go, we take ourselves — and all our internal Mess. In the *Deep Space Nine* pilot episode — 'The Emissary' — Commander Sisko may want to avoid the painful memories of the terrible battle against the evil Borg in the Wolf 359 star system, in which he lost his wife, but wherever he goes, the memories follow. Eventually he flies into the wormhole, a strange and dangerous phenomenon likely to swallow up everything, pursued by the evil Cardassian leader, Gul Dukat. Inside the maelstrom it contains, Sisko meets the prophets, who enable him to find some release from his memories and make him the Emissary to the Bajorans, while they render the pursuing Dukat ineffective.

On a smaller scale, Lucy and Edmund are being pestered, if not persecuted, by their horrible cousin, Eustace Clarence Scrubb, because of their belief in Narnia. When they seek to escape into a room with a painting of a ship hanging on the wall, Eustace follows them. All three are magically drawn into the picture where they land unceremoniously in the sea and have to be rescued, dripping wet — and this is only the start of the adventure in *The Voyage of the 'Dawn Treader'.*

For the Bible too, the adventure of Israel starts with the Israelites' escape from Egypt and the pursuit of Pharaoh's army. It resonates with the stories above in the size of the pursuers and the hopelessness of our heroes' situation, by their escape in finding a miraculous way through the very sea which overwhelms their enemy, and by the prospect of adventures still to come in the desert around Mount Sinai.

For the ancient Israelites, this event was absolutely essential as the start of their history. God created his people by and through this act. A little later, the Ten Commandments are prefaced by 'I am the LORD your

God who brought you out of the land of Egypt, out of the house of slavery' (Ex. 20:2). So this experience of having been rescued gives the Israelites a sense of both their own identity and their relationship to God as their creator and saviour.

Throughout the story, from the call of Moses through to their departure from Egypt, God takes the initiative and the people grumble and are slow to respond. So too here: as they see the pursuing Egyptians, they complain to Moses that it is all his fault and that he should have left them in Egypt (Ex. 14:11-12). In reply, Moses, as their commander, has to tell them not to be afraid, but to trust God for his deliverance (Ex. 14:13-14). Such words are easy to say, but Moses then has to act and to take the risk of failing and looking rather silly. He has to stretch his hand out over the sea and expect the water to move! What if he does so and nothing happens?

But what does happen is a mixture of both natural and supernatural phenomena: on the one hand, ordinary things occur with a 'strong east wind' blowing all night to expose the seabed, over which the Israelites can pick their way, while the Egyptians' chariot wheels get bogged down in the mud — leading to their perfectly understandable panic. On the other hand, Moses' hands splitting open the sea and the towering 'wall of water on the right and on their left' witness to the extraordinary nature of this event.

Once they are through safely to dry land and the pursuers are drowned, the Israelites' task is not completed; rather, it is only the beginning. There is still a long journey to go through the desert before a similar miracle has to be repeated for Joshua, forty years later, to permit them to cross the dry bed of the river Jordan into the promised land (Joshua 3:7-17).

Throughout the rest of the Old Testament, this act of God in bringing the Israelites through the water and saving them from their pursuing enemies is viewed as both the beginning of Israel's history and also the basis for its continuing relationship with God. Samuel, David and Solomon all look back to this at key events, recalling how God had brought them out of Egypt (see, for example, 1 Sam. 12:8; 2 Sam. 7:23; 1 Kings 8:16, 51-53). The Psalms constantly praise God for it and use it remind both God and the Israelites of the covenant they made together at Sinai afterwards (e.g., Pss. 78; 80:8; 105:43; 136:10-16).

Thus it is not at all surprising that the early Christians brought together the deliverance of Israel through the sea and their own experience of being set free through baptism into Christ. Paul says that 'our ancestors . . . were baptized into Moses in the cloud and in the sea . . . and the rock was Christ' (1 Cor. 10:1-4). Therefore, his readers must press on in their own journey of faith as they follow Christ. A few centuries later, Gregory of Nyssa interprets the crossing of the Red Sea as an allegory for the Christian being pursued by the 'passions of the soul' which seek to enslave us; they must be drowned in the waters of baptism, just as the Egyptians were, if we are to find life. But he also warns about those who try to continue with their old ways after they have set out on the Christian path (*Life of Moses,* II.121-129). The oppression and alienation which we seek to leave behind will also try to pursue us on the way, just as surely as the dark forces of Darth Vader pursue the heroes of *Star Wars.* Jesus has not just splashed down to rescue us from evil, but he calls us to enter through him as our Gateway, and to drown our old sinful ways by being baptized into him.

For Prayer and Meditation

We thank you, almighty God, for the gift of water
to sustain, refresh and cleanse all life.
Over water the Holy Spirit moved in the beginning of creation.
Through water you led the children of Israel
from slavery in Egypt to freedom in the Promised Land.
In water your Son Jesus received the baptism of John
and was anointed by the Holy Spirit as the Messiah, the Christ,
to lead us from the death of sin to newness of life.

The first part of the prayer over the water in the
baptism service from *Common Worship*

8

New Life through the Water

When you were buried with him in baptism, you were also raised with him through faith in the power of God, who raised him from the dead. . . . Put to death, therefore, whatever in you is earthly: fornication, impurity, passion, evil desire, and greed (which is idolatry). On account of these the wrath of God is coming on those who are disobedient. These are the ways you also once followed, when you were living that life. But now you must get rid of all such things — anger, wrath, malice, slander, and abusive language from your mouth. Do not lie to one another, seeing that you have stripped off the old self with its practices and have clothed yourselves with the new self, which is being renewed in knowledge according to the image of its creator. In that renewal there is no longer Greek and Jew, circumcised and uncircumcised, barbarian, Scythian, slave and free; but Christ is all and in all! As God's chosen ones, holy and beloved, clothe yourselves with compassion, kindness, humility, meekness, and patience. Bear with one another and, if anyone has a complaint against another, forgive each other; just as the Lord has forgiven you, so you also must forgive. Above all, clothe yourselves with love, which binds everything together in perfect harmony.

COLOSSIANS 2:12; 3:5-14

It is not easy to recognize that all you may have hoped for in the world is a dream. In *The Matrix,* the computer software engineer, Thomas Anderson (known as 'Neo' when on-line), is confronted by the rebels who have broken into his world. Their leader is called Morpheus, a name which suggests the idea of 'change' — and that is precisely what he offers Neo. He has to convince Neo that the world is a computer-generated illusion 'that has been pulled over your eyes to blind you from the truth . . . that you are a slave'. As Morpheus says, 'All I'm offering is the truth, nothing more', Neo has to make his decision, to choose either the blue pill or the red one; one will return him to his dream world, the other to reality. When he chooses the red pill, then Neo suddenly awakes in a watery chamber, like an incubator or a cocoon. He has been connected to lots of tubes which are extracting his electrical energy to feed the artificial intelligences which are really running the world. Painfully, he peels off the tubes, pulling them out of his body. He is then flushed out from the water to begin his new life (which his name 'Neo' hints at). Morpheus greets him with 'Welcome to the real world', but since his muscles are atrophied from lack of use, Neo has to learn everything all over again as he becomes part of Morpheus' crew.

Morpheus is a figure like John the Baptist. John also came offering a change, as he went around preaching repentance and preparing for the kingdom of God. He used immersion in the river Jordan for people to wash away their old lives and to come up from the water to begin again. After the death and resurrection of Jesus, this idea of washing and submersion was linked to his death and new life. Colossians 2:12, the start of today's passage, makes this explicit: to be baptized is to be overwhelmed, drowned and buried under the water, which is interpreted as being buried with Jesus. Then to come up out of the water is to be 'raised with him through faith in the power of God, who raised him from the dead'.

Paul uses the same idea in his classic exposition of the theology and meaning of baptism in Romans 6. 'Do you not know that all of us who have been baptized into Christ Jesus were baptized into his death? Therefore we have been buried with him by baptism into death, so that, just as Christ was raised from the dead by the glory of the Father, so we too might walk in newness of life' (Rom. 6:3-4). Baptism is a form of death, the death which we deserve to die because of our sin and selfishness, envy and oppression of others. Yet Jesus, the sinless one, enters into our world, identifies with us in his baptism and then dies for our sin on the cross. So when we are baptized into his death, it is as though we have died to that old way of life, the sin and selfishness. We cannot go back to it, any more than Neo can go back to his former existence in the computer world once he has made his decision. Instead, the tubes, the connections to the old way of life, the ties that bind us, must all be stripped away so that we can go forward into new life.

C. S. Lewis has a marvellous picture of this in *The Voyage of the 'Dawn Treader'*. After persecuting his cousins for their belief in Narnia, Eustace pursues them even through falling into the water in the magical picture on the wall. Even though he is now in Narnia too, he refuses to recognize it and continues in his old ways, being as thoroughly obnoxious and selfish as ever. Eventually he is transformed, by sleeping on a dragon's hoard, into a dragon himself; only then does he realize what his greed has done to him. This makes him into rather a better person as a dragon than ever he was as a boy, until one night he has what seems to be a very odd dream. Aslan, 'the great Lion and son of the Emperor over Sea', appears to him and takes him to a large well to be washed. But the dragon-Eustace must undress first, and twice he peels off his scales and skin to no avail, just revealing the same underneath. Eventually he has to allow himself to be undressed by Aslan, which is very painful, making a deep tear 'right into my heart'. Aslan throws Eustace into the water, where the pain is gone and he is reborn back into a boy. Then the lion dresses him 'in new clothes' and sends him back to rejoin the rest of the company. The change, however, is not immediately all-embracing. Eustace 'began to be a different boy'. He still 'had relapses . . . when he could be very tiresome. But the cure had begun' (pp. 92-99).

The early Christians often built churches by a stream or river. People who wanted to leave their old way of life would come to be baptized, arriving on the far bank in their old clothes. These would then have to be stripped off so that the candidates could enter the water to be immersed three times in the name of the Father, the Son and the Holy Spirit. This also symbolized being drowned, dying to the old life and being incorporated into the death of Christ. They would be brought out of the water on the side by the church, to be given new white robes for their new life, and then taken in to be welcomed by the rest of God's people. This symbolism continued through various practices in the history of the church, such as the custom of having special white baptismal gowns. Fonts were positioned near the entrance door in churches, some of which are big enough to immerse infants. For those who are immersed as adults, too, there is great opportunity for such dramatic symbolism.

Today's passage probably preserves some of the early teaching which was given to new converts where this exchange of old clothes, death and new robes is interpreted ethically for a new way of life. We have to 'put to death' the old earthly ways of impurity and greed, anger and slander. This is what has caused the Mess in our world — and we followed them just like everybody else (3:5-8). But now 'you have stripped off the old self' just like Eustace shedding his skin, or the first Christians their old clothes. Those who have been baptized 'have clothed yourselves with the new self', and we must 'put on' or wear the new clothes of compassion and kindness, finishing it all off, like a belt, with 'love which binds everything together in perfect harmony' (3:12-15). What is more, baptism can never be a solitary, individual thing. We are renewed in the company of others, and the new way of life breaks down the barriers of race, education and social status so that 'Christ is all and in all!' (3:11).

Starting out on this journey to new life can be painful — but so are all births. Like Neo, we are connected by so many ties that bind us to our old ways. Like Eustace, we may try to remove our own scales — but only Christ can truly cleanse us and give us his new life. But then it requires working together in the company of God's people to learn how to grow into our new clothes.

For Prayer and Meditation

We thank you, Father, for the water of baptism.
In it we are buried with Christ into his death.
By it we share in his resurrection.
Through it we are reborn by the Holy Spirit.
Therefore, in joyful obedience to your Son,
we baptize into his fellowship those who come to him in faith.
Now sanctify this water that, by the power of your Holy Spirit,
they may be cleansed from sin and born again.
Renewed in your image, may they walk by the light of faith
and continue for ever in the risen life of Jesus Christ our Lord;
to whom with you and the Holy Spirit
be all honour and glory, now and for ever. Amen.

The continuation of the prayer over the water
in the baptism service from *Common Worship*

9

Setting Out into the Darkness

Now the LORD *said to Abram, 'Go from your country and your kindred and your father's house to the land that I will show you. I will make of you a great nation, and I will bless you, and make your name great, so that you will be a blessing. I will bless those who bless you, and the one who curses you I will curse; and in you all the families of the earth shall be blessed.' So Abram went, as the* LORD *had told him. . . .*

After these things the word of the LORD *came to Abram in a vision, 'Do not be afraid, Abram, I am your shield; your reward shall be very great.' . . . He brought him outside and said, 'Look toward heaven and count the stars, if you are able to count them.' Then he said to him, 'So shall your descendants be.' And he believed the* LORD*; and the* LORD *reckoned it to him as righteousness.*

GENESIS 12:1-4a; 15:1, 5-6

In *2001: A Space Odyssey,* David Bowman has no idea of the real reason for his mission. He and Frank Poole pilot the *Discovery* towards Jupiter, believing they are on a voyage of 'discovery' and exploration. It is only after the failure of the computer and the loss of the rest of the crew that he finally comes face to face with yet another monolith in space — a counterpoint to the one which enhanced Moon-Watcher and the apes millions of years ago, only hugely bigger. Like the other monoliths, its length, width and height are in the proportions of 1 : 4 : 9, but it is over a mile high. It is totally impervious to all the instruments, radio waves and X-rays which Bowman uses to probe it; it just sits there, waiting. Eventually, Bowman decides that the only thing to do is to leave the safety of *Discovery,* and travel down to it in a small personal pod: 'I've come a billion miles — I don't want to be stopped by the last sixty' (p. 217).

Not knowing what awaits him, he sets out, hovers above the monolith and tries to land — only to find that it opens up and swallows him and his pod down into utter darkness. It is, in fact, a 'Star Gate' — and it transports Bowman across the universe in a helter-skelter ride which Stanley Kubrick filmed in an exciting whirlwind feast of colours and images, extremely adventurous for cinema of the late 1960s. Bowman realizes that this is a transport system, and goes through the equivalent of a 'Grand Central Station of the Galaxy', until he comes to rest in a synthetic environment, prepared for him by the aliens which have brought him there (pp. 225-249). All he could do was to set out — the journey and his situation have been totally out of his control: 'Logic told him that he must surely be under the protection of some controlling and almost omnipotent intelligence' (p. 236).

This theme of the hero who sets out willingly, but unknowingly, into the darkness is common in many of our stories. Similarly Dr Edwin Ransom is willing to get into the white, coffin-like box in which he is to be transported to Venus, without having any idea of how he is protected on the way or what he is to do when he gets there. As he explains to 'Lewis' the author, 'Well — simply I have been ordered there' (*Voyage to Venus,* p. 18).

Bowman and Ransom both just set out, not knowing what lies ahead. Thereafter, all they can do, in the words of the old chorus, is 'trust and obey'. This is exactly how the story of Israel begins. God takes the initiative and calls Abram to go, to leave his country and family and home (Gen. 12:1). It is never explained why God called Abram, and not any of the many others named and listed after the Tower of Babel in the previous chapter, Genesis 11. The call simply comes that Abram is to leave behind his old way of life and set out for the land God will show him in due course; but in the meantime he does not know where he is going. Most of us would have many questions or hesitations: 'Why me? Where are we going? How will we get there? Is it safe? Do I really have to leave all this behind?' We might even suggest that God sends somebody else — but all that Genesis records is simple obedience: 'So Abram went, as the Lord had told him' (Gen. 12:4).

Others may be willing to go because they want adventure, even if they are not sure where or what. Thus in Episode I of *Star Wars, The Phantom Menace,* the child Anakin Skywalker is keen for adventure and responds to the call to leave his mother and set out to train as a Jedi Knight. Similarly, Harry Potter is more than happy to answer the call from Hogwarts to leave behind life among ordinary people, known as

Muggles, and to set off, even if his journey begins by having to go through the barrier and the brick wall to get to Platform Nine and Three-Quarters, which he cannot actually see.

The history of the Christian church includes many ordinary people who responded to the call of God to leave everything behind and set off not knowing quite where they are going, but wanting to spread the gospel and help others. Thus Paul has a vision of a man from Macedonia pleading with him to 'cross over and help us', which is what determines him to leave Asia Minor and bring the Christian message first to the continent of Europe (Acts 16:9). Like Anakin Skywalker and Harry Potter, after escaping from slavery in Ireland, St Patrick first went for training, to do his theology and to become a priest. But then, when he returned home to the west of Britain, he had a dream of a man from Ireland, Victoricus, coming to him with 'the cry of the Irish', calling him to come across and take the gospel to Ireland (Patrick, *Confessions* 23) — and we can think of other Celtic saints like Columba or Chad, braving land and sea to obey their call.

Similarly, many other Christian missionaries heard the call of God and left everything behind to travel to distant parts of the globe during the great expansion of the 18th and 19th centuries. One of the most famous, Gladys Aylward, was so sure of her call that she had to push through all the 'barriers' the missionary societies and churches put up against her — and she set off for China, not really knowing where to go or how she would live. Yet she became a great source of blessing to many in that land. This stress on blessing comes five times in God's call to Abram. The call of Abram is seen by Jews as their origin, as he becomes their 'exalted father', which is what the name 'Abram' means: 'I will make of you a great nation'. But Abram's response will have universal scope and consequences, for God will bless him, and in him 'all the families of the earth shall be blessed' (Gen. 12:2-3).

But first he has to be willing to obey, to go 'as the Lord had told him', to journey out into the darkness of not knowing. St John of the Cross describes the Christian journey as responding to the call of God, but going into darkness. Conversion is the first stage, but the process of growth as a Christian leads into the 'dark night' of the senses and then of the soul and spirit, as we learn to have everything stripped away and rely on God alone.

Yet even the darkness has stars. As he enters into the Star Gate, David

Bowman's last recorded words sent back to earth are 'My God — it's full of stars' (p. 221). How Abram will become the source of blessing for all the earth is revealed to him later in a vision one night. God reveals his identity as Abram's 'shield' or protection, yet Abram demurs because he and Sarah have no children. God tells him to go outside, look up into the night sky and to count the stars — and the promise is that his descendants will be as numerous as those infinite stars. Exactly how this will happen will not be told for several chapters yet, but Abram believes God, and this is considered enough: 'The Lord reckoned it to him as righteousness' (Gen. 15:1-6). Of course, we know the story of the miraculous birth of Isaac (Gen. 21), through whom the Jews trace their descent. But Abram is not just the ancestor of the Jews, for his name is changed from 'exalted father' to Abraham, 'the father of a multitude of nations' in Genesis 17:5 — and to this day, Muslims also look to him as their forefather, while Christians see him as the spiritual father of all who share his faith in the God who calls us to set out (see Romans 4).

David Bowman set out into the darkness of the Star Gate and eventually returned to our solar system as a new creation, the 'Star-Child' (p. 255). Abraham obeys God's call, leaves everything behind and has a miraculous child to become the source of blessing for all the earth. As the children of God, we only know him as our Father because someone else obeyed his call and came to tell us. In response, can we really sit at home, going nowhere and telling no one?

For Prayer and Meditation

By faith, Abraham obeyed when he was called . . . and he set out, not knowing where he was going.

Hebrews 11:8

What is God calling you to do?
Respond to his call — and set out into the darkness.

10

Reluctant Heroes

Now the word of the Lord *came to Jonah son of Amittai, saying, 'Go at once to Nineveh, that great city, and cry out against it; for their wickedness has come up before me.' But Jonah set out to flee to Tarshish from the presence of the* Lord. *He went down to Joppa and found a ship going to Tarshish; so he paid his fare and went on board, to go with them to Tarshish, away from the presence of the* Lord. . . . *Then the men were even more afraid, and said to him, 'What is this that you have done!' For the men knew that he was fleeing from the presence of the* Lord, *because he had told them so.*

JONAH 1:1-3, 10

The words of Jeremiah son of Hilkiah: . . . Now the word of the Lord *came to me saying, 'Before I formed you in the womb I knew you, and before you were born I consecrated you; I appointed you a prophet to the nations.' Then I said, 'Ah,* Lord *God! Truly I do not know how to speak, for I am only a boy.' But the* Lord *said to me, 'Do not say, "I am only a boy"; for you shall go to all to whom I send you, and you shall speak whatever I command you.'*

JEREMIAH 1:1, 4-7

The heroes of our stories in yesterday's study may not have known where they were going — but at least they were willing to go. Others, of course, may have some idea of what they think lies ahead, and for that very reason are unwilling to go. C. S. Lewis' interplanetary voyager, Dr Edwin Ransom, may have gone happily to Venus, despite not knowing why — but this is only because of his previous experiences on Mars, or Malacandra as it is known in the Old Solar language. In the first book of the trilogy, Ransom is drugged and then knocked out as he is abducted into the spaceship (*Out of the Silent Planet,* pp. 19-22). He thinks he has been taken to Mars as a human sacrifice, so he keeps running away even from those sent to help and guide him. Eventually, he is brought face to face with Oyarsa, the supernatural being who oversees the planet, and has to explain himself. Then he discovers that his fears were groundless, and Oyarsa is as good and loving as he is powerful (pp. 139-144).

The book of Jonah is a wonderful story of an unwilling anti-hero. Jonah, whose name means 'dove', is called by God to go east to preach against Nineveh, the capital of the Assyrians. But this 'dove' is immediately terrified — and flies off in the other direction, as Jonah books a passage for Tarshish, at the far western end of the ancient world in southern Spain. Of course, one cannot escape the call and presence of God that easily, and the ship is struck by a mighty storm (Jonah 1:1-4). The sailors, frightened by the wind and waves and even more by Jonah's attempt to flee from God, throw him overboard — and eventually he is brought through the great fish to preach in Nineveh itself. Even then, things do not go according to plan, because the king and people of Nineveh repent and God decides not to destroy them at all. Jonah's preaching has been successful, despite himself — but he goes off in a sulk, complaining that this is why he fled in the first place, because he knew that God is 'a gracious God and merciful, slow to anger and abounding in steadfast love' (Jonah 4:2)!

This kind of comic anti-hero appears in much humorous science fiction also. Thus Arthur Dent is taken by Ford Prefect when he hitches a ride with the Vogon Constructor Fleet, who destroy the earth to make way for a new hyperspace bypass. Far from being grateful, he did not want to go and, like Jonah, spends all his time moaning about it — and yet he is the key to all that happens subsequently in the *Hitchhiker's Guide to the Galaxy.* Similarly, Terry Pratchett's bungling wizard, Rincewind, tries as hard as possible not to get involved in things and live an ordinary life, but, despite himself, ends up saving the Discworld on many occasions.

On a more serious level, much of *Deep Space Nine* has revolved around the role of its Commander and later Captain, Benjamin Sisko. In the very first episode, he is declared by the Bajorans' spiritual leader to have a great spiritual significance. After meeting 'the prophets' in the wormhole, he is recognized as the long-foretold 'Emissary' to the Bajorans. At first, he is very reluctant and uncomfortable in this calling, although it becomes more and more important as the years go by. In the seventh and final series, it becomes apparent that he was known and appointed for this task even before he was born and he finally comes to accept his calling.

Jeremiah was also known 'in the womb' and consecrated by God to be a prophet before he was born (Jer. 1:5). Nonetheless, when the call of God does eventually come to him, he has his excuses ready: 'I do not know how to speak, for I am only a boy'. His protestations are to no avail for God will give him the words to speak. Later, Jeremiah uses the image of having eaten the words of God before he can speak them (Jer. 15:16). However, his message of doom and judgment constantly causes him to struggle with his call, being weary of holding the wrath of God inside himself, and yet reluctant to speak out when no one will listen (Jer. 6:11).

The burden of such power and responsibility can lie heavily on those called to bear it. Thus, when the wizard Gandalf explains the importance of the Ring, Frodo the hobbit wants to give up the responsibility. After Gandalf explains that he cannot, but must travel with it to the Fire-Mountain to prevent the Enemy from obtaining it, Frodo realizes he must set off and leave the Shire. But time goes by: 'To tell the truth, he was very reluctant to start. . . . "As for where I am going," said Frodo, "I have no clear idea myself yet"' (*The Lord of the Rings*, p. 78). Similarly, in Stephen Donaldson's *Chronicles of Thomas Covenant the Unbeliever*, Covenant, who is an impotent leper in our world, is transported against his will to another Land where he has great power derived from the white gold of his wedding ring. However, he cannot use it because he does not believe in his power — and without it the Land is in peril. He is constantly torn between his own sense of unworthiness and his desire to help the people he comes to know there. It is only because of his love for them that he eventually succeeds in his struggle.

When the prophet Isaiah has his vision in the temple of 'the Lord sitting on his throne, high and lifted up', he is overwhelmed by the sense of the holiness of God as he listens to the song of the seraphim, 'Holy, holy, holy is the LORD of hosts; the whole earth is full of his glory.' Such an experience only brings home to him his own sin and inadequacy as 'a man of unclean lips' who lives 'among a people of unclean lips'. When he realizes that he has been made clean, he responds to the call of God to go back to his people: 'Here am I; send me' (Is. 6:1-8). Similarly, Ezekiel has a vision of God with the exiles by the waters of the river Chebar in Babylon, when God appears on his chariot throne — like some sort of spaceship with its 'wheels within wheels'. For him too, this experience leads to mission as he is given a scroll to eat with 'words of lamentation and woe' that he is to take to the house of Israel (Ezek. 1–3).

Such reluctant prophets are not confined to biblical times. C. S. Lewis records the moment when he finally recognized that no matter how hard he tried to flee in the opposite direction, God was confronting him: 'That which I greatly feared had at last come upon me. In the Trinity Term of 1929 I gave in, and admitted that God was God, and knelt and prayed: perhaps, that night, the most dejected and reluctant convert in all England' (*Surprised by Joy,* Geoffrey Bles, 1955, p. 215). Lewis is amazed by 'the divine humility which would accept a convert even under such terms' — and yet he then goes on to take the Christian message to the people of his own day and since, writing not just the Narnia stories and the science fiction trilogy about Ransom, but also his many other books seeking to explain Christianity in a clear and reasonable way. For all his reluctance, he became one of the most influential communicators of the gospel of the last century.

And so it is for all of our reluctant heroes. Much to his own annoyance, Jonah's preaching is successful and Nineveh's 'more than a hundred and twenty thousand persons and many animals' are saved (Jonah 4:11). Ransom, Sisko, Frodo and Covenant all have to battle with themselves, and yet eventually help to save those to whom they were sent. The struggle to hear God's word, to accept it and to take it to people who do not want to listen was not easy for Jeremiah and the other ancient Jewish prophets, any more than it was for C. S. Lewis. So why should we expect it to be any different for us? Yet God goes on calling his reluctant people to go in his name and to take his love, even to those who do not want to hear.

For Prayer and Meditation

Lord Jesus, give us ears to hear your word,
eyes to see your people's need,
and brave hearts to go where you call.

11

Turning Around

I myself was convinced that I ought to do many things against the name of Jesus of Nazareth. . . . I was travelling to Damascus with the authority and commission of the chief priests, when at midday along the road, your Excellency, I saw a light from heaven, brighter than the sun, shining around me and my companions. When we had all fallen to the ground, I heard a voice saying to me in the Hebrew language, 'Saul, Saul, why are you persecuting me? It hurts you to kick against the goads.' I asked, 'Who are you, Lord?' The Lord answered, 'I am Jesus whom you are persecuting. But get up and stand on your feet; for I have appeared to you for this purpose, to appoint you to serve and testify to the things in which you have seen me and to those in which I will appear to you. I will rescue you from your people and from the Gentiles — to whom I am sending you to open their eyes so that they may turn from darkness to light and from the power of Satan to God, so that they may receive forgiveness of sins and a place among those who are sanctified by faith in me.'

ACTS 26:9, 12-18

In their search to find the Gateway and leave behind the Mess of our world, our various heroes have had different reactions. Some are looking for adventure and set out willingly, but they do not know where they are going, while others struggle and are reluctant. More difficult still are those going in the opposite direction who have to be turned right around in order to start the journey.

Perhaps the most obvious example is the character from *Voyager* known as 'Seven of Nine, Tertiary Adjunct of Unimatrix Zero One'. She is a member of the Borg collective, the terrifying enemy comprised of individuals from many races who have been 'assimilated' and given a number of mechanical and technological implants. They are inter-connected into a hive mind, 'voices in the head', with all personal identity gone. Seven was assimilated when still only a human child, and her original name, Annika Hansen, means nothing to her; she prefers to keep her Borg 'designation', Seven of Nine. She is initially assigned to *Voyager* during a rare truce between the humans and the Borg to fight a common enemy, Species 8472. However, she becomes separated from the collective and undergoes a long and painful process of learning to be human again. Some of the crew do not trust her, while many other aliens fear her — yet she eventually responds to Captain Janeway's confidence and faith in her, becoming a valued member of the crew. She even saves her friends and the ship itself from the Borg on several occasions, as together they seek to journey back towards human space.

In fact, all of the *Star Trek* series feature this preoccupation with what being truly human means and the journey into humanity. In the original series, Mr Spock is the Science Officer, the first Vulcan to join Starfleet. In fact, he is half human, but he defied his Vulcan father, the diplomat Sarek, to go to the Academy. He too is treated with prejudice and suspicion by some humans, because Vulcans look like and are related to the Romulans, Starfleet's merciless enemy. Much of the series' conflict and humour arise through Spock's relationship with the all-too-human Dr Leonard McCoy, and Spock never totally understands humans. This human-Vulcan dynamic recurs in Enterprise, where the female Vulcan science officer, T-Pol, tries to cope with the reactions, and even suspicions, of her new human colleagues.

Similarly, in *The Next Generation*, an android, known simply as 'Data', actively seeks to become human as he establishes the rights of artificial life-forms, learns to dream and even manages to master his emotions chip. Yet his predecessors were treated with hostility by fearful humans, and his elder 'brother' Lore is evil, bringing first the Crystalline Entity to destroy humans and then setting himself up as the leader of some renegade Borg to destroy the Federation. Only with Data's help are these threats averted.

Finally, in *Deep Space Nine*, the Security Chief is a 'changeling', a liquid being who can take different forms and is known as 'Odo', which means literally 'nothing' in the local language. He learns to mimic humans and to experience human emotions like love, although he never quite gets his face right! His search to find others like him leads to the discovery that his people are the enemy, the 'Founders' of the evil Dominion. In the ensuing war, Odo plays a crucial role in Starfleet's eventual victory, but afterwards goes to help his people build a new life.

One of my favourite Christmas cards had on the outside, 'This Christmas, be like God', while inside it said, 'Become human'! For it is a fact that none of us are as God intended humans to be: our sin and selfishness, tendency to hatred, murder and oppression, which cause the Mess in the world, are evidence of that. Yet, like Data, we are always trying to become more human — even if we have problems with our emotions! Odo needed a pattern into which to form himself to learn how to shift his shape — and our pattern is Jesus of Nazareth. Yes, Jesus became human to show us what God is like — but it was also to demonstrate what it means to be truly human, so that we could be more fully what God intended us to be. In Jesus' love and compassion, we see how humans were meant to behave. In his suffering forgiveness of those who flog him and nail him to the cross, he gives us an example to follow. The famous scene in John's Gospel where Pilate parades Jesus in front of the crowd has been often painted with the title *'Ecce Homo'*, the Latin version of Pilate's words, 'Behold — the human being!' (Jn. 19:5).

What is more, says Paul, he became human because of our opposition to God: 'While we were enemies, we were reconciled to God through the death of his Son' (Rom. 5:10). As Captain Janeway separated Seven from the thoughts of the Borg collective, so God wants to take us from our collective obedience to the voices of sin in our heads, and remake us back into the unique individuals he created and loves. Jesus wants to turn us around (which is what 'convert' means) and stop us being the enemies of God, so that he can send us back to help our people.

After all, Paul should know. As he says earlier in the speech from which today's passage comes, he lived his life as a Pharisee, the 'strictest group' within Judaism (Acts 26:5). He had studied hard and worked long to try to understand the will of God, and threw himself into opposing 'the name of Jesus of Nazareth' and persecuting his followers far and wide in his zeal to keep his religion pure (26:9-11). Yet such is God's grace and mercy that even while he was on the road to Damascus to attack more Christians, Jesus appeared to him to explain that Paul was really persecuting him (26:14). It was something which became the motivating force of the rest of Paul's life and he refers to it frequently in his letters (e.g., 1 Cor. 15:8-10; Gal. 1:12-16).

Furthermore, the former enemy became the apostle, as Paul was given the mission to go to all the nations 'to open their eyes so that they may turn from darkness to light' (Acts 26:18). All his former zeal became the driving force behind his missionary journeys; all his great learning was used now to produce his letters, which have been central for the development of the Christian church and theology. Behind it all was his concern, 'as I tell you now even with tears', for those who were as he used to be, that 'many live as enemies of the cross of Christ' (Phil. 3:18). But Jesus taught us to 'love your enemies' and died forgiving those who crucified him (Lk. 6:35; 23:34).

Jesus is the true human being, who has splashed down in our world, and calls us to travel from our Mess to his Father's house. He is both the door and the way itself, so we must enter through him and follow him. We must die to the old ways which pursue us through the waters of baptism, stripping away the ties that bind and putting on his new life as we respond to his call together. Some of us may be keen for adventure, but do not know where we are going; others respond reluctantly and yet not a few are enemies who need to be turned around, converted, to head in the right direction. Whichever, God loves each and every one of us and calls us to become truly human as we shape ourselves to the pattern of his Son, Jesus Christ — and as we do this, so we begin to discover our real identity in the pilgrim people of God.

For Prayer and Meditation

'I turn to Christ.'

This simple baptismal promise is the heart of the Christian decision. What areas of your life still need to be turned to Christ?

PART 3

THE COMPANY

Now we discover that 'we are not alone'. The experience of travelling together with companions we may not have chosen enables us to explore our differences and gifts and to find life in common with others.

12

The Company

Jesus went out to the mountain to pray; and he spent the night in prayer to God. And when day came, he called his disciples and chose twelve of them, whom he also named apostles: Simon, whom he named Peter, and his brother Andrew, and James, and John, and Philip, and Bartholomew, and Matthew, and Thomas, and James son of Alphaeus, and Simon who was called the Zealot, and Judas son of James, and Judas Iscariot, who became a traitor.

LUKE 6:12-16

There is an old story told about the return of Jesus to heaven after his resurrection. After he ascended out of the sight of the disciples, he came back towards the pearly gates. As he approached, the archangel Gabriel came out to greet him and welcome him home. He was also anxious to know if Jesus' mission had been successful and enquired what the next steps might be. 'That depends,' said Jesus to Gabriel's amazement, 'on the twelve people I have left in charge.' 'Twelve!' spluttered Gabriel. 'That's not much to change the world with.' 'It is enough,' replied Jesus calmly, and passed through the gates back towards his Father.

They were indeed a motley crew. The Gospels do not even agree about the names of the twelve, and recognize the existence of other disciples too. There are various stories in the first sections of each Gospel about Jesus calling certain people to follow him — but they seem a curious choice. They come from different backgrounds, with none of the usual qualifications or leadership training, and some of them will let him down. And yet, within a few years they would be turning upside down the mightiest empire ever seen by the world at that time, and since then millions of people down the centuries and across the globe have followed their example. The effect of the church — for good and for bad — has been incalculable, and it all began with those few people being brought together. It is therefore right that after considering the various ways into our journey from the Mess the world is in, we should turn now to look at the Company we will be keeping along the way.

After all, so many of our stories also begin with a group of people around whom all the action will take place. Even those who have never seen an episode of *Star Trek* can recognize members of the crew of the starship *Enterprise,* if only from various parodies or impressions — as is obvious from the success of the comic science fiction film, *Galaxy Quest.* There is the coolly logical Vulcan Science Officer, Mr Spock, lifting one quizzical eyebrow, much to the exasperation of 'Bones', the all-too-emotional Dr Leonard McCoy. Meanwhile the broad Scots brogue of the Chief Engineer, Lt Commander Montgomery Scott, universally known as 'Scotty', announces this week's disaster which will blow up the ship unless he can work a miracle with the laws of physics in the next five minutes! Back on the bridge, there is the endless banter between the ethnically diverse Lt Hikaru Sulu and Ensign Pavel Chekov getting in the way of the communications officer, the beautiful Lt Uhura. Presiding over all of them is the famous Captain James T. Kirk, attempting to harness this motley gang into the finest crew in Starfleet. Is it just coincidence that 'kirk' is also the old Scottish name for 'church', both words being ultimately derived from the New Testament Greek adjective, *kyriak-,* meaning 'belonging to the Lord'?

A similar 'broad church' is found in the ship's crew in each of the other *Star Trek* series. *The Next Generation* began with Captain Picard assembling his crew through their 'Encounter at Farpoint', while Commander Sisko has to assemble his team to run the space station in the pilot episode of *Deep Space Nine.* In the first episode of *Voyager,* Captain Janeway not only has to pick her crew at the beginning, but also to rebuild it together with the Maquis freedom fighters they were chasing, after both crews suffer huge losses in the sudden trip to the Delta Quadrant.

Most sci-fi stories also feature a ship's Company comprised of different members — from Han Solo and Chewbacca flying the *Millennium Falcon* in *Star Wars* to Zaphod Beeblebrox and Ford Prefect in the ship *Heart of Gold,* powered by the improbability drive, in the *Hitchhiker's Guide to the Galaxy.* But it is not only ships' crews which provide these interesting groups of people. A large part of the appeal of the *Harry Potter* stories stems from the relationships of Harry Potter and his little circle of friends, especially Hermione Granger and Ron Weasley. We like to see how they are all going to get on and overcome their various differences to solve the current puzzle or problem.

In the light of these various groups, perhaps Jesus' choice of disciples is not so strange after all. Like the Starfleet captains, he gives careful consideration to them first — but even more important, according to Luke's account, was prayer. Jesus had a lot of disciples, general followers who wanted to 'learn' (which is what disciple means) from him. But he spends 'all the night in prayer to God' (Lk. 6:12) before choosing his group of twelve — rather like consulting Headquarters! Their actual names may vary, so that Thaddaeus in Matthew 10:3 and Mark 3:18 is here renamed or replaced by 'Judas son of James' (6:16), and John has other key central figures like Nathaniel or Lazarus. However, the number is crucial, always twelve, reminding us of the twelve tribes of Israel. At the last supper, Jesus says that the twelve will join him in his Father's kingdom, sitting on thrones to judge the twelve tribes of Israel (Lk. 22:30).

The mixture is no less diverse than any ship's crew. Simon is chosen to be like the 'first officer', and given a new name, 'Peter' in Greek or 'Cephas' in Aramaic, both of which mean 'rock'. Yet he will be 'rocky' or wobbly before he really becomes the solid foundation for the later church. In fact, 'Simon' was the name of one of the heroes of the Maccabean revolt, the struggle for Jewish independence in the middle of the second century BC, and other names in this list also recall other nationalist leaders like John, Matthew, and Judas. Certainly the other Simon is identified by Luke as 'the Zealot', one of the freedom fighters whose 'zeal' for the Lord led them to oppose the Romans; in the other Gospels he is called 'the Cananaean', which may have similar connotations (Matt. 10:4; Mk. 3:18). On the other hand, Matthew may be named after a hero, but he is traditionally identified with the tax collector, called 'Levi' in Luke's previous chapter, but 'Matthew' in Matthew's Gospel (Lk. 5:27-32; Matt. 9:9-13; 10:3). We might expect the sparks to fly between a collaborator like him and a Zealot, just as much as in any of our starship crews! Finally, we have Judas Iscariot, which may mean 'from Iscar' (the town Sychar or Kerioth?) but which could also be derived from *sicarius,* the Latin for 'dagger-carrier', which was how one of the groups fighting for freedom called themselves. Luke's terse comment 'who became a traitor' certainly reminds us of the dagger of betrayal within the heart of Jesus' inner circle.

This motley crew Luke now calls 'apostles', which means those who have been 'sent' in Greek (Lk. 6:13). Despite all their differences, or their suspect backgrounds or previous ways of life, they are now at the centre of Jesus' own mission. They will travel together, eat together, sleep together, listening to Jesus and watching him. For in due course, they will indeed be 'sent' to continue this mission, for which their only qualification is to have been 'with him' (Mk. 3:14). The enormity of this task would strain even Captain Kirk or Picard — but Jesus chooses them after spending all night in prayer to God, and he goes on choosing unlikely types like even you and me to carry on his mission.

Thus as we seek to respond to the call of God to enter upon the journey from the Mess of our world through the Gateway of Jesus himself, so we find that we never travel alone. We move from Captain Kirk to 'mother church'. We are part of the vast Company of men, women and children in the pilgrim people of God. Through this coming week, we shall explore what it means to be part of that Company, to travel together and to share life in common with others from very different backgrounds. Only in Christ can the barriers be broken down — yet we have also to cope with the tensions and even splits in the history of the church as we try to find our unity in diversity and see God's church grow.

For Prayer and Meditation

Almighty and everlasting God
by whose Spirit the whole body of the Church is governed and sanctified:
hear our prayer which we offer for all your faithful people;
that in their vocation and ministry
they may serve you in holiness and truth
to the glory of your name;
through our Lord and Saviour Jesus Christ, Amen.

Collect for Trinity 5, *Common Worship*

13

Travelling Together

Remember the long way that the L*ORD your God has led you these forty years in the wilderness, in order to humble you, testing you to know what was in your heart, whether or not you would keep his commandments. He humbled you by letting you hunger, then by feeding you with manna, with which neither you nor your ancestors were acquainted, in order to make you understand that one does not live by bread alone, but by every word that comes from the mouth of the* L*ORD. The clothes on your back did not wear out and your feet did not swell these forty years. Know then in your heart that as a parent disciplines a child so the* L*ORD your God disciplines you. Therefore keep the commandments of the* L*ORD your God, by walking in his ways and by fearing him. . . .*

Know, then, that the L*ORD your God is not giving you this good land to occupy because of your righteousness; for you are a stubborn people. Remember and do not forget how you provoked the* L*ORD your God to wrath in the wilderness; you have been rebellious against the* L*ORD from the day you came out of the land of Egypt until you came to this place.*

DEUTERONOMY 8:2-6; 9:6-7

From the earliest works of literature, some of the greatest stories of the world have been about epic journeys, undertaken by a small Company of people, often thrown together almost by accident, struggling together against hardships and a common enemy and forming deep relationships before they finally achieve their goal or reach their destination. In naming his film and novel, *2001: A Space Odyssey,* Arthur C. Clarke was paying homage to the ancient Homeric epic *The Odyssey,* the story of the return from Troy of one of the Greek leaders, Odysseus, as he seeks over some ten years to get home to his little island kingdom of Ithaca. Although he eventually arrives home alone, for much of the epic Odysseus is accompanied by his small ship's crew.

One of the most famous modern epics is J. R. R. Tolkien's *The Lord of the Rings,* written over a couple of decades from 1936 until the publication of its first two books in 1954. These are called *The Fellowship of the Ring,* and form the basis for the film of the same name, the first of the three films directed by Peter Jackson. The first book describes the departure of Frodo Baggins, a hobbit, from the Shire carrying the One Ring, which controls all the power of the other rings in Middle-earth. As he travels, he is pursued by the nine evil Black Riders, until he reaches the elven home of Rivendell. Here its elf-lord, Elrond, convenes a Council at which it is decided to form a group to take the Ring south: 'The Company of the Ring shall be Nine; and the Nine Walkers shall be set against the Nine Riders that are evil'. The nine are the four hobbits, Frodo, Sam, Merry and Pippin, Gandalf the wizard, Legolas the wood-elf, Gimli the dwarf and the men Aragorn and Boromir, to 'represent the Free Peoples of the World' (pp. 292-293). The whole of the second book is taken up with their hardships and travels, in which Gandalf is lost at the bridge of Khazad-dûm, until the Company is broken at the edge of the Wilderland. From here, Frodo and Sam must travel on alone to complete their mission. In his account of the travels of the Company of the Ring, Tolkien shows how the disparate, even antagonistic group of hobbits, men, dwarves and elves are formed into the Company by their shared trials and tribulations, and especially by the conflict against the evil Nine Riders.

George Lucas handles similar themes in *Star Wars.* In the original film, which is actually Episode IV of the saga, Luke Skywalker and the droids hire the ship *Millennium Falcon* with its pilot Han Solo and Chewbacca the Wookiee. As they fight together against the evil Darth Vader, rescue the beautiful Princess Leia and battle against the Death Star, so even the mercenary Han Solo cannot help becoming really involved as part of the group. Similarly in the *X-Files,* the rational and scientific Dr Dana Scully is assigned to watch and report on her FBI colleague Agent Fox Mulder, in his investigations into the bizarre and extreme cases of the paranormal and alien activity. Despite her scepticism, their shared experiences, including her own abduction, and their struggle against their faceless opponents only serve to unite them.

The story of the people of God also begins with such an epic journey, with its trials and tribulations and conflicts with opposing forces. After the Israelites escape from the oppression in Egypt and find their

Gateway through crossing the Red Sea, they have to face the wanderings in the desert of Sinai. After their miraculous deliverance from Pharaoh, they might have hoped to go straight to the promised land, 'flowing with milk and honey' — but not a bit of it. The rest of the book of Exodus and the whole of Numbers are taken up with their journey of forty years through the wilderness. Furthermore, the whole of the book of Leviticus (traditionally found between Exodus and Numbers) is about the laws and rituals which were given to the Israelites by God during their travels. Finally, Deuteronomy consists of three speeches, placed on the lips of Moses, which recap all the travels and lessons of the last forty years, culminating with his eventual death on the eve of their entry into the promised land. Thus nearly four of the first five books of the Bible, known together as the Pentateuch and revered by Jews as the Torah, or Law, are taken up with this epic journey of the people.

'Deuteronomy' literally means 'second law' in Greek, and it is usually thought to be a later book composed to remind the Israelites of their dependence upon God for their origins and for their continued existence. It may be the book found in the temple which inspires the reforms of King Josiah in 621 BC, as described in 2 Kings 22–23. Whether this is the case or not, it is clear that the book is to remind its audience of the lessons learned so painfully in the wilderness. Thus in the passage chosen for today, Moses tells them to 'Remember the long way that the LORD your God has led you these forty years in the wilderness' (Deut. 8:2). He is clear that it was God who was leading them all that time, and God who fed them with the manna and provided even for their clothes and shoes, disciplining them 'as a parent disciplines a child'. This was to teach them to rely upon him for everything and that people need not just material possessions: 'One does not live by bread alone, but by every word that comes from the mouth of the LORD' (8:3).

Throughout these chapters, Moses warns the Israelites not to become complacent, to forget God and to think that they have obtained all their wealth and security by their own strength (Deut. 8:11-20). Just as the Company of the Ring have to remember their mission and not use the Ring for their own benefit, or Luke Skywalker and Princess Leia must rely on the Force, so too must Israel trust in God. And exactly the same lesson is clear from the even longer epic of the history of the church. Like Israel, the church has known times of abundance and periods in the wilderness. Whenever the institutional church has acquired peace and prosperity, it too has often forgotten the goodness of God which has brought it to that place. On the other hand, it is often through the periods of persecution, of the struggle with evil, or in experiences of the desert that the church has really been united and Christians have rediscovered their proper relationship to God and one another.

Moses is clear that the Israelites will not keep the promised land in their own strength or righteousness. He reminds them, 'You are a stubborn people', and tells them to remember how often they were rebellious and 'provoked the LORD your God' (Deut. 9:6-7). Each of the groups in the different journeys in our stories also have to deal with those who grumble and complain and those who let the others down, and yet it is only by going through the journey together that they find their true identity and reach their goal. So too for us in the church. It is certainly not a perfect institution, and there are always others who will complain, or want to go in a different direction. But this is only to be expected from a group of human beings, seeking together to find a way out of the Mess of sin through the wilderness of this world as God guides us towards his promised land. Our only hope is to share it together, and to acknowledge who we are and where we have come from. This is why Deuteronomy stresses the importance of remembering and retelling the story. So too for us. If we want to be part of the Company and join in the Fellowship, so we must look back through the whole history of all God's people, look around at our companions and fellow travellers — and together look forward to the exciting journey to which God is calling us.

For Prayer and Meditation

Many Christians seem not to know much of the story of God's people. Why not spend some time looking at the first five books of the Bible, or get a simple introduction to the history of the church? It's an epic story, worthy of any Company!

14

Life in Common

They devoted themselves to the apostles' teaching and fellowship, to the breaking of bread and the prayers. Awe came upon everyone, because many wonders and signs were being done by the apostles. All who believed were together and had all things in common; they would sell their possessions and goods and distribute the proceeds to all, as any had need. Day by day, as they spent much time together in the temple, they broke bread at home and ate their food with glad and generous hearts, praising God and having the goodwill of all the people. And day by day the Lord added to their number those who were being saved.

ACTS 2:42-47

One of the problems faced by David Bowman and Frank Poole, the two-man crew of *Discovery* in *2001: A Space Odyssey*, was working mostly alone, taking turns to be on duty with only their computer HAL for company. By the time of the second voyage to visit the monolith around Jupiter in *2010: Odyssey Two*, the crew of the *Leonov* is much larger — seven Russians. When Dr Heywood Floyd has to be woken early from his hibernation, leaving his other two American colleagues still frozen in stasis, he looks forward to 'the "Six O'Clock Soviet", as the daily round-table conference was called', which may have only lasted about ten minutes, but which 'played a vital role in maintaining morale'. These meetings allowed for general comments and suggestions and 'good natured needling of the heavily-outnumbered American contingent'. The eight of them are squashed into the tiny common-room, and 'when he was not sleeping, much of Floyd's own time was spent in the common-room', which was decorated with pictures of Earth and other mementoes (*2010*, p. 87). When the other Americans are woken later and they all get down to their task of salvaging *Discovery* and investigating the monolith, these meetings continue to be very important, such as in the 'true confessions' episode (pp. 143-145).

Similarly, in all tales of school life, the common room plays an important part — and Hogwarts is no different, despite being a school for wizards. The Gryffindor Common Room is a vital place for Harry Potter and his friends to meet to exchange gossip, play games, share sweets and other goodies, and all the other activities which build up their sense of identity as members of their house.

The early Christian community also depended upon meeting together to build up their sense of identity. In the early chapters of Acts, we see the growth of the first Christians from a few frightened individuals huddled together behind locked doors after the crucifixion of Jesus. At first, Luke repeats the list of the apostles' names as they gather in the upper room to pray and to choose a successor to replace Judas Iscariot, so that they might be twelve once again (Acts 1:12-26). But after the power of the Holy Spirit comes upon them all at the day of Pentecost, this little group grows in confidence and numbers and they begin to become a real community, meeting in the temple and in each other's homes, as is shown in today's reading (Acts 2:46).

For a group to become a 'community', they have to share something in 'common', to meet together, sharing their hopes and fears, and becoming more united. It is a regular concern across the New Testament that the early Christians should grow together in this way. Thus Hebrews stresses the importance of meeting together as a way of encouraging each other: 'And let us consider how to provoke one another to love and good deeds, not neglecting to meet together, as is the habit of some, but encouraging one another, and all the more as you see the Day approaching' (Heb. 10:24-25). Paul, too, usually ends his letters with greetings and messages to various little groups, mentioning some individuals by name but also 'the church in their house' (Rom. 16:5; 1 Cor. 16:19).

This can also be seen in each of the different series of *Star Trek*. Social facilities are very important, as is shown by the lengths to which Commander Sisko goes when he first arrives on *Deep Space Nine* to ensure that Quark, the Ferengi, keeps his bar open, with its gaming tables and holosuites where people meet and talk and relax. Equally, Captain Janeway is rather taken back when she discovers that Neelix, who has become 'morale officer' for the crew so far from home, has turned her private dining-room on *Voyager* into a mess hall — yet time after time, its importance as a place to meet is vindicated. Indeed, there are times in *The Next Generation* when Guinan, the long-lived El-Aurian bartender played by Whoopi Goldberg, does as much pastoral care in her Ten-Forward lounge as any ship's Counsellor!

However, merely eating and drinking together is not enough. All our crews need to have briefings, to learn their orders, and to discuss what they might do in any particular situation. This happens in the observation lounge on the *Enterprise,* the briefing room on *Voyager* and the wardroom on *Deep Space Nine.* It is this combination of social activity and eating together, plus talking and learning, which builds these groups into the finest crews in Starfleet.

This is exactly the picture given to us by Luke of the early Christian church. In Acts 2:42, we have four marks of the Christian community which have been central through church history: 'They devoted themselves to the apostles' teaching and fellowship, to the breaking of bread and the prayers'.

Learning 'the apostles' teaching' is as vital as any crew seeking to understand their commander's orders. In the early church, it was the apostles, who had been 'with him', who taught the first believers the ideas which became the Christian faith. As the church grew, such teaching was increasingly given through letters and writings, which then became the books we have in the New Testament, as well as other works like the second-century *Didache,* which literally means the 'teaching'. So when we read the lessons in church, listen to sermons or share in Bible study groups, we too are devoting ourselves to 'the apostles' teaching'.

Such teaching and learning takes place in the context of a common life, the 'fellowship'. This word is often connected in the New Testament with the Holy Spirit, who is the source of our common life (2 Cor. 13:13). Such fellowship is given practical expression in today's passage by the emphasis on 'the breaking of bread'. While Acts 2:46 refers to general meals together through 'partaking of food in their homes with glad and generous hearts', the 'breaking of bread' in 2:42 as a mark of the church probably means the shared worship meal, sometimes called 'the Lord's Supper'. Its other names also reveal its significance, as 'eucharist' means thanksgiving, while the 'holy communion' brings us back again to the shared life. Finally, the mention of 'prayers' points out that the Christian community is not just another social club. The 'horizontal' relationship between human beings in church is only made possible because of our 'vertical' relationship with God. We discover that we are brothers and sisters in the family of God, because we share in the new life given to us by our heavenly Father. Therefore prayer, having communion with God, is the basis of any communion with one another.

These four elements — teaching, fellowship, breaking of bread and prayer — have been characteristics of the church in all its denominations and manifestations down through the ages. They are as vital in bringing new members into the warm fellowship as the common room meetings were for Floyd getting over his hibernation on *Leonov,* or for uniting any of our crews. But because the church is based in the love of God the Father, these four marks take it beyond any human club, and into the very life of the divine. No wonder Luke concludes that such a church was dynamic and growing, as 'day by day the Lord added to their number those who were being saved' (Acts 2:47).

For Prayer and Meditation

God our heavenly Father,
pour your grace upon your church
that in our teaching, worship and prayer
we may experience the fellowship of your Holy Spirit,
through Jesus Christ, your Son, our Lord, Amen.

15

Breaking Down Barriers

Remember that you were at that time without Christ, being aliens from the commonwealth of Israel, and strangers to the covenants of promise, having no hope and without God in the world. But now in Christ Jesus you who once were far off have been brought near by the blood of Christ. For he is our peace; in his flesh he has made both groups into one and has broken down the dividing wall, that is, the hostility between us. He has abolished the law with its commandments and ordinances, that he might create in himself one new humanity in place of the two, thus making peace, and might reconcile both groups to God in one body through the cross, thus putting to death that hostility through it. So he came and proclaimed peace to you who were far off and peace to those who were near; for through him both of us have access in one Spirit to the Father. So then you are no longer strangers and aliens, but you are citizens with the saints and also members of the household of God.

EPHESIANS 2:12-19

'We are alone in an uncharted part of the galaxy. We've already made some friends and some enemies. We have no idea of the dangers we are going to face — but one thing is clear — both crews are going to have to work together if we are going to survive. We will have to be one crew.' Captain Janeway's final speech at the end of 'Caretaker', the pilot episode of *Voyager*, sets up a major theme for the new series — how can two opposed groups be brought together? The Maquis may have seen themselves as freedom fighters, but to Starfleet they were terrorists. Thus *Voyager* was pursuing the Maquis ship when both were suddenly transported 70,000 light years into the Delta Quadrant. Both crews sustained heavy losses through this and their only hope of getting back home lies in working together on one ship, *Voyager*. However, getting both sides to accept each other and to work together as one crew is an enormous task. Not everyone can accept it, and it is only over the next few months and even years that the barriers are broken down as they strive together for the common aim of getting home.

Part of the difficulty and yet also part of the success arises from the fact that the hostility between the two groups is fairly recent. Some of the Maquis, especially their leaders, are actually people who left Starfleet to join the struggle. Longer-term hostility has to be bridged in the film of *2010*. During the time it takes for the Russian ship *Leonov* with its American passengers to get to Jupiter, the political situation on earth worsens even to the brink of war. When they eventually reach *Discovery* and restart her, both crews are ordered to separate by their respective governments back on earth and stay on their own ships. However, after the reborn David Bowman warns them of the imminent danger of staying in orbit around Jupiter, as with *Voyager*, both crews have to work together to get home. It is notable that this only happens in the film version, made in 1984 during the 'Star Wars' era of President Reagan, but not in Arthur C. Clarke's earlier novel of 1982 called *2010: Odyssey Two*.

The same motif also comes in *The Lord of the Rings*. The Company includes Legolas the elf and Gimli the dwarf, despite the deep-seated hostility between the two races since 'the Dark Days'. Although they are wary of each other at first, they gradually grow closer until they reach the elven territory of Lórien. When the local elves will only allow Gimli passage if he is blindfolded, Legolas and the rest of the Company agree to share his humiliation by also being blindfolded (pp. 362-368). After more adventures together, the elf and the dwarf 'had now become fast friends' (p. 392). Even after the Company is divided, these two are always together through the ensuing battles and trials, until eventually, after peace has been restored, they go together to visit each other's caves and woods on their way home (pp. 1014-1017).

The barriers between Jews and Gentiles in the ancient world were just as strong. The requirement for circumcision made it difficult for adult males to convert fully to Judaism. On the other hand, Jewish rituals and dietary laws made it impossible for them to eat with non-Jews. Thus Paul describes his Gentile readers as 'aliens' and 'strangers', cut off from Israel and God's promises, 'having no hope and without God in the world' (Eph. 2:12). He refers to the 'dividing wall of hostility' between them, where the word for 'wall', *fragmos,* means a partition and is connected with our words like 'fragment' and 'fracture' (2:14). Nor is this just a metaphor: in the temple in Jerusalem, there was a partition wall at the end of the Court of Gentiles, upon which notices in many languages were affixed stating that only Jews might go into the inner courts, and threatening the death penalty to any Gentiles found beyond. Thus, this 'dividing wall of hostility' was as real as the wall which separated the Communist east from the west in Berlin for several decades.

Arthur C. Clarke, writing in the early 1980s, assumed that this dividing wall would still be there in *2010*, and could not foresee the extraordinary events of 1989 when the Berlin wall was torn down. For Paul, what Christ has done is just as amazing. Jews and Gentiles might have been separated by cuts in the flesh at circumcision and the partition wall in the temple, but 'in his flesh he has made both groups into one and has broken down the dividing wall'. In place of 'the hostility between us', Jesus both 'is our peace' and is 'making peace', through proclaiming 'peace to you who were far off and peace to those who were near' (2:14-17). In *Star Wars, Episode I: The Phantom Menace,* the surface dwellers of Naboo and the Gungans who live below (who have been long estranged from each other) are united and the final word in the film is 'peace', uttered by the Gungan leader, Boss Nass.

For the Jews, 'peace' was never just the absence of war or conflict. Their word *shalom* conveys that, of course, but goes beyond it to include a sense of integrity and wholeness, of healing and well-being — all of which, says Paul, are brought to Jews and Gentiles alike, to create 'one new humanity' (2:15). This is a direct consequence of Christ's death on the cross, and now everyone, both 'near' and 'far', have 'access in one Spirit to the Father' (2:18).

The way in which we enter into this experience of the new humanity across all barriers is through the Gateway of baptism. In what has become a famous rallying-call, Paul wrote elsewhere: 'As many of you as were baptized into Christ have clothed yourselves with Christ. There is no longer Jew or Greek, there is no longer slave or free, there is no longer male and female; for all of you are one in Christ Jesus' (Gal. 3:27-28; see also Col. 3:11). Here all the major barriers in the ancient world, not just between Jews and Gentiles, but also between male and female, slave and free, are bridged in Christ. In Greek and Roman society, only free adult men were able to be proper citizens, while women, children and slaves could almost be treated as property. Yet the New Testament consistently stresses that all these barriers are broken down in Christ, as Jews and Gentiles are made one, husbands are told to love their wives, fathers to care for their children and masters to treat their slaves fairly (Eph. 5:21–6:9).

But the various groups in our stories do not accept each other immediately, and it has taken the long journey of the church to begin to see the implications of Christ's bringing us all into one humanity. Some of Paul's Jewish Christian readers wanted to circumcise their new Gentile brothers, but Paul's view eventually won the day. It took many more centuries for slavery to be abolished and even longer for women to be admitted into public ministry and for ordination. Christians must admit their responsibility for divisions in churches between black and white, and not just in South Africa, while various arguments even within denominations as well as between them still keep us apart. Yet Christ is still our peace, who has broken down 'the dividing wall'. As for Captain Janeway, 'one thing is clear': we cannot treat others as 'strangers and aliens', but accept and love them as our brothers and sisters, 'citizens with the saints and members of the household of God' (Eph. 2:19).

For Prayer and Meditation

Christ is our peace.
He has reconciled us to God in one body by his death on the cross.
Let us then pursue all that makes for peace
and builds up our common life.

What does sharing the Peace in church services mean to you? How can we take Christ's peace into a broken and divided world?

16

Turning Away

When many of his disciples heard it, they said, 'This teaching is difficult; who can accept it?' . . . Because of this many of his disciples turned back and no longer went about with him. So Jesus asked the twelve, 'Do you also wish to go away?' Simon Peter answered him, 'Lord, to whom can we go? You have the words of eternal life. We have come to believe and know that you are the Holy One of God.' Jesus answered them, 'Did I not choose you, the twelve? Yet one of you is a devil.' He was speaking of Judas son of Simon Iscariot, for he, though one of the twelve, was going to betray him.

JOHN 6:60, 66-71

After some days Paul said to Barnabas, 'Come, let us return and visit the believers in every city where we proclaimed the word of the Lord and see how they are doing.' Barnabas wanted to take with them John called Mark. But Paul decided not to take with them one who had deserted them in Pamphylia and had not accompanied them in the work. The disagreement became so sharp that they parted company; Barnabas took Mark with him and sailed away to Cyprus. But Paul chose Silas and set out, the believers commending him to the grace of the Lord. He went through Syria and Cilicia, strengthening the churches.

ACTS 15:36-41

Captain Janeway is mostly successful in persuading the Starfleet and Maquis personnel to work together on their voyage home — but not totally. One of the most recalcitrant Maquis is Seska, a young woman who is apparently Bajoran and who has been romantically involved with the Maquis leader. Seska resents Janeway and all her Starfleet rules and protocols, and starts to leak information and technology to Maje Kullah, the leader of a group harassing *Voyager* called the Kazon. When this comes to light, Seska defects to the Kazon and reveals her true identity: she is actually Cardassian, having been surgically altered to look Bajoran in order to infiltrate the Maquis. Her treachery costs her former friends dear, even allowing the Kazon to capture *Voyager* at one point; however, Seska herself dies in the battle to retake *Voyager.*

One question left hanging by the original *Star Wars* film (Episode IV) was what made Darth Vader turn to the 'dark side of the Force'. It is clear that he was originally a Jedi Knight, and yet he uses his power for evil — even killing the venerable Obi-Wan Kenobi. In the next film, *The Empire Strikes Back,* it emerges that he is actually the father of Luke Skywalker, and in *The Return of the Jedi,* he tries to turn Luke also to evil. By returning to make *Episode I: The Phantom Menace* some twenty years later, George Lucas raises the question of how good can turn to evil. One memorable picture advertising the film shows the little boy hero, Anakin Skywalker, casting a shadow which has the shape of Darth Vader, whom he will later become.

It has to be recognized that the history of the Christian church is not all sweetness and light, breaking down all the barriers. Jesus' words and deeds caused great controversy, even in his own day, which led eventually to his death. All the Gospels show the conflict developing through his ministry. In John 6, there is a long debate between Jesus and some other Jews after the miraculous feeding of the five thousand, in which Jesus gradually makes it explicit that people have to 'eat my flesh and drink my blood' (Jn. 6:54). Jesus' claim to be the 'bread from heaven' which feeds people as Moses and the Israelites were fed in the wilderness is too much for some disciples, who 'turned back and no longer went about with him' (6:66). Jesus rather wistfully and painfully asks the twelve if they also want to leave, and it is Simon Peter who declares that they have nowhere else to go, for 'You have the words of eternal life' (6:68). As Jesus looks at the twelve he has chosen, he recognizes that Judas Iscariot, even though he is still a disciple, will be the one to betray him (6:70-71). Like Seska gradually allying herself with the Kazon, or Anakin turning to evil, so Judas becomes estranged, until he finally goes out into the darkness to betray Jesus, 'and it was night' (Jn. 13:30).

Of course, not every departure leads to betrayal. Most of these disciples mentioned here who find it all too hard just withdraw and no longer go about 'with him' (Jn. 6:66). There is a bleak sadness about that phrase, which accepts the reality of those who start on the journey but abandon it along the way. C. S. Lewis recognizes this at the end of the Narnia stories, where the High King Peter has to admit 'shortly and gravely' that 'my sister Susan is no longer a friend of Narnia'. She has grown up to think that it was all childish stories and is now more interested in 'nylons and lipstick and invitations' (*The Last Battle*, pp. 123-124). So too in Bunyan's *The Pilgrim's Progress*, where Obstinate and Pliable join Christian as he leaves the City of Destruction; Obstinate turns back almost immediately, but Pliable goes with Christian for a while, only to abandon him when things get difficult and they fall into the Slough of Despond.

Furthermore, all splits do not necessarily lead to opposition. When the Company of the Ring reach the end of the Wilderland in the shadow of Tol Brandir, they must make a choice about their future route, which leads to 'The Breaking of the Fellowship'. First, Boromir tries to force Frodo to use the power of the Ring to benefit himself; although he comes to his senses shortly afterwards and tries to defend the hobbits, he soon dies, like Seska, Darth Vader and Judas. But both the film and the two books of The Fellowship of the Ring end in sorrow, as the Company is broken, and the others continue in twos or threes towards their goal by various routes, which enables them to be active in different areas (pp. 415-440).

In Acts 15:36-41, Luke recognizes that all was not peace and harmony in the early church as he records a similar split between Barnabas and Paul. After the success of their first missionary journey, Paul suggests a second round. Barnabas lives up to the meaning of his name 'son of encouragement' as he wants to give John Mark a second chance (Acts 4:36; 15:37). Paul, however, does not trust Mark, because he had left them during the previous mission in Pamphylia and turned back to Jerusalem (Acts 13:13). Unfortunately, this led to rather sharp disagreement, such that Paul and Barnabas also 'parted company'. As with the parting of the Company of the Ring, this results in two missions, as Barnabas and Mark go to Cyprus, while Paul takes Silas with him to Asia (15:39-41). The later Pauline letters suggest that there was a reconciliation since Mark is mentioned as one of Paul's team and described as 'the cousin of Barnabas' (Col. 4:10; Philemon 24); Mark is even described as 'useful in my ministry' (2 Tim. 4:11).

It is part of the grace and mercy of God that even personal disagreements and splits in the church can still have positive outcomes. We have to recognize the chequered history of the church, which has done much to overcome barriers and bring people together, and yet which has split into so many denominations and traditions — first between the eastern Orthodox and the western Catholic churches in 1054, then all the Protestant churches breaking away in the Reformation, and on to the plethora of churches today. On the one hand, this has broken the unity of the body of Christ and caused hesitations and scandal for many people both within and beyond the church. On the other, the different churches and expressions of Christianity have provided great richness and diversity, ensuring that all types of human personality and experience can find a home somewhere in the worldwide church — for we are not all the same. The next question will be how we can find our unity in such diversity and make use of the different gifts God has given us, not to separate from each other, but to travel together in our shared journey and mission.

For Prayer and Meditation

Father of all,
have mercy on those who find the journey difficult
or are tempted to turn back;
forgive us our sins and divisions
and make us one in the body of your Son Jesus Christ.

17

Many Gifts, One Crew

Now there are varieties of gifts, but the same Spirit; and there are varieties of services, but the same Lord; and there are varieties of activities, but it is the same God who activates all of them in everyone. To each is given the manifestation of the Spirit for the common good. To one is given through the Spirit the utterance of wisdom, and to another the utterance of knowledge according to the same Spirit, to another faith by the same Spirit, to another gifts of healing by the one Spirit, to another the working of miracles, to another prophecy, to another the discernment of spirits, to another various kinds of tongues, to another the interpretation of tongues. All these are activated by one and the same Spirit, who allots to each one individually just as the Spirit chooses. For just as the body is one and has many members, and all the members of the body, though many, are one body, so it is with Christ. For in the one Spirit we were all baptized into one body — Jews or Greeks, slaves or free — and we were all made to drink of one Spirit.

1 CORINTHIANS 12:4-13

Whether we look at the Fellowship of the Ring or any of our different ships' crews, they are all made up from very different people with various gifts and talents. It is this which allows for the possibility of disagreements, or even splits. Yet, at the same time, it is only through this variety of abilities that each group can function. Thus in *The Matrix,* Morpheus has gathered together a small group of followers who are the crew of his ship, *Nebuchadnezzar,* and also his team for fighting the computer matrix. Like Jesus' twelve disciples, it contains brothers — Tank, who is the trainer and operator, and Dozer, the pilot. Others, like Apoc, Switch and Mouse, go with Morpheus into the world to fight — and Cypher is the one who will eventually betray them to the evil Agents.

Similarly, in *2010* Arthur C. Clarke gives the ship's 'crew list' for *Leonov,* with the seven Russians' correct titles, names and specialisms —

propulsion, navigation, engineering structures, communications, control systems, medical life support and medical nutrition (p. 38). As the story unfolds we see how the different members' personalities somehow reflect their gifts — Max the Engineer with his practical jokes, or the Surgeon-Commander, Dr Katerina Rudenko, looking like 'the prototype of Mother Russia' (p. 50).

The same is true in each of our crews which have people with different gifts. For all their banter on the bridge of the original *Enterprise,* Dr McCoy and Spock need each other's insights and are actually good friends underneath it all. It is less obvious why robots should be built like this, yet in *Star Wars* there is the inimitable pairing of R2-D2 and C-3PO. R2-D2 is a short, barrel-like, all-purpose droid, who actually does most of the work. However, it only communicates in beeps and whistles and requires the assistance of C-3PO, a humanoid 'protocol droid', who totters around like a mechanical elderly butler, to translate. Presumably, R2-D2 could have been designed with a synthetic voice-box, but this would have missed out on their necessary complementarity and lost much of the film's humour — and paradoxically, even its humanity!

Paul is trying to make the Corinthians understand this basic lesson. This young and vibrant church is full of many gifted and talented individuals, and has already formed subgroups and factions within its community, calling themselves after Paul, or Apollos, or Peter. The first thing Paul does in the letter is to argue against this tendency for groups and splits, appealing to them 'by the name of our Lord Jesus Christ, that there be no divisions among you, but that you be united in the same mind and the same purpose' (1 Cor. 1:10-12). After dealing with many of their various questions, he returns to this theme over three chapters. 1 Corinthians 12 looks at using differing gifts in one body and chapter 14 applies this particularly to the area of worship — but in between comes Paul's great hymn to love to make the point that using any gifts without love for others is worth nothing (1 Cor. 13).

So before he gets to his 'crew list' of gifts, Paul begins by stressing the unity within the diversity. There may be 'varieties' of gifts or activities, but the very word used for 'varieties' or 'differences' really means 'distributions' — which directs our attention to the source which distributes these gifts, God himself. Paul's use of a threefold formula — 'the same Spirit', 'the same Lord', 'the same God' — reminds us of the diversity in unity of the Holy Trinity, three persons in one God. Furthermore, he is clear that these talents are 'gifts', *charismata,* which are given through the grace, *charis,* of God, rather than our own ability or possession. They are also 'services', *diakonia,* for service like a deacon's to benefit others, and they are 'activities', *energema,* literally 'energies' or operations. Therefore they are never for the benefit of the gifted person themself, but are a 'manifestation of the Spirit for the common good' (1 Cor. 12:4-7).

It is only after he has made all this clear that Paul turns to an actual list of gifts, which reads a bit like our crew lists of specialities, with 'utterance of wisdom', gifts of 'healing', or 'prophecy'. We are even reminded of C-3PO interpreting for R2-D2 with the gift of 'tongues' requiring someone else to have 'the interpretation of tongues' (1 Cor. 12:8-10)! One of the great contributions of the charismatic movement across many denominations in recent decades has been the recovery of these *charismata,* gifts of grace, and it has been good to have them used in church more frequently. However, as sometimes with new presents, people have become fixated with them, or see these as the only or most important gifts. For Paul, this list is only a selection of examples, as is made clear by a different list later in the same chapter, including other gifts like apostles and helpers or leaders (1 Cor. 12:27-30). Equally, a similar passage in Romans repeats this idea of many gifts in one body with a list which puts 'natural' gifts like administration, compassion and even giving alongside the more 'super-natural' like prophecy (Rom. 12:4-8).

For Paul, the crucial thing is not the gift, but the giver: 'All these are activated by one and the same Spirit, who allots to each one individually just as the Spirit chooses' (1 Cor. 12:11). It is like the way Father Christmas gives different presents to the children in Narnia (a shield and sword, bow and horn, a flask of healing cordial) which are 'tools not toys' to be used to help and defend others (*Lion, Witch and Wardrobe,* pp. 99-100).

This leads to Paul's favourite image of the church as 'the body of Christ', operating like a human body with its many limbs and members, yet still one body. He goes on to expand it with his almost humorous pictures of a body being all eyes or ears, or the foot feeling left out through not being a hand (1 Cor. 12:14-26). The crucial thing is that in our many and different ways, we have come out of the Mess of sin through the Gateway of being 'all baptized into one body' and 'to drink of one Spirit' (1 Cor. 12:13). In this new Company of the body of Christ, we find that our racial and social barriers — 'Jews or Greeks, slaves or free' — are broken down and instead each person has their part to play in the church as much as any of our various ships' crews. Each of us is unique, given by the grace of God our special gift, not for our own benefit that we might be pig-headed, but to use to help others for the redemption of the world.

For Prayer and Meditation

Lord Jesus Christ,
you have given to your body the church
so many gifts of grace; grant us also the unity of your Spirit
that we may use them to your praise and glory, Amen.

18

Expansion and Growth

The gifts he gave were that some would be apostles, some prophets, some evangelists, some pastors and teachers, to equip the saints for the work of ministry, for building up the body of Christ, until all of us come to the unity of the faith and of the knowledge of the Son of God, to maturity, to the measure of the full stature of Christ. We must no longer be children, tossed to and fro and blown about by every wind of doctrine, by people's trickery, by their craftiness in deceitful scheming. But speaking the truth in love, we must grow up in every way into him who is the head, into Christ, from whom the whole body, joined and knit together by every ligament with which it is equipped, as each part is working properly, promotes the body's growth in building itself up in love.

EPHESIANS 4:11-16

As the Russians and Americans in *2010* leave Jupiter in response to David Bowman's warning, they look back and see a black stain spreading across the huge planet. Suddenly they realize that it is comprised of millions of monoliths, the same shape and size as the one into which Bowman had disappeared in 2001. What is more, the monoliths are reproducing themselves by fission every two hours in 'a textbook case of exponential growth'. The Russian engineer describes them as 'von Neumann machines', devices which are capable of reproduction in the manner of living organisms. To build millions of machines to do an enormous task, 'like strip-mining the entire face of the Moon', would take centuries: however, 'if you were clever enough, you'd make just *one* machine — but with the ability to reproduce itself from the raw materials around it. So you'd start a chain reaction, and in a very short time you'd have bred enough machines to do the job in decades, instead of millennia' (pp. 264-266). At the rate the monoliths split and double, they soon cover the entire planet and trigger its ignition into a new star. In his typically scientific way, Arthur C. Clarke gives a reference in his acknowledgments to a NASA Technical Memorandum (No. 78304) for those who doubt the feasibility of such an idea as self-replicating machines (p. 296).

We began this part with the story of Jesus leaving just twelve people to change the world. If we apply this idea of self-reproduction to them, we could get amazing growth. If the original twelve disciples each made another twelve disciples in a year (just one disciple a month), and so on, with every new disciple making another twelve each year, the number would expand exponentially until it reached the present population of planet earth within just less than ten years!

Something similar happens with the growth of the followers of Paul Atreides in *Dune*. When his father is killed by his rival, Baron Harkonnen, Paul and his pregnant mother flee into the desert. Here they are befriended by the local inhabitants, the Fremen, who come to accept Paul as their 'Dune Messiah', known thereafter as Muad'dib. Too late the Baron and his adviser, the Mentat Hawat, realize how the Fremen have grown to have some 250 'sietch' communities, or 5 million people (*Dune*, p. 357). Shortly afterwards, Muad'dib and his Fremen overthrow the dominant House of Harkonnen in a big battle, and within twelve years his Qizarate missionaries have brought most of the human universe under his rule (*Dune Messiah*, p. 8).

Peter's sermon on the Day of Pentecost resulted not in just another twelve converts, but three thousand people being baptized! We studied in Chapter 14 Luke's picture of the common life of the early church and how 'day by day the Lord added to their number those who were being saved' (Acts 2:41, 47). As people leave behind the Mess and enter the Christian journey through the Gateway of baptism or conversion, so they come to join the Company — and the church grows. During this week, we have seen how growth happens through people travelling and working together, as they discover new life in common with others. The breaking down of barriers, such as those between Jews and Gentiles, or slaves and free, is also enormously attractive and provides yet more growth.

While we have to recognize that the history of the church also includes putting up barriers and having disagreements which can even lead to splits, this too can lead to further growth. After all, fission is a form of reproduction, used even at the level of amoebas. The monoliths on Jupiter doubled in thickness every two hours, and then split apart, to start growing again. Such growth by small cells, which then separate to grow new cells, has been used at various times of revival in church history, from the Methodist system of Bible classes through to the modern 'church growth movement'.

Yet church growth is never just numerical, crucial though that is. Yesterday's study showed the importance of different gifts in the life of the church. Today's passage also makes this clear. The risen and ascended Christ has given various gifts of leadership, such as apostles, teachers and prophets, to his church *not* so that the ministers can do all the work! It is 'to equip the saints for the work of ministry for building up the body of Christ' (Eph. 4:11-12). *All* Christians are involved in building the body of Christ. And while this building includes numerical growth, it is also a growth 'to maturity, to the measure of the full stature of Christ' (4:13). The word translated 'maturity' includes the sense of human fullness and perfection. We saw last week that when God was incarnate in Jesus of Nazareth, he showed us not only what he is like, but also what we are supposed to be like as human beings. Jesus Christ is the pattern for all humanity, fully and perfectly as God wants us all to be. The different gifts which God has given to his church are designed also to enable us, along our journey, to grow into being more fully human.

As people grow and become more mature, they also become more stable. A tree with few roots moves to and fro in the wind, and a boat is blown about on the waves. But a mature tree with deep roots stands before the wind, and a ship with a good anchor does not move. Paul wants his readers to have this maturity and stability so that they are not 'tossed to and fro by every wind of doctrine', by every latest bright idea which came along then — or appears now (4:14). Instead, he returns to yesterday's image of the body, and describes organic growth where every part is working properly, so that the whole body grows and develops under the guidance of the head, who is none other than Jesus Christ. This requires open and honest relationships based on trust, 'speaking the truth in love' (4:15). When each member is working together and making their contribution, then the whole body grows and develops. And finally, and supremely, Paul notes again that this whole process has to take place 'in love' (4:16).

We are now well on our way in our journey. Having left behind the Mess of the oppression and alienation of sin and entered through the Gateway of baptism and God's call, we have discovered, as in many sci-fi stories, that 'we are not alone'. We travel together as part of a Company, which may include many and different sorts of people with huge varieties of gifts. As we develop and mature individually, so the whole church grows. Now that our Company of pilgrims is established, we can look ahead to the rest of journey with its ups and downs, struggles and times of respite — for we still have far to travel.

For Prayer and Meditation

Now to him who by the power at work within us is able
to accomplish abundantly far more than all we can ask or imagine,
to him be glory in the church and in Christ Jesus to all generations,
forever and ever, Amen.

Ephesians 3:20-21

PART 4

THE CONFLICT

The journey brings us into Conflict with evil and opponents. The struggles of the spiritual life with temptation, the self and sin show our need of the Holy Spirit as we become children of God.

19

Cosmic Conflict

And war broke out in heaven; Michael and his angels fought against the dragon. The dragon and his angels fought back, but they were defeated, and there was no longer any place for them in heaven. The great dragon was thrown down, that ancient serpent, who is called the Devil and Satan, the deceiver of the whole world — he was thrown down to the earth, and his angels were thrown down with him. . . . So when the dragon saw that he had been thrown down to the earth, he pursued the woman who had given birth to the male child. . . . Then the dragon was angry with the woman, and went off to make war on the rest of her children, those who keep the commandments of God and hold the testimony of Jesus.

REVELATION 12:7-9, 13, 17

Now we are well into our journey. We have escaped from the Mess, found the Gateway and have joined the Company — so we should now be able to sit back and enjoy the rest of the ride. Except that we soon discover it is not like that at all. First, as we saw in Chapter 16, we do not always find the other members of the Company quite so congenial, and disagreements or even splits can occur. Then, as we look around, we find that we have not left the Mess behind at all; it seems to be there around us as we journey, sometimes almost getting worse. And to cap it all, if we are honest, it is not just our companions' fault or the world outside — but something inside us, still struggling with the old ways of life. Wasn't all that supposed to have been washed away in the waters of baptism and our response to God's call to enter upon the journey?

It is not as simple as that. The Christian life is not an easy ride, nor is everything sweetness and light once we are baptized and join the church. In fact, our internal conflicts may grow stronger as we realize how far from God we are and begin to try to live according to his ways. And since the church is comprised of others also struggling with their own sin and selfishness, it is hardly surprising that we find conflicts within it. It is like a hospital for those ravaged by sin, and while we may be making progress, none of us is completely healed yet. Nor is the Christian journey ever an escape from the world around us, with all its pains and hurts. In fact, we should become more and more aware of it, and find ourselves drawn into its struggles, trying to share the love of God. And then, sooner or later, we begin to wonder whether this is all linked — whether our own struggles, and the rows and pain and hurts in the church and the world, are not part of some greater cosmic conflict with evil.

This sense of a cosmic conflict is also there in most of our stories, but there are many different ways of describing it. In *Star Wars,* the obvious face of evil is Darth Vader with his black robes and face hidden behind a mask. In *The Phantom Menace,* Darth Maul appears with red skin colouring and horns, looking just like mediaeval pictures of the devil. Yet neither of them is actually the source of evil, which comes from 'the dark side of the Force'. George Lucas studied anthropology, philosophy and sociology before going to film school, and his concept of 'the Force' draws on many sources. Obi-Wan Kenobi tells Luke Skywalker that the Force is 'an energy field created by all living things. It binds the galaxy together'. Han Solo's response is sceptical, describing it as 'no match for a good blaster'! As the films progress, and we learn more of both the good and evil sides of the Force, this dualism seems quite Eastern. Certainly, the teaching of Yoda, the Jedi Master in the swamps of Dagobah in *The Empire Strikes Back* who is over 800 years old, reflects some vegetarian Zen Buddhist beliefs held by its director, Irvin Kershner.

The films also raise the question about technology. While the droids, R2-D2 and C-3PO, seem very human, the Empire's use of technology is dehumanizing. Darth Vader himself is part human and part machine — rather like the 'baddies' in *Star Trek: The Next Generation* and *Voyager,* the Borg collective, who combine organic life with mechanical implants. In *The Matrix,* when human beings lost the global war against artificial intelligence, it resulted in the computer-generated matrix which allows the machines to enslave humans for their body bioelectricity — and only a few humans like Morpheus and his crew are left to fight.

As Morpheus reveals to Neo the real struggle behind the illusion of the world, so the book of Revelation tries to tell the real story behind the cosmic conflict. After John is given various visions of heaven, he sees two 'portents' or signs — a woman and a dragon. The woman gives birth to a child, and is usually interpreted as Israel and/or Mary producing Jesus, and then also as the church itself. The dragon seeks to devour her offspring, and 'war broke out in heaven' (Rev. 12:1-7). Thus it is no coincidence that we come to the Conflict with evil in this week's studies after looking at the Company of the church. In John's vision, the archangel Michael (whose name means 'who is like God?') and his angels defeat the dragon and force him down from heaven to earth, where he wages war against 'the woman and the rest of her children', that is, the church and individual Christians (12:17). The next few chapters recount the dragon's attacks on the church, especially through various 'beasts', or Antichrist figures, culminating in great battles at the mountain of Megiddo (Har-magedon, from which we get Armageddon, 16:16) and before the holy city, at which they are defeated by a figure on a white horse, called 'the Word of God . . . King of kings and Lord of lords' (19:11-21; 20:8-10). John uses these pictures of the beasts and their city to describe the attacks by Rome and its emperors upon the early church — but he also wants his readers to look beyond their own struggles to a greater cosmic conflict with evil. Jesus has already won the battle in heaven in which we share 'by the blood of the lamb' (12:10-11). Our current trials and struggles are the 'mopping up' operation here on earth, before Christ's final triumph.

These rich and powerful images have dominated much writing, art and music over the centuries, and thus it is no surprise that they have affected our science fiction and fantasy stories too. Gene Roddenberry may have conceived a scientific and technological future without any gods or religion for the original *Star Trek,* but these themes have returned with a vengeance in the later series, especially *Deep Space Nine.* Here Starfleet has to battle against the terrible Jem Hadar, the genetically produced soldiers from the Gamma Quadrant, who fight and die for the Founders of the Dominion, whom they revere as 'gods'. Meanwhile, the Cardassian Gul Dukat goes over to the evil Pah-wraiths whom the prophets exiled from the 'celestial temple', just as Michael threw out the dragon; Dukat then becomes an Antichrist figure in an attempt to destroy both Bajor and the Federation. Such personal evil also confronts Harry Potter as he battles against the enemy 'Who Must Not Be Named' — Lord Voldemort, who killed Harry's parents and would have enslaved all the wizards were it not for Harry.

Christian writers have also reused John's imagery in stories to explain evil and the struggle. Thus John Bunyan depicts Christian doing battle in the Valley of Humiliation with a fiend Apollyon (whose name means 'destroyer' in Greek in Revelation 9:11) during his *Pilgrim's Progress.* C. S. Lewis describes the White Witch as the personification of evil in Narnia as she keeps it 'always winter and never Christmas' and enslaves its animals. Only through her battle against, and apparent triumph over, the great Lion, Aslan, does final liberation come for Narnia as she is destroyed. Elsewhere, Lewis deliberately mixes the imagery of the book of Revelation with science fiction in his trilogy about the war in the universe. The other planets in the solar system, such as Mars and Venus, are still free under the rule of the creator, Maleldil. Earth is the 'Silent Planet' controlled by a 'bent eldil', like an evil angel, up to the orbit of the moon. The other eldila have heard that the son of Maleldil has gone down to earth to struggle with the Bent One, and with the help of Dr Ransom the final battle is approaching.

Lewis warned in his preface to the *Screwtape Letters* that people often fall into one of two errors about the devil and evil — either 'to disbelieve in their existence' or 'to feel an excessive and unhealthy interest in them'. All our various stories confirm the wisdom of this warning and suggest that we should take our own experience of Conflict within and without seriously. This week of our journey will therefore take us through these struggles with evil and temptation, sin and selfishness, to consider what resources the Holy Spirit brings to protect and guide us on our way.

For Prayer and Meditation

Almighty and eternal God and Father,
you alone create and control the Universe;
Guide and protect us by your Holy Spirit
and bring us into the joy of the victory
won by your Son, our Lord, Jesus Christ, Amen.

20

Falling to the Dark Side

Jesus was led up by the Spirit into the wilderness to be tempted by the devil. He fasted forty days and forty nights, and afterwards he was famished. The tempter came and said to him, 'If you are the Son of God, command these stones to become loaves of bread.' But he answered, 'It is written, "One does not live by bread alone, but by every word that comes from the mouth of God."' Then the devil took him to the holy city and placed him on the pinnacle of the temple, saying to him, 'If you are the Son of God, throw yourself down; for it is written, "He will command his angels concerning you," and "On their hands they will bear you up, so that you will not dash your foot against a stone."' Jesus said to him, 'Again it is written, "Do not put the Lord your God to the test."' Again, the devil took him to a very high mountain and showed him all the kingdoms of the world and their splendour; and he said to him, 'All these I will give you, if you will fall down and worship me.' Jesus said to him, 'Away with you, Satan! for it is written, "Worship the Lord your God, and serve only him."' Then the devil left him, and suddenly angels came and waited on him.

MATTHEW 4:1-11

Both the opening pilot of *Star Trek: The Next Generation* and the final episode feature an apparently omnipotent being, known simply as 'Q', who puts humanity on trial with Captain Picard as the representative person upon whom all our fate rests. In the seven years between, Q appears regularly to test the Captain and to play tricks on him — and indeed he continues to do this with Sisko on *Deep Space Nine* and especially with Janeway on *Voyager.* Sometimes these are pranks, and at other times it is deadly serious, as in the trial of humanity.

Matthew and Luke also both begin their main narrative of Jesus with a 'pilot episode' featuring his baptism, followed by his testing by the devil (which is taken from their shared common source, known coincidentally to biblical scholars as *Quelle,* German for 'source', and usually abbreviated to 'Q'!). As with Picard, Jesus is here tested as the representative of the whole human race. Our fate depends upon him and his reactions. This story confronts us with the ultimate questions of good and evil, of how men and women come to choose evil — and whether Jesus can do what we cannot, and resist the temptation.

The same question of how one chooses good and evil has fascinated George Lucas throughout the *Star Wars* films. In the original film, *Episode IV: A New Hope,* we learn that Darth Vader was originally 'a good friend' of Obi-Wan Kenobi, a Jedi, but he turned to the dark side and was responsible for the betrayal and death of Luke Skywalker's father. In *Episode V: The Empire Strikes Back,* Luke has to fight and kill an image which looks like Vader in a training session in a dark cave, only to realize that the mask reveals his own face and he has been struggling with his own dark side. When he does fight Darth Vader in reality, he loses the fight and discovers that Vader is actually his father. In response, Luke chooses to throw himself off the high gantry and die, rather than go over to the dark side — but his fall is cushioned and he is caught by the *Millennium Falcon.* When the two meet again in *Episode VI: The Return of the Jedi,* Darth Vader attempts again to turn Luke to the dark side. This time, Luke not only resists the temptation, but wins the duel and then refuses to kill Vader.

With all this having been known for a couple of decades, Lucas returned to his basic question in *Episode I: The Phantom Menace,* with Anakin Skywalker, the little boy hero of the film, who still projects the shadow of Darth Vader on all the advertising hoardings. When Qui-Gon Jinn brings Anakin to the Jedi Council, there are grave misgivings about his age, and about how much fear and anger he has already learned. As the young Obi-Wan Kenobi puts it, 'the boy is dangerous' — but Qui-Gon goes ahead and trains him. When Anakin grows up in Episode II: Attack of the Clones, he disobeys Obi-Wan Kenobi's instruction and goes to Tatooine in search of the Tuskan raiders who have abducted his mother. He finds her, only for her to die in his arms — and he gives in to the temptings of his anger, slaughtering not just the men, but also the women and children. Despite the heights of his love for the lady Amidala, his inexorable slide to the dark side has begun.

Matthew and Luke stress that Jesus is 'led by the Spirit' when he goes into the wilderness to face the devil's temptations. It is no accident that it comes straight after Jesus' baptism, which ends with the 'voice from heaven' that 'this is my beloved Son with whom I am well pleased' (Matt. 3:17). This climactic revelation now forms precisely the basis for the temptations, 'If you are the Son of God . . .' It is typical of the spiritual life that the high spots are also the dangerous places from which we can fall. Yes, it is true that Jesus is the Son of God, and yes, it is true that therefore he could turn stones to bread or defy the laws of gravity — but it does not automatically follow that this is the will of God. We must be careful, especially after 'a spiritual high', not to let what seems obvious lead us astray — it might be obviously wrong!

Jesus replies with quotations from Deuteronomy about the Israelites during their forty years in the wilderness. Moses struggled with their hunger in the desert and their testing of God. Now the true Israelite replies that we do not 'live by bread alone' but by the word of God and that we must not 'put the Lord your God to the test' (Matt. 4:4, 7; see Deut. 6:16; 8:3). Finally, Moses was taken up to a high mountain from which he could see the promised land before he died (Deut. 34:1-5). Now the devil takes Jesus up and promises him the whole world if only he will worship him. For the third and final time, Jesus quotes Deuteronomy, 'Worship the Lord your God and serve only him' (Matt. 4:10; Deut. 6:13) — and the devil leaves him.

However we interpret this particular story, these temptations must have repeated themselves throughout Jesus' ministry. There will have been times when Jesus and his friends were so tired and hungry, or when the crowd were being obtuse, that the temptation to rustle up a good meal or a quick miracle might have seemed obvious. Yet when Jesus does multiply loaves and fishes, it is to feed the hungry and his miracles are to heal those in need — never for the benefit of himself or his disciples. And the temptation to use his power to go down the popular political or revolutionary route would have been more comfortable than an agonizing death alone on the cross, but the true Son of God can only serve his Father — and the children of God must do the same.

Thus the temptations are not just about a single event in the desert long ago — they reflect the day-by-day decision of Jesus to live according to God's will. In this story he recapitulates the story of Israel in the desert and succeeds where they failed. Furthermore, he also replays the story of the original temptation and fall to the dark side in the garden of Eden. Here too the temptation comes after a great spiritual high — nothing less than the creation of the universe — and turns on testing a word of God: 'Did God say . . .', whispers the serpent (Gen. 3:1). As Jesus was tempted to gain power by worshipping something other than God, so the man and the woman are tempted to eat the fruit and 'be like God' (3:5). And once again, the story is not just about a single temptation. Since 'Adam' means 'earth' and 'Eve' means 'life', they represent us all and the way men and women have always doubted what God has said and prefer to do it their own way.

C. S. Lewis has used this story as the basis for the middle volume of his science fiction trilogy, *Voyage to Venus.* The hero, Dr Elwin Ransom, is taken to Venus, or Perelandra as it is called in the Old Solar language, where another first man and woman have been created for a new pure world. Temptation comes in the guise of Ransom's old foe, Weston, who tries to persuade the woman to disobey Maleldil's one instruction by telling her of all that human beings have achieved on earth by their own initiative. The fate of the new world hangs upon the woman's decision and whether she will turn to the advice of Weston or Ransom.

In this way, all these stories become our story. Where Adam and Eve failed in the garden, Jesus succeeded in the desert. But Q has Picard on trial all through the seven years of the series, and through him the fate of the whole of the human race hangs in the balance. Anakin Skywalker has to live with the consequences of his choice for the dark side and, as Darth Vader, constantly confronts Luke with the same decision. For us too, our daily discipleship turns on the terribly simple, but terribly hard choice: to do it our way, or his way. Which it will be, depends upon you and me.

For Prayer and Meditation

Our Father in heaven . . .
Lead us not into temptation
and do not bring us to the time of trial,
but deliver us from evil.

21

Worship Me!

For the wrath of God is revealed from heaven against all ungodliness and wickedness of those who by their wickedness suppress the truth. For what can be known about God is plain to them, because God has shown it to them. Ever since the creation of the world his eternal power and divine nature, invisible though they are, have been understood and seen through the things he has made. So they are without excuse; for though they knew God, they did not honour him as God or give thanks to him, but they became futile in their thinking, and their senseless minds were darkened. Claiming to be wise, they became fools; and they exchanged the glory of the immortal God for images resembling a mortal human being or birds or four-footed animals or reptiles. Therefore God gave them up in the lusts of their hearts to impurity, to the degrading of their bodies among themselves, because they exchanged the truth about God for a lie and worshipped and served the creature rather than the Creator, who is blessed forever! Amen.

ROMANS 1:18-25

On the remote planet Pollux IV, Captain Kirk and his crew discover a Greek temple and a man who claims to be the god Apollo. He wants them to worship him and becomes angry when they refuse, abducting the attractive archaeology and anthropology officer, Lt Palamas. It emerges that Apollo is one of a race of spacefaring beings who came to earth in the classical period and who were worshipped by the Greeks because of their powers. They have waited centuries for human beings to come and find them, and now Apollo is the only survivor. When Kirk refuses to obey him, but turns the ship's weapons on his power source, Apollo finally admits that the old days of worship have gone and dissipates himself into the atmosphere.

In this classic episode, 'Who mourns for Adonais?' from the original *Star Trek* series, Gene Roddenberry as a committed atheist was trying to explain religion through the idea that the gods were visiting spacemen. The crucial point is that Apollo weakens without humans believing in him. A similar point is made in Terry Pratchett's treatment of religion on his Discworld where a god's size depends upon his worshippers. In the novel *Small Gods,* the Great God Om has become embodied as a very small tortoise, and all that keeps him from extinction is the fervent faith of the only person who actually believes in him, the humble Brutha. The irony is that his church has become all-powerful and all-demanding, running the country, waging holy wars — and even tries to martyr Brutha, spread-eagled on an instrument of torture.

The later *Star Trek* series are much more open to faith and spirituality, but are still firmly committed to resisting those who demand everything. Thus the Borg collective is seen as evil and dehumanizing, with its all-demanding commitment to the single mind of the hive. Similarly, in *Deep Space Nine* the Founders may be worshipped as gods by their genetically engineered Jem Hadar warriors, but their Dominion is aptly named — and such domination is to be resisted. In both cases, Starfleet fights to stay loyal to its ideas of human freedom.

Paul and the early church lived in the midst of lots of gods. The ancient Near Eastern religions of the Egyptians and the Babylonians were full of animal gods. Even the Israelites in the desert, after escaping the Egyptians, made and worshipped the Golden Calf while Moses was up Mount Sinai talking with God (Ex. 32). The memory of this betrayal haunts the later writers and the Hebrew Scriptures are full of warnings about the dangers of idolatry. Isaiah in particular heaps derision upon worshippers who use half a tree to make a fire and bake bread, but carve an idol from the other half to worship. The prophet's constant message is 'I am God, and there is no other' (Is. 44:9-20; 46:9). By Paul's time, the eastern animal gods have been joined by the western Graeco-Roman pantheon of the gods of Olympus, divine beings depicted in human form, with great power and often questionable morals! It is no surprise that Paul finds Athens 'full of idols' and so gives his famous sermon that the 'Unknown God', 'the Lord of heaven and earth, does not live in shrines made by human hands'. He has become known in Jesus and now requires people to turn from their idols and repent (Acts 17:16-34).

As the capital of the empire, Rome was full of temples and gods imported from everywhere. But during the first century, there also arose the imperial cult, to worship the emperor as semi-divine and to sacrifice to the state — an extremely efficient way to ensure the loyalty of so many diverse peoples. For such polytheists, another god or two makes no difference — but for monotheists this is impossible. In fact the Romans had to make special arrangements to cope with the Jews and their insistence that there was only one God. Originally, while they were still within Judaism, the early Christians were also able to shelter under these provisions, but later they were even termed atheists because of their implacable opposition to the Roman gods. This comes out in Paul's letter to the first Christians at Rome where idolatry is seen as the primary evidence of human wickedness. The power and majesty of the true God are clear to everyone from the creation, says Paul, but human beings refuse to worship him. Instead 'they exchanged the glory of the immortal God for images resembling a mortal human being or birds or four-footed animals or reptiles'. In such worship, they are 'serving the creature rather than the Creator' (Rom. 1:23, 25).

This is the basic temptation, going back as far as the garden: don't do what God says, whispers the serpent, and 'you will be like God' (Gen. 3:5). Similarly, we saw yesterday that the last temptation of Christ was to gain the world by giving in to the blandishments of the devil: 'All these I will give you if you will fall down and worship me' (Matt. 4:9). Our world may be more subtle, but, like Rome, our big cities are dominated by the towering office temples of money and business. From the 'high places' of their glass-fronted boardrooms can be seen the kingdoms of this world in all their splendour — and they can be ours if only we will give in and let them dominate our lives. Roddenberry was wrong, for atheism will not save us from idolatry. As G. K. Chesterton said, when people stop believing in God, it is not that they believe in nothing, but they end up believing in anything.

Whether it is the imperial cult, or the Borg or the Founders of the Dominion, such all-demanding gods are to be resisted, says Paul — whatever they are offering. And yes, Terry Pratchett is right, even the church can become an idol, requiring everything and being so busy about God's business that God himself is left to dwindle away. Today's passage challenges us to examine our lives, to discover what are our idols — what do we give everything to, sacrificing our time and resources, or even our children? Perhaps it is time to take a walk outside the office or even beyond the church and look up into God's wonderful creation where he has revealed his 'eternal power and divine nature' to us. In response, we can only 'honour him' and give him thanks (Rom. 1:20-21). Only then, with that primary relationship right, will we discover true human freedom.

For Prayer and Meditation

'I am the L*ORD your God.*
You shall have no other gods before me.'

Exodus 20:2-3, the First Commandment

22

The Good Spirit

> *And I will ask the Father, and he will give you another Counsellor, to be with you forever. This is the Spirit of truth, whom the world cannot receive, because it neither sees him nor knows him. You know him, because he abides with you, and he will be in you. I will not leave you orphaned; I am coming to you. . . . But the Counsellor, the Holy Spirit, whom the Father will send in my name, will teach you everything, and remind you of all that I have said to you. Peace I leave with you; my peace I give to you. I do not give to you as the world gives. Do not let your hearts be troubled, and do not let them be afraid. . . .*
>
> *I tell you the truth: it is to your advantage that I go away, for if I do not go away, the Counsellor will not come to you; but if I go, I will send him to you. And when he comes, he will prove the world wrong about sin and righteousness and judgment.*
>
> JOHN 14:16-18, 26-27; 16:7-8

To talk of 'false gods' or idols implies that there must be a true God. Equally, to be able to use 'the dark side of the Force' indicates that there is also 'the good side of the Force' in *Star Wars.* George Lucas actually came from a varied Christian background and had a mystical experience at the age of six, followed by an apparently miraculous escape from a car crash in his teens. While the dualism of the Force may appear eastern, much of what happens with its 'good side', particularly the eventual self-sacrifice of Obi-Wan Kenobi (and even Darth Vader himself), seems to owe more to Christianity. Lucas himself, in an interview, said, 'I would hesitate to call the Force God', but wants the films to make young people think about God, spirituality and morality ('Of Myth and Men', *Time,* 26 April 1999, p. 38).

Obi-Wan Kenobi is an old Jedi Knight, deeply versed in the good side of the Force, who inspires Luke Skywalker to join the mission and trains him in the Force. When they team up with Han Solo, Obi-Wan

Kenobi goes along too and keeps them company in the ship, *Millennium Falcon*. He guides and directs them, and lays down his life fighting against Darth Vader to give them time to escape. Even after his death, he continues to guide Luke, especially in the climactic battle, encouraging Luke to put aside the technology and trust the Force to enable him to attack the precise point necessary to destroy the Death Star. He also reappears in further visions to guide Luke in the subsequent films.

This theme of a 'good spirit', who accompanies and guides our heroes, teaching and instructing them, and even fighting to protect them, recurs in many of our stories. In *The Lord of the Rings,* the wizard Gandalf is rather distrusted by the good hobbits of the Shire. He has a tendency to upset things and to disturb the calm. In the film version, this is marvellously demonstrated by Gandalf's magnificent fireworks display at Bilbo's birthday party. Sure enough, he is not only behind Bilbo Baggins' departure, but many years later also inspires Frodo to set off to take the Ring on its perilous journey south. He has to teach Frodo about its powerful properties, and to protect him from using it too much. He travels with them — 'You may need my company on the Road' (p. 80) — and becomes one of the Fellowship of the Ring when it is formed (p. 293). He guides them along the way and fights for them, especially against the evil Balrog where, like Obi-Wan Kenobi, he lays down his life to permit the others to escape (p. 349). We can see much of a similar character and role as guide, teacher and protector being played by Harry Potter's headmaster, Albus Dumbledore, and John Bunyan provides Christian with similar helpers such as Faithful and Hopeful in *The Pilgrim's Progress.*

Paul's response to the idols and various gods of Rome was to direct his readers' attention to the true God, revealed in Jesus Christ. In his travels with his disciples, Jesus too played this role of being their guide and 'teacher', the literal meaning of 'rabbi'. It was through his keeping company with them that they not only learned about the kingdom of God, but began to share in it. In the debates and conflicts along the way, he has been their protector, but now he is aware the final Conflict is coming, in which, like Obi-Wan Kenobi and Gandalf, he will lay down his life for them. So here in John's account of the last supper, Jesus tries to explain all this to his apprehensive and confused followers, to prepare them for what lies ahead and to explain who will guide and protect them when he has gone.

They find all this talk of going away, 'to prepare a place for you' (Jn. 14:1-8), as worrying as the hobbits do when Gandalf is not around. So Jesus tells them he will ask the Father to give them 'another Counsellor' (14:16). Both words are particularly interesting in the Greek. 'Do you want another drink?' might mean 'a different drink', as though the first one was not good, or 'a second drink' of the same type as the last one which you enjoyed so much. Greek has two separate words for 'another' to convey this distinction, and here it is 'another of the same type'. In other words, Jesus is asking God to send them the Spirit as 'another Jesus', to be with them, guiding them and so on as he did.

Secondly, the Spirit is called the *Paraklētos* in Greek, which literally means someone 'called alongside'. Thus the Spirit is called to the disciples' side, to keep them company in the same way as when Jesus was with them. The direct translation of *paraclete* into Latin is 'advocate' which is used here in some English translations, meaning a person who is 'called alongside' in court to speak for someone, either as a defending counsel or as a supporter or character witness. The Spirit will be with the disciples, dwelling with them to stay and be in them, protecting them and speaking up for them. Thus Jesus can say that the disciples will not be left alone, desolate and 'orphaned'; since the Spirit is 'another' called alongside them like him, he can say 'I am coming to you' (14:18). No wonder another traditional translation of *paraclete* for the Holy Spirit is the 'Comforter', giving strength and encouragement to the disciples.

Furthermore, the Holy Spirit is 'the Spirit of truth' who will 'teach you everything, and remind you of all that I have said to you' (14:26). As Jesus was their rabbi, so now the Spirit will instruct them — and indeed not just the disciples. The Spirit will also 'convict' the world, proving that people have it wrong about 'sin, righteousness and judgment' and convincing them of the truth (16:8). In this way, like the other good guides, the Spirit fights on behalf of the disciples, even after Jesus has laid down his life for them. No wonder that Jesus says, 'I tell you the truth: it is to your advantage that I go away' (16:7), for this means he can send us this 'other' helper, guide, teacher, comforter and protector — who is all and more than Obi-Wan Kenobi, Gandalf and all the others could ever be, for he is none other than the Holy Spirit of God.

For Prayer and Meditation

Holy Spirit of God,
accompany us on our journey,
encourage us with your comfort,
teach us by your wisdom,
and protect us by your power,
that we may come ever to be with Jesus, Amen.

23

Shields Up!

Be strong in the Lord and in the strength of his power. Put on the whole armour of God, so that you may be able to stand against the wiles of the devil. For our struggle is not against enemies of blood and flesh, but against the rulers, against the authorities, against the cosmic powers of this present darkness, against the spiritual forces of evil in the heavenly places. Therefore take up the whole armour of God, so that you may be able to withstand on that evil day, and having done everything, to stand firm. Stand therefore, and fasten the belt of truth around your waist, and put on the breastplate of righteousness. As shoes for your feet put on whatever will make you ready to proclaim the gospel of peace. With all of these, take the shield of faith, with which you will be able to quench all the flaming arrows of the evil one. Take the helmet of salvation, and the sword of the Spirit, which is the word of God. Pray in the Spirit at all times in every prayer and supplication.

EPHESIANS 6:10-18

Whenever the *Enterprise* encounters a dangerous situation either from a natural space phenomenon or a hostile ship, the siren sounds and the 'red alert' signs light up as the first officer, Commander Riker, calls out, 'Shields up!' Starfleet spaceships are protected by deflector shields which provide a localized distortion of space. These energy fields protect the ship and its crew and deflect enemy fire, although under sustained and repeated attack, their efficiency will gradually deteriorate. If the shields are damaged, the ship is an easy target for an enemy to destroy. Thus, defensive armour alone is not enough. The ship must have offensive weapons as well. Phasers — from Phased Energy Rectification — replaced earlier lasers, but still look like a beam of light, fired either in a steady stream, or in bursts from the phaser cannon on the *Defiant*, the warship that protects *Deep Space Nine.* Phasers, however, cannot be fired when travelling faster than light, so in these situations, photon torpedoes are extremely useful, which produce matter-antimatter explosions.

Such deflectors and phasers are, of course, just the science fiction version of the swords and shields beloved of little boys for thousands of years. George Lucas cleverly brought the two together in the light-sabres which can only be used by the Jedi Knights in *Star Wars.* The swish and the buzz of these laser-like swords in the duels ensured a ready market in plastic replicas — and it is said that Ewan McGregor would vocalize his own sound effects when filming as the younger Obi-Wan Kenobi in *The Phantom Menace,* simply out of the habits learned from playing with one as a child many years ago!

This interface between a scientific or magical weapon and basic swords and shields is also seen in the wizards' wands of Harry Potter and his friends. They can even be used for having wizards' duels, and disarming someone by knocking their wand out of their hand is crucial to stop them doing magic. The wizard's staff is equally important in *The Lord of the Rings,* as is seen in the duel between Gandalf and Saruman with all the special effects in the film! Later, Gandalf orders Saruman's staff to break itself when he removes him from the Council (p. 607).

Paul also uses swords and shields as an image for the spiritual Conflict with evil. He stresses that Christians are struggling not with human enemies, 'flesh and blood', but 'against the cosmic powers of this present darkness, against the spiritual forces of evil in the heavenly places' (Eph. 6:12). It is a very powerful image, recalling the dark side of the Force, or the huge space battlefleets of Darth Vader's Empire or the Dominion in *Star Trek* — but far more real, and much more malevolent. No human being could hope to stand against such assaults in their own strength. So Paul tells us to not just to 'be strong' as some English translations lamely put it, but to 'be made strong' in the Greek, to 'be empowered' by the strength of God's power (6:10). We dare not seek protection in our own resources, but we must 'put on', 'be clothed in' — using the same word as in the baptismal imagery for new clothing we studied in Chapter 2 — the 'armour of God' (6:11). This, too, is a poor translation, for it evokes ideas of mediaeval knights' metal outfits, decorating castle hallways, which are purely defensive, like a tortoise retreating into its shell. However, the Greek word means 'all the weapons' — *panoplia,* giving us the English 'panoply' — which includes all the equipment of a soldier of that time, both light body armour and his offensive weapons too.

Furthermore, it is actually 'God's armour' which we are to wear, not our own. Isaiah describes the Lord himself wearing 'righteousness like a breastplate' and a 'helmet of salvation' (Is. 59:17; see also 11:4-5). The book of Wisdom, written during the period between the Old and New Testaments, says that 'the Lord will take zeal as his whole armour', and then goes on to describe once again the 'breastplate of righteousness', as God will take 'justice as a helmet . . . holiness as an invincible shield and sharpen stern wrath for a sword'. All creation will join him in the battle, with lightnings and hailstones, floods and winds directed against evil-doing (Wisdom 5:17-23). It sounds as dramatic as any battle from the special effects department in our films!

Paul draws on these pictures for his account of a Christian putting on God's armour for the Conflict here in terms of the equipment of a first-century soldier (Eph. 6:13-18). The 'belt' around the waist was to gather up the tunic and to stop you from tripping over its folds in the rapid movement of battle. In spiritual warfare, it is the 'belt of truth' which stops Christians tripping up, as we are honest and make sure that there is nothing we might stumble over (6:14). The breastplate was to protect the chest and the vital internal organs; the job of guarding our hearts falls to 'righteousness'. From the leather sandals of the legionary to today's army boots, the importance of proper footwear to give stability and manoeuvrability is recognized, and we are to be grounded upon 'the gospel of peace' (6:15). To protect the head — our thoughts, ideas and imagination — is the task of the 'helmet of salvation', that saving wholeness which comes from the healing of the gospel.

Finally, we come at last to the sword and shield, both of which are used in attack and defence, as the sword blocks an opponent's swipe or the shield presses hard against him. Thus the shield of 'faith' is to protect us against 'all the flaming arrows of the evil one', quenching his doubts and questions as a wet leather shield put out incendiary attacks — and yet at the same time, faith can be used to push back any incursions (6:16). Nimble use of 'the sword of the Spirit, which is the word of God' can both parry the enemy's blow, and make a thrust at his heart — as we saw Jesus using his knowledge of Deuteronomy to answer the devil during the temptations. And of course, the best use of weapons of attack and defence depends on being in constant communication with headquarters, so Paul concludes, 'Pray in the Spirit at all times' (6:18).

Some people today are uncomfortable with mention of evil or ideas of spiritual warfare, dismissing it as mediaeval imagery. However, our films and stories witness to new variations on the basic images of good and bad, while the pain of our struggling world demonstrates the reality of evil all too clearly. As the battles with the Borg and the Dominion forced Starfleet to develop the *Defiant* class of warship, so we cannot hope to confront evil, or even survive, without the protection of the armour of God. And like using any weapons, we need to practise — with or without the sound effects!

For Prayer and Meditation

Soldiers of Christ, arise, and put your armour on,
Strong in the strength which God supplies, through his eternal Son.
Stand then in his great might, with all his strength endued;
And take, to arm you for the fight, the panoply of God.

Charles Wesley (1707-88)

24

Resistance Is Not Futile

But I say, walk by the Spirit, and do not gratify the desires of the flesh. For the desires of the flesh are against the Spirit, and the desires of the Spirit are against the flesh; for these are opposed to each other, to prevent you from doing what you would. But if you are led by the Spirit, you are not under the law. Now the works of the flesh are plain: immorality, impurity, licentiousness, idolatry, sorcery, enmity, strife, jealousy, anger, selfishness, dissension, party spirit, envy, drunkenness, carousing, and the like. I warn you, as I warned you before, that those who do such things shall not inherit the kingdom of God. But the fruit of the Spirit is love, joy, peace, patience, kindness, goodness, faithfulness, gentleness, self-control; against such there is no law. And those who belong to Christ Jesus have crucified the flesh with its passions and desires. If we live by the Spirit, let us also walk by the Spirit.

GALATIANS 5:16-25

'Resistance is futile!' is the chant of the Borg when they invade a starship and start to assimilate its human and other crew members into members of the collective. On the unique occasion when Captain Janeway makes a shaky alliance with the Borg against their common enemy, Species 8472, she asks for a single Borg drone to be stationed on *Voyager* as their representative. 'Seven of Nine, Tertiary Adjunct of Unimatrix Zero One', as she is snappily known, has only the vaguest recollection of her human origins, having been assimilated at the age of six, and continues to assert the Borg maxim that 'resistance is futile!' in her confidence that Janeway and the crew will be assimilated in due course after this temporary alliance ends.

And yet, the reverse happens. When Seven's neurotransceiver is disabled and her link to the collective severed during *Voyager*'s escape, her human immune system starts to reject the Borg technological implants. Eventually the ship's doctor manages to remove 82 per cent of the hardware and restore an increasingly attractive human appearance — but the internal struggle is much harder. Seven has heard countless voices in her head for most of her life, and now she feels terribly alone. She has had no human social contact and understands nothing of eating or drinking, humour or facial expressions, friendship or love. Sometimes, her Borg ways assert themselves almost despite herself, contacting the collective, or disobeying Janeway to kill a wounded member of Species 8472. And yet, gradually, with the encouragement and support of the captain and the holographic doctor (who has his own problems with human beings!), she slowly recovers her humanity and becomes a trusted and valued member of the crew.

So far this week, we have seen the reality of evil and conflict, with the temptation to fall to the dark side or worship all-demanding false gods and systems. To help us in the struggle, we have the good and true Spirit together with the weapons and equipment of God himself. The problem is that the Conflict is not just 'out there', in outer space or the higher heavens, but we also face an internal struggle deep within our own hearts. Like the wooden horse, taken into Troy with armed Greek soldiers hidden inside, we are pregnant with the seeds of our own destruction through our sin and selfishness. We cannot simply escape the Mess, for we carry it within us. When we go through the Gateway of baptism, it may drown the old enemy, but it does not wash out all his ways. Conversion is never a single complete event, but takes place over the rest of our journey as we learn to 'walk by the Spirit' (Gal. 5:16). As with Seven of Nine, being separated from evil restarts our spiritual immune system and it begins to reject the implants of sin, making us gradually more truly human as God wants us to be.

The internal struggle of good and evil features in many of our stories. In *The Next Generation,* Lore is Data's 'elder brother', another android created before Data, but shut down because of his evil tendencies. When he is reactivated, he makes alliances with Starfleet's enemies, most notably with the Borg, and even manages to get Data to join him by turning off the ethical subroutines in Data's programming. When Lore orders Data to kill Captain Picard, the android's ethical subroutine is rebooted — and once again he saves the day. In an early episode of the original series, significantly entitled 'The Enemy Within', Captain Kirk suffers a transporter malfunction which duplicates him as two people — his good half and his bad half. The latter gets drunk on Saurian brandy, tries to rape his female assistant and fights everybody in sight before the two are reintegrated. There is also the 'mirror universe' visited both by Kirk and his crew, and also by various members of *Deep Space Nine,* populated by evil and scheming versions of themselves. Similar struggles with 'the enemy within' can be seen in the temptation for Bilbo to want to see the Ring again; as he reaches for it around Frodo's neck, so his face changes to become like Gollum, wanting to hold on to 'my preciousss' Ring (p. 248).

Paul is clear that becoming a Christian 'reboots our ethical subroutines' but there is still a struggle between the two sides, which he calls 'the desires of the flesh' and 'the desires of the Spirit'. Each is opposed to the other and tries to prevent us doing what 'we would' (Gal. 5:17). Thus, the Spirit tries to restrain our sinful desires, while the flesh hinders our good impulses. Therefore, we are faced with perpetual choices, day by day, or even second by second, and we have to learn to 'walk by the Spirit' on our journey. The tense used here in the Greek depicts not a single action, but a present and continuing habit: 'walk — and go on walking' (5:16). But it is not a simple dualism, for we are 'led by the Spirit' and not 'under the law' and so the works of the flesh become increasingly 'plain' and obvious to us (5:18-19). The negative side of Kirk with his drunkenness, sexual lusts and fighting manifests several of the 'works of the flesh', and his colleagues soon realize that this is not the real Kirk. Paul spells out a similar list of immorality, idolatry, quarrelling, fighting, and indulgence in excess — and that 'those who do such things shall not inherit the kingdom of God' (5:19-21).

We cannot learn to avoid these overnight, any more than Seven can stop being Borg, but we can begin the process. What the Christian journey produces in us is 'the fruit of the Spirit' — and fruit takes time to grow. New habits have to be learned, and they become slowly ingrained through the choices we make as we 'walk by the Spirit' day by day. As we are guided by the Holy Spirit and learn to use the weapons and equipment of God, so we start to change. We will not be perfect immediately, but we should begin to manifest the 'patience, kindness, goodness, faithfulness, and gentleness' which come from a spiritual 'self-control' — and this results in a 'love, joy, and peace' which no law could ever produce (5:22-23). As Seven of Nine demonstrates, resistance is *not* futile, and the change away from evil becomes extremely attractive!

For Prayer and Meditation

Reflect upon each of the fruit of the Spirit — 'love, joy, peace, patience, kindness, goodness, faithfulness, gentleness, self-control'; how can you learn to 'walk by the Spirit' and encourage their growth?

25

The Spirit of Adoption

But you are not in the flesh; you are in the Spirit, since the Spirit of God dwells in you. Anyone who does not have the Spirit of Christ does not belong to him. . . . For all who are led by the Spirit of God are children of God. For you did not receive a spirit of slavery to fall back into fear, but you have received a spirit of adoption. When we cry, 'Abba! Father!' it is that very Spirit bearing witness with our spirit that we are children of God, and if children, then heirs, heirs of God and joint heirs with Christ. . . . [T]he creation itself will be set free from its bondage to decay and will obtain the freedom of the glory of the children of God. We know that the whole creation has been groaning in labour pains until now; and not only the creation, but we ourselves, who have the first fruits of the Spirit, groan inwardly while we wait for adoption, the redemption of our bodies. . . . No, in all these things we are more than conquerors through him who loved us. For I am convinced that neither death, nor life, nor angels, nor rulers, nor things present, nor things to come, nor powers, nor height, nor depth, nor anything else in all creation, will be able to separate us from the love of God in Christ Jesus our Lord.

ROMANS 8:9, 14-17, 21-23, 37-39

At the start of *Star Wars,* Luke Skywalker lives with his uncle and aunt, who will not let him leave to become a pilot. When he follows after the runaway droids, they lead him to Obi-Wan Kenobi, who says Luke's father was his 'good friend'; he then becomes like a surrogate father to Luke in introducing him to the Force. After his death, Obi-Wan appears to Luke to direct him to another father-figure in the over-800-year-old Jedi Master, Yoda, who prepares Luke for his duel with Darth Vader. Only when Luke loses his duel does he discover that Vader is actually his real father who fell to the dark side. When they meet and fight again at the end of *The Return of the Jedi,* Luke defeats Darth Vader, but refuses to kill him; in return Vader dies saving Luke from the evil emperor, and

Luke gets a vision of Darth Vader transformed back into Anakin Skywalker as his real father in heaven, with Obi-Wan Kenobi and Yoda.

Many of our stories have similar themes of parenting and adoption in the Conflict of good and evil. In the *X-Files*, FBI Agent Fox Mulder discovers that his enemy, the sinisterly unnamed 'Cigarette Smoking Man', was actually a close friend of Fox's dead father and may even have had a relationship with his mother; Fox has to rely on his boss, Assistant Director Skinner, for protection and guidance. Like Luke, Harry Potter also lives with his uncle and aunt who will not tell him the truth about his parents and how they were killed by the evil Lord Voldemort. Later, at Hogwarts School for Wizards, Harry is hiding from the escaped prisoner, Sirius Black; Black ends up rescuing Harry, revealing that he was the 'best friend' of his father and is Harry's godfather who now wants to take care of him (*Prisoner of Azkaban*, pp. 152, 277). Finally, *The Lord of the Rings* begins when Bilbo Baggins has his 'eleventy-first birthday'. He had 'adopted Frodo as his heir' when he was ninety-nine, and now Frodo has his thirty-third birthday on the same day as Bilbo is 111: 'He comes of age and into his inheritance today' (pp. 33, 42). With that inheritance comes the Ring, and so Frodo has to set out on his great adventure.

Thus all of these stories turn on fatherhood and adoption, which have major implications for the rest of the world in the Conflict with evil. As this week draws to its close today, we find the same theme in Paul's climactic account of the spiritual life in Romans chapter 8. He begins with the triumphal statement that 'there is now no condemnation for those who are in Christ Jesus' (8:1), but goes on to describe the struggle between living 'according to the flesh' and 'according to the Spirit' in terms similar to yesterday's study (8:2-8). Next, Paul takes his account to a higher level, well away from any hint of dualism — like that found in the dark and good sides of the Force — in the relationship of the flesh and the Holy Spirit, by asserting, 'But you are not in the flesh; you are in the Spirit, since the Spirit of God dwells in you' (8:9).

He describes Christians with the same phrase, 'led by the Spirit', as yesterday (8:14; see Gal. 5:18) — but goes much further by saying that 'all who are led by the Spirit of God are children of God'. Our human parents may have been tempted by the dark side like everyone else this side of the garden of Eden, but we have received 'the spirit of adoption'. Jesus always prayed to God as his father, 'Abba' in Aramaic; so 'when we cry, "Abba! Father!" it is that very Spirit bearing witness with our spirit that we are children of God' (8:15-16). When we pass through the Gateway of baptism, we do not just find a new Company — but a whole new family as brothers and sisters of the one true Father in heaven. Furthermore, if we are adopted as children, then like Frodo, we also have an inheritance to come, as 'heirs of God and joint heirs with Christ' (8:17).

This is an incredible statement which changes everything. We do not worship false idols, but the true God, who gives us his Spirit and protects us with his own armour. But we do not face the spiritual struggle in our own strength or as just his soldiers. He has made us nothing less than his own children and raised us to share the inheritance won by his Son, Jesus Christ. Furthermore, the whole cosmic Conflict is somehow bound up with our struggle. The Mess and the problems of the world are part of 'its bondage to decay', waiting and 'groaning in labour pains' as we too 'groan inwardly while we wait for adoption, the redemption of our bodies' (8:21-23). Just as the fate of the whole of Middle-earth hangs upon what Frodo will do with his inheritance of the Ring, or the freedom of all wizards depends on Harry Potter, so too we are part of creation and its liberation is bound up with ours.

God holds the vast and beautiful interstellar nebulae in being by his love, just as much as the movement of atoms at the microcosmic level — and yet somehow he has linked all the universe to the creation of conscious beings who are free to respond to his love, like you and me. That is what the Conflict is all about — and it is so important that God did not even withhold his own Son, but 'gave him up for all of us' (8:32). It is because of this extravagant love in the heart of God the Father, in creating us in the first place and in letting his Son die so that we could be redeemed and adopted back as his children, that Paul can rise to the heights of eloquent trust at the end of this passage. Yes, evil is a reality and there truly is a cosmic struggle going on, but in it we are 'more than conquerors' not because of anything we can do, but 'through him who loved us'. Therefore whatever the enemy throws at us, whatever disasters or difficulties we may encounter or opponents we may face, ultimately nothing 'in all creation will be able to separate us from the love of God in Christ Jesus our Lord' (8:37-39).

These studies have demonstrated why our journey through life can never be an easy ride, because it entails facing the ultimate realities. Part of the attraction and fun of so many science fiction TV episodes is the weekly conceit that 'the fate of the universe is in our hands'. But as we have traced the biblical story from the cosmic struggle through our individual choices and back again, we have seen that this is not because of our own importance, but because of the love of God for his universe and for us. With such a destiny calling us, it is vital that we must now turn to how we find our way through the journey.

For Prayer and Meditation

Eternal Lord of heaven and earth,
thank you that you have made us your children;
guard us in our struggles and guide us on our journey,
that we may join with all creation
to sing your praise and glory,
through him who has redeemed the universe,
your Son, our Lord Jesus Christ, Amen.

PART 5

FINDING THE WAY

The journey continues — but how do we find the right way through the highs and lows? The valleys and the mountaintops, the joys and the dark places cause us to seek spiritual guidance and direction.

26

Ups and Downs

Ahab told Jezebel all that Elijah had done, and how he had killed all the prophets with the sword. Then Jezebel sent a messenger to Elijah, saying, 'So may the gods do to me, and more also, if I do not make your life like the life of one of them by this time tomorrow.' Then he was afraid; he got up and fled for his life, and came to Beer-sheba, which belongs to Judah; he left his servant there. But he himself went a day's journey into the wilderness, and came and sat down under a solitary broom tree. He asked that he might die: 'It is enough; now, O LORD, *take away my life, for I am no better than my ancestors.' . . . He got up, and ate and drank; then he went in the strength of that food forty days and forty nights to Horeb the mount of God. At that place he came to a cave, and spent the night there. Then the word of the* LORD *came to him, saying, 'What are you doing here, Elijah?' He answered, 'I have been very zealous for the* LORD, *the God of hosts; for the Israelites have forsaken your covenant, thrown down your altars, and killed your prophets with the sword. I alone am left, and they are seeking my life, to take it away.'*

1 KINGS 19:1-4, 8-10

We are half way through our journey. The Company is now well established and we have been bloodied in Conflict along the way. By now, like on any long journey, we may have begun to settle into a routine, perhaps even got a little bored — but also we will probably have begun to notice a pattern of ups and downs. This is most obvious, of course, on a long sea voyage. For a sailing ship, the periods of flat calm are not only boring, but no progress is made. When the wind blows, the ups and downs are literally so, climbing up the peaks of the waves and down into the troughs between them. In the midst of a storm, this can be terrifying and exhilarating all at the same time. The spiritual life is often described as like a journey, and it too has its periods of calm and its ups and downs. The quiet periods may be restful or they may be boring, but when the wind of the Spirit starts to blow, get ready for ups and downs, both exciting and not a little frightening sometimes! At these sorts of times, it is good to have a good sense of direction, or a pilot onboard who knows the way, or decent maps and charts, and to pray for the occasional glimpse through the clouds of what lies ahead — and these are the themes we must now explore.

Since the time of Homer's *Odyssey*, this rhythm of a journey has provided stories with momentum and interest. Thus in *The Voyage of the 'Dawn Treader'*, Caspian and the children sail east from Narnia through the Lone Islands, beyond the magician's island of the Dufflepuds and even to the World's End, experiencing both terrible storms and hot, flat calm along the way. So too for the heroes of *2001: A Space Odyssey*. Here the vast tracts of space between the planets are such a boring calm that the best way to travel is to be frozen in a hibernation unit! Yet there are the high points too, both frightening and exhilarating, such as the struggle with HAL the computer over the AE35 antenna providing their link with earth (which HAL shuts off), or the discovery and entry into the black monolith which is the Star Gate. Similarly in *2010: Odyssey Two*, the American crew members sleep in stasis, while the others experience the firestorm of braking around Jupiter's atmosphere and they all have to pull together to save themselves and escape at the end.

As a walker, I have enjoyed many long hikes, and while plodding along the flat is much easier, the ups and downs are what makes it interesting. High places are good for seeing the way ahead, while valleys can be either soothing and pleasant, or full of trees or rivers which make it difficult to find your way through. John Bunyan uses all these images in *The Pilgrim's Progress*, as Christian struggles up the Hill Difficulty, after which he gets a view of the Delectable Mountains, from which, in due course, he will be able to see all the way to the gates of the Celestial City. In between, he must fight Apollyon the Destroyer in the Valley of Humiliation and struggle through the Valley of the Shadow of Death. In *The Lord of the Rings*, the converse seems often to be the case, as mountains are the places of conflict with evil. Thus Frodo is attacked by the Black Riders on Weathertop, and the Company of the Ring cannot cross over the Misty Mountains and have to go under them, where Gandalf is lost fighting the Balrog, before the final conflict with evil in the mountains of Mordor, especially inside Mount Doom. On the other hand, it is in the valleys that places of rest and healing are found, like Lorien and

Rivendell. The films beautifully recreate all these places with the magnificent scenery of New Zealand's mountains and valleys.

The geography of ancient Israel-Palestine was dominated by mountains and valleys. The high places were scoured bare by the wind and elements, and such topsoil as there was would tend to be washed down into the valleys, often irrigated by a little stream. Thus agriculture would take place on the valley floor, and cities would be built on the hilltop for protection, with the scrubland in between used for pasturing flocks. In the deserts of Judea, Sinai and the Negeb, the mountains could be high, awesome places — but dry valleys could become a death-trap in the event of a flash-flood.

Such considerations influenced both the physical travels of God's people and also their spiritual journey. The forty-year wanderings through the wilderness of Sinai with its ups and downs has had a profound influence on the rest of Israel's history and faith. It was up in the cloud on the heights of Mount Sinai that Moses met God and received the Ten Commandments (Ex. 19:16-25); yet when he descended to join the people again, he discovered that they had turned to idolatry, worshipping the Golden Calf — so that Moses in his anger smashed the tablets at the foot of the mountain and destroyed the Calf (Ex. 32:1-20).

Going from a spiritual high to the depths of despair was also the experience of Elijah. After three years of spiritual conflict against King Ahab and the worship of Baal brought in by his foreign Queen Jezebel, Elijah challenges Baal's priests to a final contest on the top of Mount Carmel. Four hundred and fifty priests call on Baal all day without a response, except for Elijah's mocking that perhaps Baal is on holiday or in the toilet (1 Kings 18:27)! When God answers Elijah's prayer with a lightning bolt setting alight his sacrifice, despite it having been soaked with water, it produces a thunderclap of faith for the Israelites, who kill all Jezebel's priests, and the rainstorm which ends the drought (18:40, 45).

Yet despite all this high excitement on the mountain, one threat from Jezebel a few days later is enough to plunge Elijah right down into a suicidal depression; he flees into a desert valley and wants to die (19:1-4). God could have reminded him of the power he had witnessed a few days previously, or given him another demonstration — but instead gently arranges for him to be fed by an angel, and then sends him on a long journey back to the roots of his faith (19:5-8). Elijah retraces the steps of the ancient Israelites with a forty-day journey into the wilderness, until he comes to Mount Horeb, another name for Sinai. Here God asks, 'What are you doing here?' — and such is his patience that he lets Elijah tell him his self-pitying tale that 'I alone am left' not once but twice (19:10, 14). In between, Elijah does get his demonstration of the power of God in the earthquake, wind and fire — but the Lord is not to be found in them. Only after enduring the 'sound of sheer silence' does Elijah hear the 'still, small voice' of God reassuring him that it is not all over, that there are still plenty of true believers left in the Company of Israel, and that Elijah still has work to do for the Lord (19:15-18). From the heights of victory on Mount Carmel through the valley wilderness of despair, it is a long climb back up to rediscover his spiritual roots on Mount Sinai — but it was worth it. Restored, renewed and given a new vision of what lies ahead, Elijah heads back down to face the next stage of the Conflict with the false god and his prophets.

Thus we must not be surprised if we have our ups and downs in our journey with the Company of the church and in our Conflict along the way. There will be great spiritual triumphs — and times of utter despair. Sometimes we will be forging ahead with a clear vision, and at other times we may have to retrace our steps or rediscover our calling. Like Elijah, we will need to be given some guidance along the way, to spend some time both in silence and talking to God, and in his mercy he will restore our vision and send us back into the tasks he has ahead for us. These are the themes, therefore, which we shall explore together this week.

For Prayer and Meditation

Breathe through the heats of our desire
Thy coolness and thy balm.
Let sense be dumb, let flesh retire;
Speak through the earthquake, wind, and fire,
O still small voice of calm.

J. G. Whittier (1807-92)

27

The Master

Paul, an apostle of Christ Jesus by the will of God, for the sake of the promise of life that is in Christ Jesus, To Timothy, my beloved child: Grace, mercy, and peace from God the Father and Christ Jesus our Lord. I am grateful to God — whom I worship with a clear conscience, as my ancestors did — when I remember you constantly in my prayers night and day. Recalling your tears, I long to see you so that I may be filled with joy. I am reminded of your sincere faith, a faith that lived first in your grandmother Lois and your mother Eunice and now, I am sure, lives in you. For this reason I remind you to rekindle the gift of God that is within you through the laying on of my hands; for God did not give us a spirit of cowardice, but rather a spirit of power and of love and of self-discipline.

2 TIMOTHY 1:1-7

In *The Phantom Menace,* a younger Obi-Wan Kenobi (played by Ewan McGregor) appears as the pupil of an older Jedi Knight, Qui-Gon Jinn, and goes with him to the planet Naboo to sort out a trade conflict there. They then land unexpectedly on Tatooine, where they meet the boy Anakin Skywalker, whom Qui-Gon senses is 'strong in the Force'. Despite Obi-Wan's hesitations and the Jedi Council's objections, Qui-Gon starts to train Anakin. After Qui-Gon's death, Obi-Wan Kenobi continues with Anakin's training, but in Episode II: Attack of the Clones Anakin disobeys his master's instructions. Thus he begins the process by which he eventually becomes the dark lord, Darth Vader. Years later, the older Obi-Wan Kenobi similarly takes Anakin's son, Luke Skywalker, and starts to train him; after Obi-Wan's death, he appears in a vision to Luke and sends him to his own teacher, Yoda, a Jedi Master over 800 years old who lives in a swamp on Dagobah. While Yoda agrees that Luke is also strong in the Force, he has difficulties teaching him — not least because of Luke's overconfidence. Eventually, with his training still unfinished, Luke ignores Yoda's warnings and goes off to fight Vader immediately — with almost disastrous consequences.

Many of our stories contain similar partnerships where a young person is trained by an older master. In *Star Trek: The Next Generation,* Dr Crusher has her bright young son Wesley on board. In an early episode, 'Where no one has gone before', the *Enterprise* is hurled across the galaxy, and it is Wesley who realizes that the cause is a mysterious visitor, who calls himself the Traveller. The Traveller is so impressed that, before he departs, he advises Captain Picard that Wesley is a genius, like Mozart. The Traveller appears a second time to help Wesley rescue his mother from a collapsing parallel universe where she was sent after one of Wesley's experiments went wrong! Finally, his third appearance right at the end of the series helps Wesley decide to leave Starfleet and they set off together to explore the universe. Similar themes of advice and guidance from a wiser master recur in the way Gandalf advises Bilbo and Frodo, or how Albus Dumbledore, head-master of Hogwarts, teaches and trains the young Harry Potter.

After the 'still, small voice' allowed Elijah to repeat his tale of woe, as we saw yesterday, God gave Elijah a new task of anointing kings and reassured him that at least seven thousand true Israelites would be left who had not worshipped Baal. Elijah's immediate response is to set out in obedience — and his first action is to find Elisha, who is ploughing. Elijah throws his mantle over Elisha, who interprets this as a call to follow the master (1 Kings 19:19-21). Elisha then learns the ways of God from being with and observing Elijah, until the day when other prophets warn him that 'today the Lord will take your master away from you'. Elisha insists on following his master to the edge of the river Jordan, which they cross when Elijah hits it with his mantle to reveal dry land, repeating Moses' feat at the Red Sea. Elisha asks his master to let him 'inherit a double share of your spirit', and then he watches Elijah being taken into heaven. He returns to the river Jordan, picks up Elijah's mantle, strikes the water and walks across on dry land to continue the task of calling Israel and its kings to the worship of the true God. No wonder the other prophets declare, 'The spirit of Elijah rests on Elisha' (2 Kings 2:1-15). Even though the word 'mantle' is hardly used in English any more for an over-garment, none the less it is still used when someone picks up a master's task or abilities, and 'the mantle falls upon them'.

As Qui-Gon found Anakin and Obi-Wan found Luke in Tatooine, so

Paul found Timothy in Lystra, in modern Turkey. His mother and grandmother were Jewish believers, but his father was a Greek, so Paul took Timothy and initiated him by circumcision (Acts 16:1-3). Timothy followed Paul on his missionary journeys and learned from him, becoming a key 'co-worker' (Rom. 16:21), someone Paul can describe as 'my beloved and faithful child in the Lord' (1 Cor. 4:17). He is even linked with Paul as a writer at the start of some letters (2 Cor. 1:1; Phil. 1:1). The New Testament contains two letters written by Paul, or in his name by a later disciple, to Timothy, who is now a church leader in his own right. Here Paul still calls him 'my beloved child' and reminds him of his mother and grandmother; he recalls their time together and prays for him 'night and day' (2 Tim. 1:2-5). We saw a couple of weeks ago the importance of spiritual gifts in the Company of the church (1 Cor. 12). Here Paul uses the same word, *charisma,* as he urges Timothy 'to rekindle the gift of God' which he received when Paul laid hands on him (v. 6). Finally, in an echo of last Saturday's passage on 'the spirit of slavery' and 'the spirit of adoption' (Rom. 8:15), Timothy is reminded that God did not give him a spirit of cowardice but of 'power and love and self-discipline' (2 Tim. 1:7).

We may not all consider ourselves 'strong in the force' of God, or want to inherit the mantle of Elijah, yet there is a lot we can learn from one who is older and wiser, or more experienced in the spiritual life than ourselves. When I was a student and a young Christian, we were encouraged to join 'Paul and Timothy' pairs with more experienced Christians (sometimes even a year or two older!) to learn from regular prayer and Bible study together. This is actually a form of spiritual direction, which has been long practised especially within the religious orders, where a novice will go to an older monk for guidance and advice. Because we are all 'novices' in the spiritual life, many in the wider church have found such regular guidance from a more experienced Christian valuable throughout their lives.

As we saw last Wednesday, the true director is, of course, the Holy Spirit, who is 'called alongside' us, to guide, encourage, comfort and teach us as Jesus did the early disciples (Jn. 14:16-18). But we need human encouragement too, and so often the Holy Spirit brings his guidance through an older brother or sister in Christ. Such spiritual direction is a particular calling of many monks or nuns, which they offer to lay people, seeing them on a regular basis several times a year for conversation and prayer. However, it need not be as formal as this. Part of the task of Christian ministers is to give their people direction in their spiritual journey, and many clergy long to do this more than the paperwork or administration which clogs up their diaries! Often an older or retired member of the congregation, who cannot do as much as they used to, could be used as a great spiritual resource for others in this way. The problem with your own minister or someone from your own church is that they may be too close, and sometimes we can benefit from the detachment of someone further away, whom we see from time to time — as Wesley Crusher saw the Traveller occasionally. Another useful way for many is to belong to a small cell group of three or four people, who may meet perhaps monthly for a few hours, or a couple of times a year for a day or two. Such groups can provide a safe setting where we can open up to each other, listen and be listened to, share ideas and read the Scriptures, pray and be prayed over.

People may often try all of these different contexts and methods in the course of their spiritual journey, but they all share similar activities such as conversation and discussion, advice and guidance, Bible study, prayer and listening in silence to one another and to God. In these ways, we can grow in the spiritual life and begin to find the way through on our journey. Sometimes we may be impatient and go rushing off or ignore the advice, like Luke Skywalker — but a wise guide will go on praying for us and help us to sort it out later. In due course of time, we may find others coming to us for guidance, which is when we need to be under direction ourselves all the more. And there is great joy in seeing those who have been our 'children in Christ' pick up the mantle, stir up their gifts — and go off to save the universe!

For Prayer and Meditation

Think about the ways and the people to whom you turn for spiritual advice and direction, and those who come to you. Are there more or different things you could try doing? Why not discuss it with your minister, or read a book about it?

28

Page the Oracle

Does not wisdom call, and does not understanding raise her voice? . . . 'Take my instruction instead of silver, and knowledge rather than choice gold; for wisdom is better than jewels, and all that you may desire cannot compare with her. I, wisdom, live with prudence, and I attain knowledge and discretion. The fear of the LORD *is hatred of evil. Pride and arrogance and the way of evil and perverted speech I hate. . . . I walk in the way of righteousness, along the paths of justice, endowing with wealth those who love me, and filling their treasuries. The* LORD *created me at the beginning of his work, the first of his acts of long ago. . . . And now, my children, listen to me: happy are those who keep my ways. Hear instruction and be wise, and do not neglect it. Happy is the one who listens to me, watching daily at my gates, waiting beside my doors. For whoever finds me finds life and obtains favour from the* LORD*; but those who miss me injure themselves; all who hate me love death.'*

PROVERBS 8:1, 10-13, 20-22, 32-36

'The Matrix cannot tell you who you are,' Trinity explains to Neo after his first trip back into the world which he used to think was real, but now sees as a computer-generated illusion. For real answers, they have to visit the Oracle, who made the prophecy about the coming One, who they hope is Neo. She has been 'with us from the beginning,' says Morpheus, 'a guide to help you find the path'. So they take him to see her in a flat, containing a sitting-room full of other hopefuls. Morpheus tells Neo, 'I can only show you the door. You have to walk through it.' When he is invited into her presence, he finds a black woman, smoking and cooking in a kitchen, with the Latin for 'Know Thyself' on the wall. She examines his mouth, eyes and hands, and warns him of the difficult choices which lie for him on the journey ahead.

In this scene from *The Matrix,* the figure of the Oracle draws on a number of strands, most obviously the ancient Greek oracle at Delphi.

Here, too, there was a waiting-room with the text 'Know Thyself' in Greek on the wall, an inner sanctum full of incense smoke, and a priestess who spoke in riddles, often capable of several interpretations — which was useful when the future turned out unexpectedly. Thus King Croesus, encouraged by the oracle that if he invaded his neighbour 'a great kingdom would be lost', did invade — and lost his own kingdom! In the *Hitchhiker's Guide to the Galaxy*, our heroes steal the latest spaceship, *Heart of Gold*, equipped with 'improbability drive', and travel across the galaxy to find out who is really running the universe. It transpires that there is an old man with a cat in a shed on a deserted planet, whom people come and ask whether they should do this or that. The fates of billions rest upon his totally random answers, which the enquirers then go and put into action.

The ancient Jewish prophets often brought messages from God which they called 'oracles' — see particularly the prophecies of Isaiah. However, in other books of the Hebrew Scriptures, the idea of the wisdom of God becomes personified in the female figure of Wisdom. The book of Proverbs has many pithy, short sayings, and even some riddles, about the wise thing to do or the right path to take, but chapter 8 gives a long speech to Wisdom herself. Like the Oracle, she has been 'from the beginning' when God created her first of all (8:22). Her words are neither random, like the old man in *Hitchhiker's Guide*, nor riddling like the Greek priestess, but they are the wisdom which comes from the 'fear of the LORD' (8:13). Her instruction is better than 'silver', 'choice gold' or 'jewels' and people should seek to fill their treasuries with her advice, not the illusions of this world (8:10-11, 21). She hates evil, pride and lies and wants kings and rulers to govern rightly by her precepts in the 'way of righteousness, along the paths of justice' (8:13-20). Like Neo, a wise person will be examined by her and listen to her, coming daily to wait at her door — and this is the path which leads to 'life and obtains favour from the LORD' (8:34-35).

If we are to find our way through our spiritual journey, we too will need wisdom to follow the 'way of righteousness'. But while God's instructions are neither riddling nor random, nor are they simply texts written on the wall. We must desire wisdom, seek after her and answer her call — and this may come in a whole range of ways, natural and supernatural.

As the crews in *Star Trek* 'boldly go' where none have gone before in the journey into outer space, much of the interest comes from their personal, internal journeys. Here they tend to consult three sources of wisdom — their friends, trained professionals and even religious guides. It is the friendships between Kirk, Spock, McCoy and the others which often show the way forward. In *The Next Generation,* the *Enterprise* has a lounge bar on the tenth deck right at the front of the ship, hence its name Ten-Forward. Keeping bar there is Guinan, a female El-Aurian who is at least some 500 years old. Sensitively played by Whoopi Goldberg, Guinan is prepared to listen, and to understand all who prop up her counter, from the android Data trying to be human to Bajoran Ensign Ro who needs help to face her anger. In this way, Guinan complements the official ship's Counsellor, Deanna Troi. Being half-human and half-Betazoid, Troi has empathic abilities which are combined with her professional training to enable her to help all on board with general advice, or sets of counselling sessions. Similarly, the young ensign Ezri Dax who becomes the Counsellor on *Deep Space Nine* has to integrate her basic training with the wisdom of eight lifetimes when she receives an emergency 'joining' with the long-lived Dax symbiont. Finally, for all the technological and scientific wizardry of the future, Captain Sisko begins to appreciate the religious dimension through his experiences with the 'orbs of the prophets' on Bajor; meanwhile, Lt Worf leaves the *Enterprise* to go off to the monastery on Boreth to seek a vision of Kahless, the original Klingon warrior and spiritual leader, when his faith is failing and he loses his way.

All three of these sources — friends, professionals and religious — are important for us as we seek wisdom and guidance along the way. Part of the reason why we travel in the Company of the church is the encouragement and support we receive from our brothers and sisters. Facing challenges together and meeting new situations forces us to rely on each other, and often God can bring us his wisdom through the words of a friend. Our church may not contain people as long-lived as the centuries of Guinan or the many lifetimes of Dax, but older and more experienced Christians should be a natural source of advice and wisdom. Empathy, the ability to put yourself in someone else's shoes and really understand how they are feeling, is crucial for anyone seeking to guide or help others. There is also a right and necessary place for counselling and those who have been professionally trained to listen and understand others. Many Christians can grow in their spiritual life by understanding more of their own human development, their upbringing and family, and all that goes to make up the unique person God wants each of us to be.

Last, whatever advice or guidance we may receive from all these different sources, it needs to be brought under the gentle and peaceable wisdom of God. Christians believe that the Wisdom and the Word of God have become human in the person of Jesus, who was created first and has been 'with us from the beginning' (Prov. 8:22; Jn. 1:1). Whether it is going off to a monastery, seeking a renewed vision or trying to understand a spiritual experience, our search for wisdom will always lead us back to Jesus, who is both the Door and the Gateway where we start, and the guide along the way. As Morpheus explained to Neo after the visit to the Oracle, 'There is a difference between knowing the path and walking the path'. Jesus is 'the pioneer and perfecter of our faith', 'the beginning and the end' (Heb. 12:2; Rev. 22:13) — and he will guide us on better than any oracle as we turn to him in prayer, silence and study in the days ahead.

For Prayer and Meditation

Lord Jesus Christ,
Wisdom and Word of God:
may we hear your words
and know your wisdom,
that we may walk the path to your Father.

29

Phone Home

Rejoice in the Lord always; again I will say, Rejoice. Let your gentleness be known to everyone. The Lord is near. Do not worry about anything, but in everything by prayer and supplication with thanksgiving let your requests be made known to God. And the peace of God, which surpasses all understanding, will guard your hearts and your minds in Christ Jesus. Finally, beloved, whatever is true, whatever is honourable, whatever is just, whatever is pure, whatever is pleasing, whatever is commendable, if there is any excellence and if there is anything worthy of praise, think about these things.

PHILIPPIANS 4:4-8

When Morpheus and his companions enter the illusory world produced by the computer Matrix, they keep in touch with their ship by telephones. Morpheus first contacts Thomas Anderson, as Neo is known inside the Matrix, by sending him a mobile phone. He then gives him very detailed instructions down the cell phone to help Thomas to escape — but Thomas gets frightened and drops the phone, allowing the evil Agents to capture him. Whenever members of a *Star Trek* crew are transported into a new or strange world, they keep in touch with their ship through their communicators. In the original 1960s series, these early communicators look eerily like our later mobile phones, even down to the flip-up covers into which they speak. By the later series, crew members have 'com-badges' on their uniforms which allow them to talk to each other or get instructions from their ship simply by pressing them. The com-badges also allow the ship's computer to keep a constant lock on their position, ready for any eventuality.

Luke's Gospel portrays Jesus as the man of prayer, constantly in touch with his Father. At every significant moment of Jesus' ministry, Luke notes that 'he was praying' — at his baptism, 'all the night' before he chose the disciples and at his transfiguration (Lk. 3:21; 6:12-13; 9:28-29). Despite, or perhaps because of, the 'great crowds who gathered to listen or to be healed', Jesus 'would withdraw to deserted places and pray' (Lk. 5:15-16). No wonder that when the disciples observe him praying, they ask him to teach them to pray too (Lk. 11:1). If Jesus needed to keep in contact and ask for instructions before he did anything, how much more do we need to do so on our journey? Just like the crews in our stories, we need to keep in constant communication with base.

This is true for our crews in their daily routine — but even more so when something goes wrong. Starfleet's communicators and combadges signal their exact location in case the crew need an emergency 'beam-out' back to the ship. When Morpheus and his colleagues are in trouble, they phone their 'operator', a freeborn human called Tank, to reprogramme things around them when necessary, or to provide them with a way out — 'Tank, I need an exit — fast!' When the young extraterrestrial is left behind on earth, afraid, alone and 'three million light years from home' in the film *ET*, he turns to the ten-year-old Elliot with the stammered request, 'Phone home'; together, they construct a rudimentary communications system, which eventually brings help.

So too Paul instructs his readers not to 'worry about anything' because 'the Lord is near'. If we are in constant contact with the 'operator' of the whole universe, then indeed we have good reason not to worry. Instead, says Paul, 'with prayer and supplication, let your requests be made known to God' (Phil. 4:5-6). The first word, for 'prayer', covers the whole general area of prayer, but the second, for 'supplication', indicates specific 'needs' or necessity. There are some people who feel uneasy about bothering the Lord of the cosmos with our minor concerns — yet such is his love for us that he wants our 'requests to be made known'. Jesus, too, is quite clear about this; often his first words when someone came to him was to ask them to be specific: 'What do you want me to do for you?' (Mk. 10:51). Even sinful human beings 'know how to give good gifts to your children', rather than nasty surprises like a stone when asked for bread, or a snake instead of a fish. So too, our heavenly Father wants to 'give good things to those who ask him' (Matt. 7:11). In this broken world, God wants to help all those in need and so our prayers must never be just for ourselves, but for all his children, especially the poor and hungry, the oppressed and the refugee. But this is not a reason for ignoring our own needs — and often, as God answers our prayers, so he sends us out to be the answer to someone else's.

The problem occurs when we lose contact with base. Neo drops the mobile phone which Morpheus sent him, and gets captured by the evil Agents; another of the crew, Cypher, who wants to go back to his old life in the Matrix, actually throws his away — which allows the Agents to track them. During *Discovery*'s long journey in *2001: A Space Odyssey*, the astronauts keep contact with earth via an AE35 antenna which must be focused on the ever diminishing globe. When HAL the computer starts to go wrong, he causes the AE35 unit to go off target, so there can be no communication with Mission Control — and no reply (pp. 135-163).

Unfortunately, prayer can be like that for many. Our focus can slip, our mind goes off target, and we do not know whether we have been heard, much less receive any response. As the astronauts have to check their communication unit, so too we need to examine ourselves. Do we really believe that God can love us and wants to answer our prayer, or is there perhaps some sin or resentment which is holding us back? In *The Lord of the Rings*, when Pippin looks in the Palantir, an ancient 'seeing stone', with all the wrong motives, he is almost engulfed by the evil he has contacted (pp. 614-617). Thus Paul goes on to stress that prayer needs to be in the context of thinking on 'whatever is true, honourable, just, pure' and so forth (Phil. 4:8). Having examined ourselves, however, it may be that we can find no reason from our side for the apparent silence. Some Christians teach that such unanswered prayer is always the person's fault, rather than God's lack of response, and this can cause them further pain or hurt. But God is not a cosmic telephone answering service for us to manipulate at will, and there are times in all relationships when we walk quietly together in silence. And if that is difficult, seek the advice and help of a wise spiritual guide, or someone to sit with you in the stillness.

For Paul, the crucial thing to remember is that 'the Lord is near' — whether we feel his presence or not. This is the only basis upon which we are not to worry, but to bring our prayers and needs to God. And he also tells us to do it 'with thanksgiving' for all that God has already done for us. As we reflect on God's goodness, so too we may 'rejoice in the Lord always' and begin to know 'the peace of God which surpasses all understanding' and let it guard our hearts and minds in Christ Jesus (4:4-7).

For Prayer and Meditation

'Ask and you will receive, that your joy may be full.'

John 16:24

Phone home — it's a local call from here!

30

Strength in Silence

Why do you say, O Jacob, and speak, O Israel, 'My way is hidden from the Lord, *and my right is disregarded by my God'? Have you not known? Have you not heard? The* Lord *is the everlasting God, the Creator of the ends of the earth. He does not faint or grow weary; his understanding is unsearchable. He gives power to the faint, and strengthens the powerless. Even youths will faint and be weary, and the young will fall exhausted; but those who wait for the* Lord *shall renew their strength, they shall mount up with wings like eagles, they shall run and not be weary, they shall walk and not faint. Listen to me in silence, O coastlands; let the peoples renew their strength.*

ISAIAH 40:27–41:1

Propping up Quark's bar on *Deep Space Nine* is usually a large, wrinkled alien, a Lurian by the name of Morn. He wears a heavily padded outfit, and looks very strong — but he is also the silent type, and seldom speaks; he just sits there, quietly drinking. However, he is enormously popular and is almost like a mascot for Quark. When he is absent, bar takings drop by more than four per cent, so Quark replaces him with a hologram! It is only when Morn supposedly dies that his real secret emerges — that he has concealed in his second stomach a quantity of liquid latinum, the most valuable substance in the universe, the profits of an old bank robbery. In return for Quark's help in getting rid of his former associates who were after his wealth, Morn regurgitates some treasure from within to give to a delighted Quark.

We noted yesterday that it is not uncommon for us to lose contact with base, to let our focus slip off target and to find that our prayers seem to meet with a cosmic wall of silence. The prophet Isaiah addresses such people who feel that 'my way is hidden from the Lord'. In response, he reminds them of the nature of God, 'the everlasting God, the Creator of the ends of the earth'. As such, God cannot 'faint or grow weary' (40:27-28). It is part of being human, even for strong young men, that we get tired and exhausted (40:30). Isaiah is addressing the Jews towards the end of their exile in Babylon. After a generation of captivity away from Jerusalem, it is no wonder that they feel that God does not answer their prayers and they are growing weary. It must have seemed that all contact had been lost. Yet Isaiah brings words of 'comfort' to God's people, to remind them of the everlasting nature of the word of God and of his love for his people like a gentle shepherd (see Is. 40:1-11). God 'gives power to the faint, and strengthens the powerless' (40:29). This is good news, and our immediate reaction is to want to know how we can restore contact and get access to this power, so that we can have eagles' wings, or 'run and not be weary'. Isaiah's answer is clear: 'Those who wait for the LORD shall renew their strength'. So often we want a quick and easy answer — and we do not like waiting. Yet that is the source of this power. People can 'renew their strength', but we have to learn to 'listen to me in silence' (40:31–41:1). We need to be quiet, like Morn, and then we can reach the treasure which is hidden deep within us.

Yesterday, we looked at keeping communication lines open, especially making our needs known to God by our specific requests. However, in all relationships there is 'a time to speak and a time to keep silence' (Eccl. 3:7) and this is just as true for prayer. In the *Star Trek* universe, it is the Vulcans who have learned this best. Mr Spock will be very quiet and concentrate in order to gather his strength when a particular task is required. Another young Vulcan officer, Tuvok, resigned from Starfleet because of the illogical and emotional nature of his human colleagues and devoted himself to the rigorous Kolinahr discipline instead. After making a long pilgrimage on foot across the Vulcan desert to Mount Seleya, Tuvok returns to Starfleet where he serves on *Voyager*. During its long journey home, Tuvok's mental and spiritual disciplines prove invaluable. He teaches Vulcan meditation techniques to a Betazoid crewman, Suder, to enable him to cope with his violent emotions. He instructs the Ocampan, Kes, in silence before a candle flame to help her develop her latent mental abilities.

Similar techniques have long been used in many religious traditions to help a person find inner stillness or for meditation. Many eastern techniques have become popular in western countries in recent years, including attention to body posture and breathing. Yet such things are as old as the Psalms, where there is also this concern for stillness and silence: 'Be still, and know that I am God!' 'For God alone my soul waits in silence, for my hope is from him' (Pss. 46:10; 62:5). This contemplative tradition runs throughout Christian history, especially in the writings of people like St John of the Cross, or the *Cloud of Unknowing.* One important difference is the Christian emphasis upon knowing God. It is not just a relaxation technique to 'empty the mind' or clear your thoughts. In fact, in the cosmic Conflict, an empty mind can be a tempting invitation to evil influences, so our silent prayer must keep a focus on the goodness of God. None the less, simple techniques like using a candle and paying proper attention to your body posture or your breathing can be very helpful. Many people find that confessing their sins, hurts or anxieties while breathing out and then taking in the comfort and strength of 'the breath of God', the Holy Spirit, on the in-breath can be very helpful. This rhythm of breathing can also be linked to simple mental prayers like the Jesus prayer — 'Lord Jesus Christ, son of the living God, have mercy on me a sinner' — or repeating phrases from Scripture.

Tuvok rejoined Starfleet as result of his pilgrimage, while the Klingon, Lt Worf, went to stay at the monastery on Boreth to seek a vision of Kahless, the long-dead Klingon spiritual leader, when he had lost contact with his roots. Even though the Kahless who came to him turned out to be a clone manufactured by the priests, somehow it still resulted in Worf's faith and energy being restored. Going on quiet days and retreats can be another way for us to recharge our spiritual batteries and rediscover our roots in God. For those who are not used to it, the invitation to silence can be rather daunting, or even frightening. This is why it is usually undertaken with a retreat leader or spiritual director, who will listen to your experiences and give guidance or instructions. A retreat can be totally silent, for days or even weeks, except for regular, usually daily, individual conversations with the director. Alternatively, it may be a weekend away with a group, with little talks or homilies, and the times of silence interspersed with walks and services. Some retreats include creative activities, like painting or pottery, as another way to reach your inner depths and express them before God.

All of these are different ways of realigning our focus and getting back on target. We can all, young and old alike, 'faint and grow weary' — but, like Morn, we have treasure hidden within us. It is through stillness and silent prayer, at home or on retreat, alone or in company, that we can begin to reach the depths of our being — and be touched by the love of God.

For Prayer and Meditation

Be still, and know that I am God!

Psalm 46:10

If you have been on retreat, spend some time in silence recalling the experience, and bring the peace into the present; if not, why not spend the time finding out what is available — and booking one?

31

The Guidebook

But as for you, continue in what you have learned and firmly believed, knowing from whom you learned it, and how from childhood you have known the sacred writings that are able to instruct you for salvation through faith in Christ Jesus. All Scripture is inspired by God and is useful for teaching, for reproof, for correction, and for training in righteousness, so that everyone who belongs to God may be proficient, equipped for every good work.

2 TIMOTHY 3:14-17

The *Hitchhiker's Guide to the Galaxy* is precisely what it says — a guide. As Ford Prefect explained to a bemused Arthur Dent, just after rescuing him from the demolition of the earth, 'It tells you everything you need to know about anything. That's its job' (p. 44). It even contains the ultimate answer to 'life, the universe and everything' — the number 42; now all we need to do is to find the right question to which that is the answer! Actually, it is not quite as informative as it claims, since Arthur discovers that the entry for 'Earth' contains the one word, 'harmless' — and even Ford's fifteen years of research on earth has only updated it to 'mostly harmless' (p. 52). But a guide can be extremely useful on a long journey, and the *Hitchhiker's Guide* becomes essential for our heroes as they travel around. When Gene Roddenberry and his colleagues produced the writer's guide with all the background notes for *Star Trek: The Next Generation,* it was known as 'the bible'. The 'bible' for *Deep Space Nine* was just nineteen pages long, but contained all the basic descriptions of the station and the characters. Because they came from the creators of the series, these bibles had to be followed in the practical tasks of writing and producing all the episodes.

Some Christians treat the Bible as though it is the final guide to 'life, the universe and everything'. However, like the *Hitchhiker's Guide,* it cannot contain all the details about everything; on the other hand, because it comes from the creator of the universe, it contains all we need to know for its particular purpose, 'to instruct you for salvation'. This is why Paul encourages Timothy to 'continue in what you have learned' (2 Tim. 3:14-15). The Jews were particularly zealous for the law, not in any legalistic sense, but with a passionate devotion, as Psalm 119 makes clear: 'Oh, how I love your law! It is my meditation all day long.' This is because it had a practical purpose in guiding their lives: 'Your word is a lamp to my feet and a light to my path' (Ps. 119:97, 105).

But first we have to be able to see the light. At the start of *The Lord of the Rings,* when Gandalf throws the ring on the fire, Frodo is amazed to discover 'lines of fire' forming the 'letters of a flowing script'. Because they are Elvish, he cannot read them, but Gandalf translates them and discovers that this is indeed 'the One Ring to rule them all' (pp. 63-64). Translation is not always so easy. When Captain Sisko brings a very old Bajoran inscription back to *Deep Space Nine,* his Science Officer struggles to translate it. One phrase might mean that the Bajorans are to 'suffer horribly', or just 'eat fruit' — and the difference is quite important!

Timothy is more fortunate, since he has known the sacred Scriptures 'from childhood' (3:15). Since he has a Greek name, a Greek father and lived in the Greek city of Lystra in Asia Minor, he would have been taught the Hebrew Scriptures in the Greek translation we call the Septuagint, which lies behind many of the Old Testament quotations in the New Testament. We too should be grateful for the work of Bible translators over centuries, who have now produced so many different versions in English. Some of them are very close to the original Greek and Hebrew, while others are more of a paraphrase and easier to read. It is important that we use a modern translation in our Bible reading, because English words do change their meaning over time, and we should compare different translations to help us grapple with what the text is saying.

Once we have read the translation, we have to work out what the text actually means, to interpret it for our lives today. This is particularly important for any text from a different culture or time from our own. In another episode of *Deep Space Nine,* 'Destiny', a priest tries to stop an experiment to communicate through the wormhole to the other side because of an ancient prophecy which he interprets to be about the destruction of the 'celestial temple'. In fact the experiment is a success and keeps the wormhole open — which is then seen to be a fulfilment of an alternative interpretation of the prophecy.

Unfortunately, church history is also full of different interpretations of some Bible passages, especially from some of the more colourful sections of books like Revelation. It is therefore very important that we check our reading of Scripture against the interpretation of others, so that we can understand it properly. Many people use Bible notes daily to help them with their reading, like those produced by the Bible Reading Fellowship. Commentaries are also very useful, but they can range from extremely detailed analysis of the original texts to a simple devotional retelling of the story. Again, it is worth trying a few to see which might best suit your needs. This book is itself an attempt to help people read the Bible regularly — and a similar mixture of study and application can be found in the *People's Bible Commentary,* also published by BRF.

At Hogwarts, Hermione Granger is always accompanied by a large pile of books which she has borrowed from the library. While Harry Potter and the others may sometimes mock her as a swot, her reading habits come in extremely handy for solving various mysteries such as finding Nicolas Flamel, the maker of the philosopher's stone (*Philosopher's Stone,* p. 161) or getting the recipe for the 'polyjuice potion' (*Chamber of Secrets,* pp. 122-124). Then all they have to do is to go and follow the instructions. Paul is equally clear that the Scriptures are for our 'instruction' (2 Tim. 3:15). Furthermore, they are not the instructions for 'life, the universe and everything' like the *Hitchhiker's Guide,* but 'for salvation through faith in Christ Jesus'. The Bible is 'inspired by God', literally 'God-breathed', to be 'useful' for some specific purposes — teaching, reproof, correction and training in righteousness (3:16). These are all very practical, and make it clear that the Bible is a guide for our journey. If we read it regularly, it will help us to grow in our understanding, to be taught the way we should go, and to put us right when we make mistakes, or go the wrong way.

Finally, no amount of reading, interpretation or instruction is any good if it is not then put into practice and acted upon. Gandalf and the Company of the Ring spend some time by the lake outside the entrance to the Walls of Moria, trying first to find the door, then to read the inscription, to translate it and to work out what 'speak, friend, and enter' actually means. Gandalf tries speaking every charm and spell he knows but the door remains shut fast, and no amount of force can open it. It is only when he actually obeys the instruction, and speaks the single word 'friend', that the doors open magically to welcome them — just in time to avoid capture by the monster in the lake (pp. 321-326). Our passage concludes that the purpose of Scripture is equally practical, so that we 'may be proficient, equipped for every good work' (3:17). Both words 'proficient' and 'equipped' mean ready or fitted for the task — and for us, the task is to complete our journey of faith as we obey its instructions, let it speak to us as a friend and open itself up to us.

The Bible is essential to help us find our way through life and the universe, even if not everything else. We need to read it and interpret it, using all the skills we may have and the assistance from others through things like commentaries or Bible reading notes. But most important of all, we must actually follow the guide and go and put it into practice — and then we may begin to find the 'ultimate answer', even better than *Hitchhiker*'s '42', on our journey.

For Prayer and Meditation

Blessed Lord,
who caused all holy scriptures to be written for our learning:
help us so to hear them, to read, mark, learn and inwardly digest them
that, through patience and the comfort of your holy word,
we may embrace and forever hold fast the hope of everlasting life
which you have given us in our Saviour Jesus Christ.

The Collect for Bible Sunday, *Common Worship*

32

Dreams and Visions

Peter, standing with the eleven, raised his voice and addressed them, 'Men of Judaea and all who live in Jerusalem, let this be known to you, and listen to what I say. Indeed, these are not drunk, as you suppose, for it is only nine o'clock in the morning. No, this is what was spoken through the prophet Joel: "In the last days it will be, God declares, that I will pour out my Spirit upon all flesh, and your sons and your daughters shall prophesy, and your young men shall see visions, and your old men shall dream dreams. Even upon my slaves, both men and women, in those days I will pour out my Spirit; and they shall prophesy."'

ACTS 2:14-18

At the end of his long *Space Odyssey* to meet the monolith around Jupiter and of his even longer journey through the Star Gate, David Bowman suddenly finds himself in a 'vision' of a normal hotel suite — except that it turns out to be as real and 'solid as anything he had ever seen'. Eventually, he gets into bed: 'Within seconds, he had passed beyond the reach of dreams. So, for the last time, David Bowman slept' (*2001*, pp. 241-249). His mind is then analysed and he becomes the Star-Child. In *2010: Odyssey Two,* he appears to Dr Floyd to warn him of Jupiter's impending destruction — but Floyd and the others struggle to work out whether it was real or a dream (*2010*, pp. 214-220). In *2061: Odyssey Three,* Floyd has a dream of the monolith, during which his consciousness is 'echoed' by HAL and stored with Bowman in the monolith itself; later, a vision of Floyd appears to his grandson (*2061*, pp. 219-220, 257-266, 291-292).

As an atheistic humanist, Gene Roddenberry was concerned to take his original *Star Trek* on the journey into outer space. However, in *The Next Generation,* the journey into inner space is of more interest, especially with people like Deanna Troi, the ship's Counsellor, aboard. When the *Enterprise* is stuck in a spatial rift in the episode 'Night Terrors', the crew are deprived of normal sleep and dreams, and descend into depression and madness; only Troi's deciphering of her nightmares saves them all. After Roddenberry's death, the producers' interest in spiritual themes develops further. The android, Data, discovers that he has a dream programme and, in a dream, meets his 'father', the scientist Dr Noonian Soong who created him in his own image. Later Data experiences waking nightmares, about which he consults a hologram of Freud. Eventually, Data realizes that they are the clue to the way the ship and its crew are being devoured by 'interphasic leeches'. In one of the last episodes of the final season, Wesley Crusher is encouraged to undertake a Native American 'vision quest', which leads to him leaving Starfleet to explore the galaxy with the Traveller.

These themes of guidance and being saved through dreams recur regularly through *Deep Space Nine.* Benjamin Sisko has various visions of the prophets and dreams about Bajor and its past. Through them, he comes to understand the wormhole, receives guidance about excavating Bajor's past and is warned to save Bajor from the coming war with the evil Dominion. Similarly, during *Voyager*'s long journey home, the Native American First Officer, Chakotay, undertakes several vision quests, while the former Borg drone, Seven of Nine, has visions of her childhood as her humanity reasserts itself.

Dreams and visions are used repeatedly in the Bible for guidance, understanding and saving people. It is through his dream of the angels' ladder bridging the gulf between heaven and earth and his night struggle with God that Jacob becomes Israel, the father of the nation (Gen. 28:10-22; 32:22-32). His son Joseph's dreams may have been very annoying to his brothers at first, but eventually his interpretation of Pharaoh's dreams of seven fat cows and seven thin cows saves not only Egypt from the famine, but his father Jacob and all the family too (Gen. 37–47). It is in a dream that Solomon asks God for wisdom, and receives the promise of wealth and honour also (1 Kings 3:5-15). The prophets like Amos and Ezekiel regularly have daydreams, or see visions of things like a 'bowl of fruit' or a 'valley of dry bones', which are interpreted as guidance, warnings or encouragement for Israel (Amos 8:1-2; Ezek. 37). Daniel has dreams and 'night visions' of the future of God's people in the midst of the eastern great empires (Dan. 7–8), as well as being able to interpret the dreams of the Persian king, Nebuchadnezzar, which leads to both Daniel and God's people being saved (Dan. 2–4). In

The Matrix, the whole world is a computer-induced dream, and the human race is saved by Neo, Morpheus and the crew of their ship, which is called *Nebuchadnezzar* in an obvious link to the dreams in Daniel.

In the New Testament similarly, dreams are used to guide and save people. In a dream, Joseph discovers that Mary's child is actually 'conceived from the Holy Spirit' and will be called Jesus, which means Saviour, 'for he will save his people from their sins' (Matt. 1:20-21). Dreams warn the wise men to go home a different way, instruct Joseph to take Mary and Jesus to Egypt to avoid Herod, and eventually to return to live in Nazareth (Matt. 2:12, 13, 19). Even Pilate's wife is warned in a dream that Jesus is 'innocent' (Matt. 27:19). In Acts, Peter is guided by day-dreams or visions to go to Cornelius and accept Gentiles into the church, and is saved from prison in what seems to him to be a dream (Acts 10:10-16; 12:6-11). Meanwhile, Paul first takes the gospel into Europe in response to a vision of a man from Troas asking for help, and is reassured by God in other dreams (16:9-10; 18:9-10; 27:23-24).

Thus it is not surprising on the day of Pentecost that Peter interprets what is happening as a fulfilment of Joel's prophecy that 'young men shall see visions, and old men shall dream dreams'. But whereas in Old Testament days, only prophets and leaders might expect to have such revelations, now in the 'last days' God is pouring out his Spirit upon everybody, young and old, men and women, free and slaves alike (Acts 2:17-18). It is not because they have been drinking spirits early in the morning that they are seeing such amazing things, it is God guiding and saving through his Holy Spirit.

After all the important work of Freud, Jung and many psychologists and therapists since, we now know more of how important dreams are, and that people deprived of dream-sleep will go mad, just like the crew of the *Enterprise.* As they were for Data or Seven of Nine, dreams can be important ways of retrieving some of our childhood memories or experiences. Equally, we may sometimes find an answer or resolve a difficult problem with which we have wrestled in the day only by sorting it out in our dreams. If this is true as a normal human process, it is even more to be expected that, as we go to sleep in an attitude of prayer, perhaps after saying the night service of Compline, God may guide us in our dreams, or bring us healing.

But dream imagery is very difficult to interpret, as is clear from both our science fiction and Bible stories. It is rare that the people or objects in our dreams actually represent themselves; often, they may stand for parts of our own personality and thoughts of which we may have been unaware until now. Sometimes it is helpful to write them down immediately upon waking during a particular period of decision making, while other Christians include them within a daily journal. Discussing them with a wise counsellor or spiritual director can also be helpful. Bunyan's entire *Pilgrim's Progress* is presented as a dream he had, and in it Christian visits the 'House of the Interpreter', where various visions are explained to him. If it is by God's Spirit that we 'dream dreams and see visions', it is by that same Holy Spirit that we should seek to understand and interpret what God may be saying to us.

Thus our dreams and visions need to be put into the context of the whole of this week's study as we have sought to find our way through the highs and lows on our journey of faith. Like so many of the characters in all our stories, we need guidance and direction along the way. This can come in many forms through spiritual direction or wise counselling, in spoken prayers or silent meditation, by reading the Bible and in our dreams. And because we are not yet whole, we can get it wrong or take the wrong direction — so it is important to bring all these ways together and let them balance each other under the guidance of the Holy Spirit. He will protect us in the Conflict and enable us to Find our Way — and will bring us to times of rest and healing as we go.

For Prayer and Meditation

God our Father, Lord of day and night,
speak to us in the dark and guide us by your light,
that we may come to the unclouded vision of your glory.

PART 6

HEALING AND FEEDING

After five weeks on the road, we need to find resources and repairs. Where can we find rest and healing, food and drink, to restore us in body, mind and soul?

33

Oases

The Lord *is my shepherd, I shall not want. He makes me lie down in green pastures; he leads me beside still waters; he restores my soul. He leads me in the paths of righteousness for his name's sake. Even though I walk through the valley of the shadow of death, I fear no evil; for you are with me; your rod and your staff, they comfort me. You prepare a table before me in the presence of my enemies; you anoint my head with oil; my cup overflows. Surely goodness and mercy shall follow me all the days of my life, and I shall dwell in the house of the* Lord *for ever.*

PSALM 23

When Frank Poole wakes up at the start of *3001: The Final Odyssey,* he slowly recalls the last thing he remembers — 'spinning helplessly in space' (*3001,* p. 13), after he had been knocked off *Discovery*'s hull by HAL while trying to repair the AE35 antenna and re-establish their contact with earth. Now he is in a hospital bed, and as he is slowly brought back to health, fed and cared for, he learns what really happened — that the failure of his spacesuit had caused him to be rapidly frozen and that he has drifted out among the edges of the solar system for a thousand years. Poole's new life, and his reunion with his colleagues, David Bowman and HAL still stored in the monolith, form the climax of Sir Arthur C. Clarke's extraordinary sequence of novels, but first he has to rest and recuperate.

Our journey may not be as long as Poole's, but there will be many times along the way when we need to stop for repairs and restoration, for healing and recovery — or just for a break! One of the good things about travelling in a Company is that responsibilities can be shared around and we do not have to be 'on duty' all the time. The Conflict with all that opposes us along the way will mean that, however much we use the armour of God, we will suffer pains and hurts and things get broken, so healing and repairs will be necessary. In addition, Finding our

Way through all the ups and downs, even with all the proper guidance and instructions we discovered last week, can still be very tiring and we need opportunities to recover our strength — which will be our concerns for this week.

Many of our stories include resting at such an oasis along the way. When the children first enter the frozen wastes of Narnia under the White Witch, they are taken by a friendly beaver into his house on a dam. Here they find Mrs Beaver, busy doing the mending, and they enjoy a delightful meal together in the warmth. Mr Beaver explains more of what is happening and then, duly strengthened, they all set off back into the snow (*Lion, Witch and Wardrobe,* pp. 68-81). Similarly, on their later *Voyage of the 'Dawn Treader'*, they come to Aslan's table on an island at the World's End, where 'those who have come so far' may rest and eat a wondrous banquet (pp. 170-172).

In the Middle-earth of C. S. Lewis' friend, Tolkien, the elf-houses in the valleys play a similar role. Bilbo Baggins goes to the house of the elf-lord, Elrond, at Rivendell on his first journey: 'His house was perfect, whether you liked food, or sleep, or work, or storytelling, or singing, or just sitting and thinking best, or a pleasant mixture of them all. Evil things did not come into that valley' (*The Hobbit,* p. 48). Bilbo returns to Rivendell at the end of this journey, to recuperate after defeating the dragon Smaug, and eventually retires there after his eleventy-first birthday. Frodo wakes up there after his battle with the Black Riders, and is overjoyed to see Bilbo again. Here the Fellowship of the Ring is formed and sent out on their journey to battle the Dark Lord, and Frodo returns here on his way home (*Lord of the Rings,* pp. 235-297, 1022-1024). Equally, the elf-realm of Lórien is also an oasis of rest and healing for the Company after their battles in Moria and the grievous loss of Gandalf (pp. 372-388).

The Psalmist could be describing any of these oases in what has become arguably the most famous psalm of all, said by people alone and frightened or together in great joy, at weddings and funerals, in disasters and celebrations. We saw at the start of our journey that John's Gospel describes Jesus as the Good Shepherd, both the Door and the Way for the sheep. The image of a shepherd caring for his sheep was frequently used for God's relationship with his people in ancient Israel. The shepherd usually had to feed his sheep on the dry scrubland at the edges of the wilderness, but occasionally they might find a valley, watered by a stream. Wherever water is found in Israel-Palestine even today, grass springs up alongside — and the Psalmist draws on a memory of lying on such 'green pastures . . . beside still waters' to paint a marvellous picture of the rest he finds in God. It may be a tough journey, but God is the shepherd who 'leads' us along the right paths, and who also 'leads' us to the quiet oasis. Here indeed is rest and healing as 'he restores my soul' (Ps. 23:1-3).

The writer knows the dangers of the journey and the Conflict along the way all too well. Some of the rift valleys in that area of the Middle East can be very deep and dark where the sun rarely penetrates. An old Hebrew idiom uses 'deadly' or 'of death' to indicate the 'greatest', so the 'valley of the shadow of death' really means the valley with the deepest and darkest shadows (v. 4). Such places would be where robbers or wild animals might lie in wait, and the shepherd would have only his 'rod and staff' to protect the sheep. The Psalmist is confident in the armour of God, that his 'rod and staff' are enough to protect and comfort us in the 'deepest darkness', as some modern Bible versions more correctly translate it. Yet it is true that experiences of death and bereavement are often the darkest times on our journey, and to know that God is with us even 'in the valley of the shadow of death' is such a comfort that the old translation will always be used.

Finally, as at Aslan's table or in the elf-houses, food is also important for the Psalmist. God is our genial host, preparing a table, even in the presence of enemies, like death and evil. Such is his protection and generosity that it is more like a party. In such hot climes, people would anoint their heads with perfumed oil, to provide coolness and healing as it evaporated, spreading its fragrance around; meanwhile, so much wine is poured out here that it spills over the cups (v. 5). Such 'goodness and mercy' of God are our companions along the way and follow us 'all the days of my life' as we dwell in the presence of God for ever (v. 6).

However, that brings the temptation to stay in the oasis itself forever. In *The Pilgrim's Progress,* Christian stays at the House Beautiful, where he is given fine food and wine, and allowed to rest and sleep. But then he is taken to the armoury and given the weapons and armour of God, and a view of the Delectable Mountains to which he is travelling, before being sent back out on the journey. Caspian and the children find three Narnian Lords asleep at Aslan's table, who never made it to the World's End, and the Lotus-Eaters tempt Odysseus' crew to give up their odyssey and stay in their pleasant land for ever. Even Captain Janeway is sometimes anxious that her weary crew will give up trying to get home and settle on a nice planet in the Delta Quadrant, like the one inhabited by humans descended from people abducted from earth as long ago as 1937.

Oases and pleasant valleys are wonderful gifts from God along our journey. Many Christians make an annual retreat at a religious community, where they can rest, catch up on some sleep, enjoy wholesome food and have time to pray. Such places do indeed restore the soul, and we shall learn more of them in the coming week as we look at the themes of healing and feeding. But we must not forget that they are only oases along the way, not our destination. The continuing Conflict with evil, whether in the form of a wicked witch, greedy dragon or dark lord, must be pursued and our journey completed at the World's End, if we are ever finally to get back home. So let's enjoy the rest, restore our souls and get ready to complete the task as the Good Shepherd leads us through his valleys — and beyond to his kingdom.

For Prayer and Meditation

I remember a house where all were good to me, God knows.

Gerard Manley Hopkins, *In the Valley of the Elwy*

Think of places that have been oases on your journey; do you need to go on retreat, or rest for repairs and encouragement?

34

The Healer

As soon as they left the synagogue, they entered the house of Simon and Andrew, with James and John. Now Simon's mother-in-law was in bed with a fever, and they told him about her at once. He came and took her by the hand and lifted her up. Then the fever left her, and she began to serve them. That evening, at sundown, they brought to him all who were sick or possessed with demons. And the whole city was gathered around the door. And he cured many who were sick with various diseases, and cast out many demons; and he would not permit the demons to speak, because they knew him.

MARK 1:29-34

During a survey mission from *Deep Space Nine* into the Gamma Quadrant, Dr Julian Bashir finds a planet which once had a thriving culture, now decimated by disease. The oppressive Dominion, angry at the people's defiance, sent this upon them as an 'example to others'. Everyone is born with the 'blight' — coloured lesions on their skin; when these 'quicken' and turn red, the people die slowly and painfully. There is no cure, and all their 'hospital' can do is to administer poison to people at their quickening to allow them to die peacefully and quickly. As a doctor, Bashir is appalled, accusing them of being murderers, and starts some research, confident that he will find a cure within a week or two. When he does not, he becomes quite depressed and has to face the consequences of his own arrogance as the woman he was helping dies in a painful childbirth. However, her child is born without the blight; Bashir may not have found a cure, but he can vaccinate pregnant women to produce a new healthy generation (see the episode 'The Quickening').

Dr Bashir may not be able to cure everything, but medicine in *Star Trek*'s optimistic future has improved unimaginably. Dr McCoy — known as 'Bones' — on the original *Enterprise* may be a crusty old doctor with a sharp tongue and a debatable bedside manner, yet even he seems to achieve minor miracles in sickbay most of the time. By *The Next Gen-*

eration, Dr Crusher is able to thaw three people who had been cryogenically frozen as soon as they died (from heart disease, cancer, cigarettes and alcohol!) in the twentieth century, and bring them back to full health. When *Voyager*'s doctor is killed in the shift to the Delta Quadrant, the ship's Emergency Medical Hologram is activated, a computer-generated doctor programmed with all medical knowledge. Although he is not designed for long-term use, the doctor develops his own programme and becomes a valued member of the crew.

Healers play an important role in many of our stories, from Lucy being given a healing cordial in Narnia to the redoubtable Madam Pomfrey, matron of the hospital wing at Hogwarts who has to help Harry Potter recover after most of his adventures. This is also a hugely important aspect of Jesus' ministry. In Mark's account of the start of Jesus' ministry, it was this aspect which ensured he was immediately noticed by the people. After calling his first disciples, Jesus enters the synagogue in Capernaum to teach — but he is immediately confronted by a man 'with an unclean spirit'. When Jesus restores the man to health, it is no surprise that his 'fame' begins to spread through 'the surrounding region' (Mk. 1:21-28).

Jesus, however, is aware of a more immediate and local need. If you visit Capernaum today, you can still see a little stone house next to the synagogue. It was covered by a small church in the fifth century because it was believed to be the home of Peter and Andrew, between the synagogue and the harbour. Here Jesus retires with his disciples, but before he can rest, he goes to the bedside of Peter's mother-in-law and heals her from her fever (1:30-31). She then gets up to serve them a meal — but the word is out, and soon a crowd gathers at the door. The Sabbath would end at sunset, which is when people would be allowed to travel and work again, and carry burdens, including the sick. As soon as they can, people bring their loved ones who are diseased or oppressed to Jesus — and he heals them (1:32-34).

Some of the ancient Hebrew prophets performed healings, such as Elijah healing the widow's son at Zarephath or Elisha curing Naaman the leper (1 Kings 17:17-24; 2 Kings 5). Isaiah saw it as part of the calling of the servant of God to bear our infirmities and carry our diseases, that 'by his bruises we are healed' (Is. 53:4-5). In Matthew's version of the healing of Peter's mother-in-law, he sees Jesus fulfilling this prophecy (Matt. 8:17). All the Gospels stress the importance of healing in Jesus' ministry. Thus in Mark, this passage is followed by accounts of the healing of a leper (1:40-44), a paralysed man (2:1-12), a man with a withered hand (3:1-6), the woman with the flow of blood and Jairus' daughter (5:21-43), a deaf man with speech difficulties (7:31-37), two blind men (8:22-26 and 10:46-52), as well as several people with unclean spirits (1:23-27; 5:1-20; 7:24-30; 9:14-29) and the general summaries of Jesus' healing ministry as in 1:34 (see also 1:39; 3:10; 6:13, 56).

Thus it is clear that this was a major part of Jesus' ministry. The crucial element which links all these stories together is his love for people in need — but beyond this there is great variation, and we should be cautious about forcing it all into one neat pattern. Sometimes the phrase used is to 'make clean'; other words are more medical, using 'heal', *therapeuō,* which gives us the English word 'therapy', and also the verb 'doctoring', *iatr-,* from which all our '-iatrics' words come. Just as commonly, however, the word is to 'save', *sǭzō,* to make whole in the broadest possible sense. There is similar variation about the people's faith: sometimes those healed are told, 'Your faith has made you well' or 'saved you' (5:34; 10:52), while on other occasions it is the faith of friends or family (2:5; 5:23). Mark says that the unbelief in Nazareth meant that Jesus could only heal a few people there, while the father of the boy with a dumb spirit cries out, 'I believe, help my unbelief!' (6:5-6; 9:24). However, on other occasions, faith is not mentioned, so we must be careful not to prescribe how healing takes place, or blame those who are not healed for their lack of faith.

What this study shows is that healing is more about who Jesus is than about what we might do. Jesus heals because in him God embodies his love in human form and because he is the Lord of all life. Tolkien makes a similar point in *The Lord of the Rings;* after the siege of Gondor and the Battle of Pelennor Fields, three grievously wounded bodies are carried to the Houses of Healing at Minas Tirith — the Lord Faramir, the Lady Eowyn and Merry the Hobbit — but they seem beyond help. But the saying goes 'The hands of the king are the hands of the healer, and so shall the rightful king be known.' Then it is that Aragorn comes and heals them as only a true king can (p. 897). In Jesus of Nazareth the 'true king' has indeed come, bringing in the kingdom of God, and 'the hands of the king are the hands of the healer'. He longs to make us whole and well, to save and heal us — and what is more, he wants to heal others through us.

This is why Christians down through the ages have been involved in caring for the sick and working for their healing. Both the church's healing ministry and its work in founding hospitals and medical missions are responses to the commission of the true Healer, Jesus Christ. There need be, and should be, no conflict between these two forms of healing. For on our own planet, we are all afflicted with the 'blight' of sin, from which only Christ can cleanse us. Some are called, like Dr Bashir, to respond in medical research or to work as doctors and nurses, while others may find that they become the 'hands of the healer' as they seek to be 'the hands of the king', praying with people in the name of Jesus of Nazareth, the Saviour and Doctor of our souls and bodies.

For Prayer and Meditation

Almighty and everliving God,
whose Son Jesus Christ healed the sick
and restored them to wholeness of life:
look with compassion on the anguish of the world
and by your healing power
make whole both individuals and nations,
through our Lord and Saviour Jesus Christ.

Collect for 8th Sunday Before Easter,
Alternative Service Book 1980

35

Regeneration Cycles

Come to me, all you that are weary and are carrying heavy burdens, and I will give you rest. Take my yoke upon you, and learn from me; for I am gentle and humble in heart, and you will find rest for your souls. For my yoke is easy, and my burden is light.

MATTHEW 11:28-30

For in one place it speaks about the seventh day as follows, 'And God rested on the seventh day from all his works.' . . . So then, a sabbath rest still remains for the people of God; for those who enter God's rest also cease from their labours as God did from his. Let us therefore make every effort to enter that rest.

HEBREWS 4:4, 9-11

In the gloom of the cargo bay on *Voyager*, some sinister Borg green lights circle and flicker. In one alcove stands a crew member motionless, with eyes shut and apparently barely conscious — and yet, for Seven of Nine, such regeneration cycles are actually what keeps her alive. Even though much of her human physique has been restored, she still needs Borg regeneration in the way the rest of the crew need sleep, and it is during these cycles that she is restored and replenished. Similarly Odo, the shape-shifting constable of *Deep Space Nine*, needs to return to his natural state of a gelatinous liquid every day. While others on the station sleep, he practises changing his shape and then recuperates in his bucket! On one occasion, when he is trapped in a turbo lift with Counsellor Troi's mother, Lwaxana, and cannot return to regenerate, his body starts to break down. Mrs Troi, who normally has about as much tact as a wild Klingon Targ beast, sensitively makes a bowl from the folds of her dress to hold him and keep him safe until he is himself again.

Yesterday, we saw that Jesus is the true Healer, because he is also the true King, the Lord of all life. Now we move from the healer to the healing he offers us in its broadest sense. The Gospels are full of physical healing miracles — and these still attract the most attention when people are healed today. But in the Bible, health is always much more than just physical, and this was an unusual view at the time. The Greeks had a dualistic concept of the soul inhabiting a body, which sometimes led to a denigration of the physical realm, and such approaches have had a great influence on Christian thinking down the centuries and still today. However, right from the stories of the creation of Adam and Eve, mixing the dust of the physical universe with the breath of God, human beings are seen in the Bible as a psychosomatic unity, where body, soul, mind and spirit are all joined in one living being.

Thus for the ancient Hebrews, *shalom,* or 'peace', included all these elements of health and wholeness in peaceful and right relationships with our own selves, with one another and with God. This is exemplified in the story of the paralysed man let down by his friends through the roof to reach Jesus, who first tells him 'Your sins are forgiven' — and only then does he go on to heal his physical disability, so that he can 'get up and walk' (Mk. 2:1-12). This is not to say that the man was being punished for his sin by his paralysis, a common view of sin and sickness rejected by Jesus in John 9:2-3; rather it is a recognition of the need for healing in all its dimensions, spiritual and physical. It is the healing of wounded hearts and minds and of broken relationships with God and one another that Jesus offers as much as, or even more than, physical healing.

This is why he calls all who are weary from their labours and tired from the burdens they carry along our journey to come to him (Matt. 11:28). When an ox or cattle was tired or weak, it would be yoked next to a stronger animal, which could take more of the burden, or a younger beast could learn from a more experienced one in the same way. So Jesus invites us to 'take my yoke upon you', to let him be alongside us, letting him share the burden and learning from him — and then 'you will find rest for your souls' (11:29). He is indeed the loving master, who makes sure the yoke sits easily and that the burden is not too heavy (11:30). In this way we too will find regeneration, as much as Seven of Nine or Odo. As we travel through life on our Christian pilgrimage, we will need times to rest and recuperate; we will need physical healing for our hurts and pains; and we will need sleep to cure our wounds and anxieties. Ultimately, 'regeneration' actually means being 'born again' and it is to new birth and new life that Christ the healer calls us.

Frodo the hobbit is wounded by a Black Rider in his fight on Weathertop. He becomes increasing weary and starts to fade away, as the blade fragment in his wound takes effect: '"My master is sick and wounded", said Sam angrily. "He needs rest".' There follows their headlong flight to the ford, where Frodo is borne on an elf-horse, pursued by the Riders. Finally, they reach the house of Elrond at Rivendell, where Frodo sleeps for several days before regaining his strength and finding healing after the evil splinter is removed (*Lord of the Rings,* pp. 212, 227, 235-238). Similarly, after Gandalf has sacrificed himself in the battle against the Balrog, he is borne up on eagle's wings by Gwaihir the Windlord to Lothlórien 'where the days bring healing not decay' and he slowly recuperates to a new life as Gandalf the White (p. 524). We too have been grievously wounded in our Conflict with evil and need to be healed. The 'splinter' of sin is lodged deep within us and we need to be regenerated, born again to new life in Christ.

Some people talk of being 'born again' as just a single event at the start of their Christian journey. We do indeed come to Christ for healing and forgiveness, restoration and wholeness, and take his yoke upon us. But as Seven of Nine and Odo remind us, regeneration is a continuing process throughout our lives. The principle of the sabbath rest is built into the universe by God himself, 'who rested on the seventh day from all his works' (Heb. 4:4). We need to sleep every day to restore our bodies and to worship together at least every week to refresh our spirits. But we must also press on towards the 'sabbath rest' which 'still remains for God's people' (4:9). Hebrews reminds us that the journey is not yet finished — and that, paradoxically, we must 'make every effort to enter that rest' (4:10). The sabbath rest with God in heaven is our ultimate destination on our journey — and it will require 'effort' to reach it. Along the way, we will be weary, and pick up other burdens, or acquire more wounds. So we will need to come to the true healer, whose 'yoke is easy and burden light', for regeneration and healing, so that, like Frodo or Gandalf we can rejoin the Company, return to the Conflict and complete the journey until we enter finally into God's promised sabbath rest.

For Prayer and Meditation

Be present, Living Christ, within us,
your dwelling place and home,
that this house may be one
where our darkness is penetrated by your light,
where our troubles are calmed by your peace,
where our evil is redeemed by your love,
where our pain is transformed in your suffering
and where our dying is glorified in your risen life.

Jim Cotter, *Prayer at Night's Approaching,*
Cairns Publications (5th edition), 1997

36

The Exorcist

Just then there was in their synagogue a man with an unclean spirit, and he cried out, 'What have you to do with us, Jesus of Nazareth? Have you come to destroy us? I know who you are, the Holy One of God.' But Jesus rebuked him, saying, 'Be silent, and come out of him!' And the unclean spirit, convulsing him and crying with a loud voice, came out of him. They were all amazed, and they kept on asking one another, 'What is this? A new teaching — with authority! He commands even the unclean spirits, and they obey him.' At once his fame began to spread throughout the surrounding region of Galilee.

MARK 1:23-28

The struggle between good and evil in *Star Wars* comes to its climax at the end of *The Return of the Jedi* in the confrontation as Darth Vader brings his son, Luke Skywalker, to the Emperor. We already know that anger, fear and aggression lead to the dark side. Now the Emperor seeks to turn Luke to the dark side by encouraging him to fight them: 'Release your anger, your hatred'. While Luke does pick up his light-sabre to fight initially, he soon refuses to oppose evil with anger, preferring instead to appeal to what little of the good side there is left in his father. The result is that Vader comes to protect his son even at the cost of his own life, but evil is finally overthrown.

Similarly, Harry Potter has to face the Dementors, the guards of the wizards' prison of Azkaban. They are 'among the foulest creatures that walk this earth . . . soulless and evil' and the only defence against them is to conjure up a Patronus, a protector produced by a 'positive force, a projection of . . . hope, happiness.' When Harry is about to be consumed by them, he is saved by a Patronus who takes the form of a stag, previously used by Harry's long-dead father (*Prisoner of Azkaban*, pp. 140, 176, 300).

In the last couple of days, we have seen how Jesus is the true healer who restores us to wholeness in every dimension of life. This must also include spiritual sickness and oppression from evil. While physical illness is not a direct result of sin, the nature of human beings — a psychosomatic unity, according to the Bible — means that emotional and spiritual factors will affect our physical well-being. This is increasingly recognized in modern medicine, which now takes a more holistic approach to health. We cannot face our dark sides by fighting them or seeking to repress them with anger but only by bringing them out into the light. Only true hope or happiness can fill the soulless void which oppresses so many in the world today, and positive emotions are very important in much counselling. But in the end, both Luke and Harry needed more than positive feelings as their protector came in the form of a father to ward off evil.

Jesus comes as our true king with 'the hands of the healer' to set us free from all that oppresses us, and he is able to do that because he is the true Son of his heavenly Father. In Mark's Gospel, Jesus' identity as Son of God is hidden from human beings all through his ministry. It is only when he dies that he is finally recognized by someone who is not even one of God's people, but is a Roman soldier: 'Truly this man was the Son of God' (Mk. 15:39). However, in the spiritual realm both his identity and his role as a healer and protector are accepted right from the start of his ministry. The first incident after he has called his disciples occurs in the synagogue at Capernaum where he confronts an unclean spirit, who knows that he is 'the Holy One of God' who has the power to destroy evil (Mk. 1:24). To everyone's amazement, Jesus 'commands even the unclean spirits, and they obey him', and so the man is healed spiritually (1:27).

The healer with the power over evil is an important figure in many of our stories. When the Company of the Ring has to do battle with the evil orcs in the Mines of Moria, it is upon Gandalf the wizard that they must rely, and eventually he falls to his doom on the bridge, protecting them from the monstrous Balrog (*Lord of the Rings,* pp. 341-349). When he returns as Gandalf the White, he heals Theoden, King of Rohan, by breaking the spell of Saruman and Wormtongue which has enslaved him and his land for too long. At first the old king is a tired and stiff figure, but as he is set free so he begins to stand 'proud and erect' again and to recover his former authority (pp. 536-541).

So too it is with Jesus' power over evil forces which enslave and dehumanize people. As he came to restore wholeness to those afflicted by physical ailments, so he also confronts spiritual sickness. A few chapters later, Mark recounts the story of the man possessed by a 'legion' of evil spirits in the country of the Gerasenes (Mk. 5:1-20). As with the other unclean spirit, so too they recognize who he is, 'Jesus, Son of the Most High God' (5:7). After Jesus has removed the evil spirits from the man and healed him, people are amazed by the change in him, as he, like Theoden, is back 'in his right mind' (5:15). Then this begins to have an effect on his community, as first people are in awe and then the man goes about the local towns, proclaiming what Jesus has done for him (5:16-20).

In our stories too, spiritual sickness and evil oppression affect people's communities — and their removal leads to healing not just for individuals but also for their lands. The overthrow of the evil Emperor at the end of *The Return of the Jedi* brings liberation and great joy to many worlds, from the jungle party of the furry Ewoks to the vast crowds in the big city. The healing of Theoden also allows both his land and people — the Riders of Rohan — to be free to join Gandalf and the Company in their Conflict with evil. C. S. Lewis makes the same point in his story of how King Caspian's son, Prince Rilian, has been enslaved for ten years by a wicked witch until Eustace and Jill set him free from the Silver Chair to which he is bound each night. Then the evil spell is broken on Rilian himself, and the Earthmen who inhabit the Under-land also wake from their enchanted service to the witch (*The Silver Chair,* p. 146).

Too often today, Christians are divided between two extremes about the oppression of evil, from those who see demons everywhere and want to cast out the 'spirit of sloth' from someone who cannot get up in the morning, to others who consider evil to be an impersonal consequence of our political and social structures. What is interesting from our films and stories is how they agree with the Bible that this is a false dichotomy. Oppression and evil are real, and can afflict both individuals and nations, through natural and supernatural means. We have learned that from our own recent history which has contained both sick people and evil leaders like Hitler or Pol Pot. But Christ is our true healer, who has won the victory over evil and who has come to make us whole and set us free from all that spoils his father's creation.

As we travel in the Company of the church and face the Conflict with evil, we will have to deal with spiritual sickness as well as physical or emotional. We may be called to care for people who feel oppressed, perhaps through counselling or through properly authorized ministry and prayer for deliverance. At the same time, we shall be called to join with those who are seeking to set whole nations free from oppressive regimes or international structures like world debt which enslave so many millions of God's children. In both cases, however, we cannot go out in our own strength, but only to bring people to Jesus who, because he is the true Son of his Father, is our patron and protector, our liberator and the healer of all.

For Prayer and Meditation

Lord Jesus Christ, Son of the Most High God,
where we hurt, touch us,
where we suffer, heal us,
and where we are oppressed, free us,
so we and all the world may praise your Father
here on earth and in heaven above, Amen.

37

Desert Springs

From the wilderness of Sin the whole congregation of the Israelites journeyed by stages, as the LORD commanded. They camped at Rephidim, but there was no water for the people to drink. The people quarrelled with Moses, and said, 'Give us water to drink.' Moses said to them, 'Why do you quarrel with me? Why do you test the LORD?' But the people thirsted there for water; and the people complained against Moses and said, 'Why did you bring us out of Egypt, to kill us and our children and livestock with thirst?' So Moses cried out to the LORD, 'What shall I do with this people? They are almost ready to stone me.' The LORD said to Moses, 'Go on ahead of the people, and take some of the elders of Israel with you; take in your hand the staff with which you struck the Nile, and go. I will be standing there in front of you on the rock at Horeb. Strike the rock, and water will come out of it, so that the people may drink.' Moses did so, in the sight of the elders of Israel. He called the place Massah and Meribah, because the Israelites quarrelled and tested the LORD.

EXODUS 17:1-7

The planet Arrakis is an arid world of great deserts, ravaged by sandstorms and winds. It is no wonder that everyone calls it 'Dune'. Like everywhere in the universe, here water is essential to life — but there is so little of it. The semi-nomadic people of the planet are called Fremen and they have evolved an entire culture around the scarcity of water. Their dwellings are insulated to prevent moisture evaporating and outside they wear 'still suits' which enclose the body and recycle any perspiration. Water is the most precious commodity. At death, the body must be recycled as 'the water belongs to the tribe.' When Paul Atreides cries for a dead friend, the Fremen are astonished, for tears are 'giving water to the dead', the highest honour. The deserts are inhabited by enormous sandworms which produce the melange spice, which not only lengthens life, but also enables the space navigators to cross the vast interstellar void. Despite all the difficulties, therefore, the Fremen still travel out across the deserts in search of worms and spice and have learned how to find and conserve moisture, simply in order to survive.

When Wesley Crusher is about to leave the *Enterprise* to enrol at Starfleet Academy, the episode 'Final Mission' describes his last journey with Captain Picard, where they crash-land on the desert moon of Lambda Paz. Their first task is to find shade and water. After a long trek through the sands, they find a cave with a fountain — but it is protected by a forcefield. Dirgo, the pilot, tries a frontal assault with his weapon, which only results in his being killed and the Captain seriously injured. Wesley develops a new relationship with Picard, who was a close friend of his dead father, as he struggles to keep him alive and to work out a way to gain access to the water. Unsurprisingly perhaps, he only manages to do this in 'the nick of time', and he preserves Picard's life until they are rescued.

After the ancient Israelites escape from the Mess of slavery in Egypt through crossing the Red Sea, they have to journey through 'the wilderness of Sin', the area around Mount Sinai. Even today it is an arid desert and finding water for both the people and their flocks to drink would have been difficult (Ex. 17:1). It is not surprising, therefore, that they soon start to quarrel with Moses, and to blame him for bringing them out here to die (17:2-4). They doubt God's promise and want to 'test' his ability to keep them alive. The paradox is that water is there around them. As for Picard and Wesley, it is under the rock, where what rainfall there is seeps through the limestone and collects in pools. When Moses asks God for help, the Lord reminds him of the staff which Moses used to strike the water of the Nile in the plagues of Egypt (see Ex. 7:20). Now a blow from this staff opens the rocks, and allows the water to spring out for the people to drink (17:6). Moses names the place Massah, which means 'test', and Meribah, or 'quarrel' (17:7) — but the Israelites do not learn the lesson. Instead, they spend the next forty years wandering through these deserts, quarrelling and testing God, barely surviving until they finally reach the promised land.

On our journey through the wilderness of this world, many Christians are like the Fremen. We learn to cope on very little. Our baptism may have been a refreshing experience of water once, but now we plod on, just recycling our perspiration. No wonder this sometimes leads to testing and quarrelling among members of the Company, in the church as much as it did among the Israelites. Yet the paradox is that there is water close by, hidden in the rock. Paul also relates the journey of the Israelites to our Christian life, saying that they 'all passed through the sea and were baptized into Moses . . . and all drank the same spiritual drink'. It is his interpretation of the water from the rock which is crucial: 'For they drank from the spiritual rock which followed them, and the rock was Christ' (1 Cor. 10:1-4). Christ is the rock upon which we stand, but Christ is also the rock which accompanies us on the way. And within this rock are collected great reservoirs of spiritual refreshment. There are times on our pilgrimage when we have to stop sweating along, and rest on the rock. Like Wesley, we cannot force our way into the fountain, but as we quietly listen to stories of our father, so we will learn to drink from the rock of Christ.

In *2061: Odyssey Three,* Heywood Floyd once again travels out into space, this time to meet a large rock 'the shape and size of the island of Manhattan' whose course brings it through our solar system every seventy-five years — Halley's comet. As it is heated by the sun, so jets of water vapour and chemical start to erupt, giving it the characteristic comet's tail — and the largest geyser is nicknamed 'Old Faithful' (*2061,* p. 22). Floyd is invited to go on the maiden voyage of a new space-liner, the *Universe,* and to land on the comet. Later, when they are actually on Halley's comet watching the geyser erupt, Floyd becomes part of the plan to redirect the flow of melting ice crystals into *Universe*'s fuel tanks, using its water to power the starship's drive and to enable them to cut across the solar system in three weeks to rescue the *Galaxy,* their sister ship, which is stranded on the moon, Europa.

On a hot day over a thousand years after the desert wanderings, two descendants of the ancient Israelites, a Samaritan woman and a man from Nazareth, meet by a well at noon. Jesus asks her for a drink of water, despite the estrangement of their two peoples, and replies to her astonishment by offering her 'living water'. When she, who is used to sweating along by herself, points out rather testily that he has 'no bucket', Jesus tells her that 'those who drink of the water I will give them will never be thirsty. The water I will give will become in them a spring of water gushing up to eternal life' (Jn. 4:7-14). As Paul Atreides becomes 'the Dune Messiah' and changes the planet's climate to bring rainwater to the Fremen, so Jesus our Messiah brings us the living water from his father above. Hidden in him are unlimited reserves of spiritual resources which he longs for us to access, to bring us life and refreshment. We cannot force our way to the fountain, but we must let it well up within us. Then, just like the geyser, Jesus is 'faithful' and will give us his power to 'save the Galaxy' as we complete our journey to his father's kingdom.

For Prayer and Meditation

'Lord, give this water, so that I may never be thirsty'.

John 4:15

Make the Samaritan woman's prayer your own.

38

Food for the Journey

The Passover, the feast of the Jews, was near. When he looked up and saw a large crowd coming toward him, Jesus said to Philip, 'Where are we to buy bread for these people to eat?' He said this to test him, for he himself knew what he was going to do. Philip answered him, 'Six months' wages would not buy enough bread for each of them to get a little.' One of his disciples, Andrew, Simon Peter's brother, said to him, 'There is a boy here who has five barley loaves and two fish. But what are they among so many people?' Jesus said, 'Make the people sit down.' Now there was a great deal of grass in the place; so they sat down, about five thousand in all. Then Jesus took the loaves, and when he had given thanks, he distributed them to those who were seated; so also the fish, as much as they wanted. When they were satisfied, he told his disciples, 'Gather up the fragments left over, so that nothing may be lost.' So they gathered them up, and from the fragments of the five barley loaves, left by those who had eaten, they filled twelve baskets. When the people saw the sign that he had done, they began to say, 'This is indeed the prophet who is to come into the world.'

JOHN 6:4-14

Important though it is, water alone is not enough to keep us alive and well on the journey. As they draw near to the end of their journey towards Mount Doom, the hobbits are getting very tired and Sam is worried about Frodo's lack of strength. Water is not enough: 'At the end of a long nightmarch, and after bathing and drinking, he felt even more hungry than usual', so Sam sends Gollum to look for something to eat, and he returns with two small rabbits. Sam finds a few herbs and stews the rabbits, in a touching concern to strengthen Frodo. And indeed, it has the desired effect: 'It seemed a feast' (*Lord of the Rings,* pp. 678-681). Of course, a real feast is how it all began, with Bilbo's eleventy-first birthday party for all the hobbits, 'a *very* pleasant feast . . . rich, abundant, varied and prolonged' (p. 41) — and Peter Jackson had great fun re-creating Bilbo's party for the film version. This is also how it will be at the end of it all, when '1420 in the Shire was a marvellous year' in which the children born were 'fair and strong', the fruit 'so plentiful' and 'the vines were laden' and the beer so good that 1420 'became a byword' (pp. 1061-1062). And yet, somehow, this little meal of 'herbs and stewed rabbit' which they eat along the way seems even more special as it fortifies our heroes just before they face the ultimate struggle on Mount Doom.

Israel never forgot how Moses had fed the people in the wilderness with water from the rock, and with quails and the manna, the white bread which appeared each morning with the dew (Ex. 16:13-20). After Jesus has promised the Samaritan woman living water springing up to eternal life, he too has to provide some food as well. It is the Passover, 'the feast of the Jews', when they recalled the Exodus from Egypt, and Jesus has gone out into the hill country beyond Galilee. Yet even here, the crowds will not leave him alone (Jn. 6:1-4). As always in this Gospel, Jesus takes the initiative, and he asks Philip what they should do about feeding them. Philip, unfortunately, fails this 'test' by thinking only on the human level and replies that 'six months' wages would not buy enough bread' (6:7).

Instead, Andrew brings forward a little boy with his packed lunch of five barley loaves and two fish. Barley loaves were the cheapest bread at the time, eaten by the poor, and the fish are not fresh from the lake, but *opsaria,* dried or pickled. No wonder he asks, 'What are they among so many people?' (6:9). Yet as the two small rabbits and a few herbs seemed a feast to the hobbits, so now this little offering becomes the basis for the multiplication of the loaves and fishes into an over-abundance for everyone.

On the starship *Enterprise* and *Deep Space Nine,* hunger is a thing of the past, thanks to the Federation's advanced technology which has produced 'replicators'. These simple machines are found in each crew member's quarters, as well as in major public places for gathering and eating. They take a basic raw food stock and reconstruct its atoms into whatever food has been ordered, and serve it up almost immediately, hot or cold, in similarly replicated containers. Afterwards, the glass or china and the leftovers are simply recycled back into the stock of raw material.

So too here, the basic material of the boy's offering is taken by the one through whom all things were created, and transformed into enough for five thousand people to enjoy, 'as much as they wanted' (6:11). This cannot help but remind us of the Israelites collecting up the manna 'as much as they needed' (Ex. 16:18). And as for the leftovers, they are collected into twelve baskets — one for every tribe of Israel (Jn. 6:13). Thus as the hobbits' wilderness feast both recalled the party at the beginning and anticipated the abundance of the end of the story, so this miraculous feeding in the Galilean hills also recalls the way Israel was fed at the beginning of her story and looks forward to the celebrations at the end when the Messiah would come. No wonder the people look at what Jesus has done and exclaim, 'This is indeed the prophet who is to come into the world' (6:14).

Each of the stories about Harry Potter ends with a great school feast, with lots to eat and fun to be had by all, leading up to the great final judging of house points to determine who has won the Cup this year. So too the Hebrew prophets looked forward to the coming of the Messiah as an abundant feast, when the harvest will be so great that 'the threshing floors shall be full of grain, the vats shall overflow with wine and oil'. Even nature itself will join in: 'In that day the mountains shall drip sweet wine, the hills shall flow with milk and all the stream beds of Judah shall flow with water' (Joel 2:24; 3:18; see also Amos 9:13-15). The day of God's final judging is not to be feared, but to be celebrated, as his people are vindicated, the hungry are fed and the oppressed finally set free. The five thousand who shared in this banquet of bread and fish would have seen this miraculous multiplication as an anticipation of that great Day to come, and Jesus as the prophet.

In the *Hitchhiker's Guide* books, Ford Prefect and Zaphod Beeblebrox also give Arthur Dent a foretaste of the End when they take him to *The Restaurant at the End of the Universe.* This is constructed in a time bubble at the end of the universe, which allows diners to watch the final cataclysm while eating, and then brings them back afterwards! Because of the way compound interest rates mount, a small down payment of a penny in your own time results in a large sum at the End to pay for your meal. While Arthur is there, even the long-expected, and much overdue, prophet Zarquon manages to appear just as everything ends.

Thus this extended picnic for the crowd is so much more than just a miracle of multiplication. It is set at a crucial time, at the Passover, the 'feast of the Jews'. That feast looked back at the way God provided for his people at the start when they left Egypt, along the way in their travels, and looked forward to the final Messianic banquet. So too, in its own way, the little meal of 'herbs and stewed rabbits' strengthened the hobbits on the way, as well as recalling Bilbo's original party and anticipating the final abundance in the Shire. So for us, as we travel along our journey, there will be times when we are tired and hungry, and need to be fed by Jesus our guide. These occasions will give us the ability to go on, because they also remind us of how we started and give us a glimpse of the celebrations still to come. All of this, because of one little boy's offering — and the way Jesus 'gave thanks' over it (Jn. 6:11).

For Prayer and Meditation

Guide me, O thou great Redeemer,
Pilgrim through this barren land;
I am weak, but thou art mighty;
Hold me with thy powerful hand:
Bread of heaven,
Feed me now and evermore.

W. Williams (1717-1791)

39

Soul Food

For I received from the Lord what I also handed on to you, that the Lord Jesus on the night when he was betrayed took a loaf of bread, and when he had given thanks, he broke it and said, 'This is my body that is for you. Do this in remembrance of me.' In the same way he took the cup also, after supper, saying, 'This cup is the new covenant in my blood. Do this, as often as you drink it, in remembrance of me.' For as often as you eat this bread and drink the cup, you proclaim the Lord's death until he comes.

1 CORINTHIANS 11:23-26

After Gandalf falls to his doom fighting the evil Balrog, the Company of the Ring rest and recuperate in the elf-land of Lórien where Galadriel and Celeborn make them welcome. When it is time to resume their journey south, the elves bring them gifts of food and clothing for the way ahead. The food consists of very thin cakes of brown meal. They are told that it is '*lembas* or waybread, and it is more strengthening than any food made by Men'. They must eat only a little at a time, and it will sustain them 'when all else fails' (*Lord of the Rings*, pp. 389-390). Sure enough, over the days and the miles ahead, the *lembas* keeps Sam and Frodo alive as they travel south, and they are still eating it as they climb even into the shadow of Mount Doom (pp. 628, 955).

In *The Next Generation*, the Borg capture and assimilate Captain Picard to make him their mouthpiece, Locutus, as they attempt to convince Starfleet that 'resistance is futile'. Picard is rescued by his faithful crew and his body is returned to human form. His mind, however, is a different matter and he is plagued by bad memories and doubts. While the *Enterprise* is being repaired in spacedock, Picard returns to the family home at Labarre in France, his first visit in twenty years. His elder brother, Robert, still tends the ancestral vineyard and their childhood arguments resurface, leading to a fight in the mud. As they realize how ridiculous this is, they start laughing, and return home to celebrate their restored relationship over a bottle of fine vintage — and unreplicated — wine. As Picard, now fully recovered, returns to lead his repaired ship again, Robert gives him a bottle of the 2347 vintage with the instruction 'Don't drink it alone'. Eventually, we see Picard share it several episodes later with the Head of State of the planet Malcor with whom they have just made first contact.

Bread and wine are often seen as somehow symbolic of both God's bounteous provision and all human life and work. Both wheat and grapes are fruits of the earth, but they need to go through the processes of human labour to become food and drink. Yet they are also different. Bread is such a staple food across all time and space that it reminds us of all the farmers and producers who provide us with these essentials of life. Wine, on the other hand, speaks of joy and celebration, of family and friends. The Psalmist thanks God that he makes plants grow 'to bring forth food from the earth, wine to gladden the human heart . . . and bread to strengthen the human heart' (Ps. 104:14-15). These two aspects are brought home in the two examples from our stories. The elf-food is called *lembas,* which means 'waybread' — bread to strengthen the travellers on their 'way'. Without it, they would have starved and fallen exhausted along the roadside. Meanwhile, Robert Picard's fine wine is not to be drunk alone — but is consumed in a celebration of friendship in the meeting of a planet's inhabitants with space travellers for the first time.

Thus it is not surprising that these same two elements, bread and wine, are at the heart of the most central and sacred act of Christian worship — the holy communion. Here, all we have been considering this week about renewal and restoration, healing and feeding come together in this simple meal, which gives us food for body and soul, spiritual as well as physical nourishment, and brings us into communion with God and one another.

Paul preserves in his first letter to the Corinthians the earliest account of the last supper and the institution of the holy communion. While he is writing in the 50s of the first century, only some 20 years after the death of Jesus, he uses the technical words for passing on a tradition: he 'received' and 'also handed on' this account (1 Cor. 11:23), which suggests that it is very ancient indeed, going right back into the earliest period of the church. It is right, therefore, that it has been at the heart of the eucharistic prayer over the bread and wine in most Christian liturgies over the centuries. In this brief account we see the four simple actions which are still performed in every communion service — taking, thanksgiving, breaking and giving.

First Jesus 'took a loaf of bread' and then 'he took the cup also'. We have already seen how these two elements represent and encapsulate human life and work. As Jesus took them, so he set them apart for the worship of God. So too, as we bring bread and wine to a communion service, we are giving back to God all our life and work for him to bless and to use to renew us. However, in the words Jesus says over these elements, he gives them a new meaning — that 'this is my body' and 'this cup is the new covenant in my blood'. As we set bread and wine apart for God, they become for us the body and blood of Jesus.

Second, Jesus 'gave thanks' over them. This would probably have been in the form of a Jewish blessing, 'Blessed are you, O LORD God, King of the universe', drawing upon Psalm 104 quoted above. The word for 'having given thanks' is *eucharistesas,* which gives us the word 'eucharist', another name used for the communion (1 Cor. 11:24). It also occurred in yesterday's passage when Jesus gave thanks over the bread and fish (Jn. 6:11) — and look what the result of that was! As we give thanks to God for his mercy and generosity to us, so we multiply our blessings and open ourselves to receive his goodness to us and all his creation.

Next Jesus 'broke' the bread in order to share it. If the loaf remains all in one piece, it may look very pretty — but no one can eat it. The grain of wheat must 'fall into the earth and die', be broken open for the new shoots to grow into the wheat plant (Jn. 12:24). So too the one loaf must be broken for everyone to have a part of it, and the wine must be poured out for us to drink. This phrase 'breaking of bread' has also been another name for the communion from the time of the early church (see Acts 2:42). It may be a painful image, but we must also be 'broken' and 'poured out' if God's broken world is to find his healing and refreshment.

Last, Jesus gave the bread and the wine to his disciples, and told them to 'do this in remembrance of me'. There must a giving and receiving for anything to happen. It does not matter how much the wheat and grapes grow and the bread and wine are produced, or what actions and words are said over it, if it is not given to me. And there is no point in any of that, if I do not receive it and take it into myself, to let it nourish and restore me. Furthermore, like Picard's vintage wine, it cannot be consumed alone — for the very meaning of communion is 'union with'. In receiving holy communion, we have union with God who feeds us and we have union with one another with whom we feed and drink.

Finally, Paul reminds us what this bread and this cup mean as we 'proclaim the Lord's death' — the body and blood of Christ. The bread which is broken speaks to us of Jesus' body broken upon the cross, and the wine poured out recalls his blood pouring from his wounds. This is where this week's studies and our whole journey draw near to their climax. The oases for rest and recuperation, the healing of our body, mind and spirit, the waters springing up for new life and the abundant provisions for the journey are only possible because of the self-sacrifice of the one who gives them to us and gave himself for us. As the elves gave the *lembas* as bread for the way, and Robert Picard gave wine for sharing with others, so Christ feeds us and gladdens our hearts on our journey. But now that journey is bringing us to its climax, where we discover that all his gifts come from his giving of himself for us upon the cross.

For Prayer and Meditation

Blessed are you, Lord God of the universe;
through your great goodness we have this bread and wine to share,
which earth has given and human hands have made;
it will be our spiritual food and drink.

PART 7

GREATER LOVE

As we reach Jerusalem, so we follow Jesus from his entry into the holy city through betrayal and self-sacrifice to the Cross and tomb.

40

The Return of the King

The next day the great crowd that had come to the festival heard that Jesus was coming to Jerusalem. So they took branches of palm trees and went out to meet him, shouting, 'Hosanna! Blessed is the one who comes in the name of the Lord — the King of Israel!' Jesus found a young donkey and sat on it; as it is written: 'Do not be afraid, daughter of Zion. Look, your king is coming, sitting on a donkey's colt!' His disciples did not understand these things at first; but when Jesus was glorified, then they remembered that these things had been written of him and had been done to him.

JOHN 12:12-16

Our journey is drawing closer to its climax. It seems quite a long time ago now that we first struggled to leave behind the Mess of sin and our old way of life and found the Gateway of baptism and the call of God to set out on this pilgrimage. We soon found that we did not travel alone, but as a member of the Company of the church in all its richness and diversity. We have experienced Conflict and been wounded in the battle with evil and through the difficulties of Finding the Way with all its ups and downs. And yet, we have also enjoyed the oases and the times of Healing and Feeding to sustain us as we go. As the city comes in sight and we draw near to the end of our journey, so we might begin to look forward to the happy ending.

After all, this is how many of our stories end — in triumph and glory. The third part of *The Lord of the Rings* is entitled *The Return of the King,* and it all ends with the crowning of Aragorn, and the praise he gives to the hobbits for their part in the travels and the struggles (pp. 989-990, 1003-1004). Similar happy scenes of great celebration greet the heroes at the end of *The Phantom Menace, Star Wars,* and *The Return of the Jedi.* Throughout his time on Venus, Dr Ransom has heard much about the King, as he has sought to save the newly created woman on that planet from falling into the temptation to ignore Maledil's commands while separated from her King. When she and the King finally arrive on the mountain top, Ransom is overcome with awe: 'It was hard to think of anything but the King' (*Voyage to Venus,* p. 190).

So too it is as Jesus comes to Jerusalem for what will be his last week. The 'great crowd' is in Jerusalem for the feast of the Passover. The ancient Jewish historian Josephus says that over two million people would come to the holy city for this event each year, a cast of extras which would strain the budget of any of our films, even if they were generated by computers! They hear of Jesus' arrival and they go out to greet him, waving some 'branches of palm trees' and shouting 'Hosanna' (Jn. 12:12-13). The Greek words used here for 'branches' and 'palm' are rare, but they also occur in the accounts of two other triumphal entries into Jerusalem. During the middle of the second century BC, Jerusalem was ruled by the Graeco-Syrian dynasty of several kings called Antiochus who sought to eradicate Jewish faith and worship. After Antiochus III desecrated the temple, Judas Maccabeus led a successful revolt and was able to rededicate the temple in 164 BC — and he was greeted by processions of people, waving 'palm branches' (2 Maccabees 10:7). Some years later in 142 BC, his brother Simon recaptured the citadel of Jerusalem from Antiochus VI, and this was also celebrated with 'palm branches' (1 Maccabees 13:51).

When the crowds took 'palm branches' to greet Jesus as he entered Jerusalem, they were acclaiming him as much a hero as the Maccabeans. Furthermore, they sang verses from Psalm 118, with its cry of 'Hosanna', which means 'Save us, O Lord', saluting the conquering hero: 'Blessed is the one who comes in the name of the Lord — the King of Israel' (Jn. 12:13, quoting Ps. 118:25-26). We saw last Friday that when Jesus fed the crowd in the wilderness during the previous Passover, they interpreted it as a sign of the messianic abundance, and called him 'the prophet who is to come' (Jn. 6:14). Now at another Passover, they are ready to crown him King.

Yet sometimes, the return of a king can be quite difficult, especially if things have changed in the meantime. Aragorn may be crowned king at the end of *The Return of the King,* but when they enter Minas Tirith earlier, Gandalf counsels Pippin to say nothing about the coming king: 'If he comes, it is likely to be in some way that no one expects' (p. 784). Similarly, when Odysseus eventually arrives back home after his great journey in the *Odyssey,* he finds the palace full of suitors who want to marry his wife and become king in his place. He disguises himself as a beggar, and only his faithful dog recognizes who he truly is.

Jesus too is well aware of the dangers of being recognized as king, when the city is under the control of the Roman emperor. Nor does he want to be greeted as a conquering hero or be pushed into the role of the warrior liberator like the Maccabean leaders, whom some Jews hoped the Messiah would emulate by leading the armed struggle against the Romans. Like Aragorn, he comes 'in some way no one expects', by going to find a young donkey, rather than the proud and warlike horse any coming king ought to ride (Jn. 12:14). John sees this as a fulfilment of Zechariah's prophecy of the coming peaceful king: 'Lo, your king comes to you, humble and riding on a donkey'. He even omits Zechariah's comment that the king is 'triumphant and victorious' (which is yet to come) and changes the instruction to Jerusalem from 'rejoice greatly and shout aloud' to 'fear not' (Jn. 12:15; see Zech. 9:9). No wonder 'his disciples did not understand these things at first' — but John is writing with the hindsight of someone who has thought long and prayed hard to understand it all many years later (Jn. 12:16).

The king has come, but not as expected, nor yet ready to reveal himself in all his glory. In the frozen Narnia under the power of the evil witch, the children are having tea in the warmth of the dam house when Mr Beaver tells them that 'Aslan is on the move'. They do not understand, and ask who Aslan is. 'Why, don't you know? He's the King. He's the Lord of the whole wood, but not often here, you understand. . . . But the word has reached us that he has come back' (*Lion, Witch and Wardrobe,* p. 74). Then the children begin to realize that great things lie at hand which they do not yet comprehend.

It is the same for us at the start of this week. Our King has returned, but not quite as expected — so will he be welcomed? The most difficult battle of our whole journey still lies ahead as we face the climax of all we have been through. Yet Jesus' curious choice of riding on a lowly donkey warns us that this story may not follow quite the usual pattern of the conquering hero. So all we can do is to stay close and follow him, listen and watch, for 'something wonderful' is about to happen.

For Prayer and Meditation

Ride on! ride on in majesty!
In lowly pomp ride on to die;
Bow thy meek head to mortal pain,
Then take, O God, thy power, and reign.

H. H. Milman (1791-1868). A hymn traditionally sung on Palm Sunday to commemorate Jesus' entry into Jerusalem.

41

A Good Clear-Out

Then they came to Jerusalem. And he entered the temple and began to drive out those who were selling and those who were buying in the temple, and he overturned the tables of the money changers and the seats of those who sold doves; and he would not allow anyone to carry anything through the temple. He was teaching and saying, 'Is it not written, "My house shall be called a house of prayer for all the nations"? But you have made it a den of robbers.' And when the chief priests and the scribes heard it, they kept looking for a way to kill him; for they were afraid of him, because the whole crowd was spellbound by his teaching.

MARK 11:15-18

When Odysseus finally makes it back to Ithaca after his long years of travelling, he finds that most people presume him to be dead. His house is overrun with young men who are consuming all his food and wine, helping themselves to his possessions and trying to persuade his wife Penelope to marry one of them. When he finally gets his old bow back in his hands, he reveals his true identity and has to clear them all out of his house.

After his first great adventure, poor old Bilbo similarly gets back home to Bag End from defeating the dragon Smaug only to find that he too is presumed dead — and he has just missed the auction where most of his things were sold. His cousins, the Sackville-Bagginses, are even 'busy measuring his rooms to see if their own furniture would fit' and he has to clear them out of the house and establish his true identity to get his possessions back (*Hobbit,* pp. 276-277). Something even worse awaits Frodo and Sam on their return from defeating evil at Mount Doom. The Shire, their beautiful hobbit land, has been taken over by ruffians who have taken all the produce and chopped down the trees. When they get to Bag End, they find that Saruman the evil wizard, whom Gandalf and they expelled from Rohan and Orthanc earlier, has occupied it, together with his servant Wormtongue. Saruman is killed by Wormtongue, who then is shot by some hobbit archers — but they still have to put things right. '"I shan't call it the end, till we've cleared up the mess," said Sam gloomily. "And that'll take a lot of time and work."' In fact, the task of clearing up is such that it becomes known as the 'Scouring of the Shire' (*Lord of the Rings*, pp. 1035-1058).

Finally, when Commander Sisko first arrives on *Deep Space Nine*, it is a total mess: the Cardassians, who occupied it before, destroyed everything when they left and now Sisko has to try to get it working again as well as cope with the infighting of the newly liberated Bajorans. Constable Odo arrests a young Ferengi, Nog, for stealing, whose uncle, Quark, is about to give up running his bar because he will not be allowed to cheat and make huge profits under Starfleet control. In the midst of it all, Sisko finds himself having an out-of-the-body experience with one of the orbs of the prophets; Kai Opaka, the Bajoran spiritual leader, recognizes Sisko as the promised 'Emissary', the title of this pilot episode. When Sisko discovers the wormhole to the Gamma Quadrant, Opaka realizes that it is the Celestial Temple, created and inhabited by the prophets.

For Jesus, it is the other way round. He is the Messiah, also long promised by the ancient prophets, and he comes to find the temple first — and then follows this by the task of clearing it out. As he does so in this little passage, several themes emerge which relate to our stories. According to Mark, this incident takes place on the day after Palm Sunday, after Jesus has been greeted as the King 'coming in the name of the Lord'. It is only to be expected that Jesus goes here first. Even today, the temple mound in Jerusalem is a site of pilgrimage for all the three major monotheistic world faiths — Jews, Christian and Muslims alike — and a major tourist attraction, with its large share of stalls selling pictures and mementoes.

As a pious Jew from the north, Jesus would go to the temple first to worship and pray — but he is horrified by what he finds. As Bilbo and Odysseus come home to find all their possessions being sold or consumed, so Jesus is outraged by 'those who were selling and those who were buying in the temple' (Mk. 11:15). As with the auction at Bag End, no doubt it was legal: most people would arrive with Roman or Greek coins which could not be used in the temple because of the graven images they carried of the emperor or others, and so these had to be exchanged for the official and acceptable temple coinage — at a 'reasonable' rate. Equally, most people would have come to offer a sacrifice, and there were strict rules about what made animals acceptable for the priests. Instead of bringing your own, therefore, it was much safer to buy approved animals and birds at the temple. On the other hand, you do not have to be a Ferengi like Quark to recognize this as a golden 'business opportunity' to make a good profit! So Jesus sees these sellers as little more than the ruffians and thieves in our stories, and shouts out the words of an earlier prophet, Jeremiah, that 'you have made it a den of robbers' (Jer. 7:11). Like the 'scouring of the Shire', he clears it out, turning over their tables, and stopping their trade of carrying things through the temple courts (11:15-17).

Secondly, Jesus recognizes that the temple is a 'house', just like Odysseus' palace or Bag End, and he wants to reinstate its proper owner — God himself — and its correct function as a 'house of prayer for all the nations'. As the Bajoran prophets lived in the wormhole, or the 'Celestial Temple', so God was perceived to dwell in the innermost sanctuary of the temple, the Holy of Holies, where only the High Priest was allowed to go once a year. From this inner point outwards, access was granted in a sequence of strictly controlled courts: the Court of Priests surrounded the shrine, with the Court for Jewish men beyond that, and the Court for Jewish women further back still. Non-Jews, the Gentiles or the 'nations', had to make do with the very outermost courts, and we still have preserved some of the notices warning them of the death penalty if they go further into the temple itself. 'All the nations' do indeed come to visit the temple — but all they are allowed to do is to buy things, or watch from afar, so Jesus protests that the temple is 'a house of prayer for all the nations' (11:17).

Not surprisingly, this action does not go unchallenged. When Bilbo appeared back at Bag End it took years of 'legal bother' to establish his identity (*Hobbit,* p. 276) and Odysseus too had to prove his claim against the suitors' families (which he did in the time-honoured fashion of a good drubbing in battle!). For Sisko, this issue is also back to front. He thinks he knows who he is as a Starfleet officer, and is rather taken aback by the Kai's recognition of him as the Emissary. So too the Jewish temple authorities, 'the chief priests and scribes', are rather taken aback by this young preacher from up north and his dramatic action. Much as they would like to destroy Jesus, they are powerless to act for the moment because of the crowd (Mk. 11:18). Later they return to question him, precisely on this question of identity: 'By what authority are you doing these things?' (Mk. 11:27-33).

As the children travel with the beavers towards the Stone Table, there are increasing signs that 'Aslan is nearer': Father Christmas is able to appear at long last with presents for everyone, the snow starts to melt and snowdrops and crocuses begin to shoot up. Winter in Narnia is coming to an end, and with it the witch's power as she has to abandon her sledge and continue on foot. However, this only makes her more and more angry as she heads for the final confrontation (pp. 99-112).

Thus Jesus is 'the one who comes in the name of the Lord' and he comes to put everything right again. He clears out the 'thieves' from the temple, reclaims it as a 'a house of prayer for all the nations' and begins to let his true identity finally be known. But none of the messes at the end of our stories were cleared up without a fight — and for Jesus, the storm clouds are gathering as the opposition begin to make their preparations.

For Prayer and Meditation

Lord Jesus Christ,
come in the name of the Lord,
cleanse our hearts of all greed,
and teach us to pray
that all nations may know your true identity.

42

Betrayal

> *Then one of the twelve, who was called Judas Iscariot, went to the chief priests and said, 'What will you give me if I betray him to you?' They paid him thirty pieces of silver. And from that moment he began to look for an opportunity to betray him. . . . While they were eating, Jesus said, 'Truly I tell you, one of you will betray me.' And they became greatly distressed and began to say to him one after another, 'Surely not I, Lord?' He answered, 'The one who has dipped his hand into the bowl with me will betray me. The Son of Man goes as it is written of him, but woe to that one by whom the Son of Man is betrayed! It would have been better for that one not to have been born.' Judas, who betrayed him, said, 'Surely not I, Rabbi?' He replied, 'You have said so.'*
>
> MATTHEW 26:14-16, 21-25

In *The Matrix,* when Neo joins the Morpheus group on board the *Nebuchadnezzar,* he meets a character called Cypher. Cypher is getting 'tired of this war' and tells Neo that he wishes he had taken the blue pill, and stayed in the computer-generated illusory world. Instead, he is drinking heavily, and is dismissive of Neo: 'So you're here to save the world'. Later, when he goes back into the world of the Matrix, Cypher meets an Agent over a meal of rare steak and fine wine; even though he knows they are illusions, they still taste better than the real rations back on the ship. The blood dripping from the steak hints at the cost of the deal Cypher is doing with the Agent. He wants to return to live in the Matrix world with a new identity, to be rich and 'someone important' — and the Agent smiles and agrees, 'Whatever you want'.

When Morpheus takes Neo to see the Oracle, Cypher deliberately drops the mobile phone, their way of keeping in touch with the ship, into a dustbin. This enables the evil Agents to track them and spring their trap, capturing and torturing Morpheus. Cypher escapes back into the ship, where he shoots Tank and takes over as the operator. He then kills three members of the crew and tells Trinity that he used to love her, but now is going to pull the plug on her and Neo, leaving them stranded in the Matrix, before he 'goes back to sleep' in the illusion. His last words are 'I don't believe it', before Tank, who was wounded rather than killed, shoots him and he dies. But the damage has been done: Morpheus is being beaten up by the Agents, and the *Nebuchadnezzar* itself is being attacked by sentinel machines.

The 'inner member' who turns traitor seems to be a crucial figure in many of our stories. Sirius Black is Harry Potter's godfather and a very close friend of his parents, yet he is thought to have betrayed them to the evil Lord Voldemort, so he has been in the wizards' prison of Azkaban for the last twelve years. When he escapes and comes to Hogwarts, it is not, as everyone thinks, to attack Harry, but to expose the real traitor, Peter Pettigrew. Peter had been the 'Secret-Keeper' for James and Lily Potter, but betrayed where they were hiding to Voldemort, who killed them and nearly killed Harry too (*Prisoner of Azkaban,* pp. 263-276).

Similarly, Michael Eddington is a trusted security officer and colleague of Sisko on *Deep Space Nine.* However, he becomes increasingly disenchanted with Starfleet, and betrays them by joining the Maquis freedom fighters, including taking with him a lot of important equipment. Meanwhile Seska had already infiltrated the Maquis as a Cardassian spy; when she finds herself on *Voyager* with the others in the Delta Quadrant, she betrays both crews to the Kazon warriors, who let her join them instead. She continues to keep in touch with Jonas, yet another traitor on *Voyager,* who sends her information. In *The Empire Strikes Back,* Lando Calrissian, an old friend of Han Solo, is forced to betray him to Darth Vader.

All of these stories reflect on the archetypal betrayer, Judas Iscariot. We saw several weeks ago when the Company was chosen, that 'Iscariot' might mean from the town of Sychar or Kerioth, but that some people link it with the *sicarii,* the Jewish 'dagger-carriers' who were freedom fighters, like the Maquis. Certainly, his other name, Judas, recalls the great liberator, Judas Maccabeus. These hints have caused some people to speculate that Judas was someone who thought that Jesus was going to bring in the kingdom of God by leading a revolt against the Romans. When Jesus did not follow up the temple cleansing by starting the insurrection, perhaps Judas got disillusioned, or thought he could force Jesus' hand by getting him arrested.

Immediately before Judas goes to the chief priests, Jesus is anointed with some precious ointment (Matt. 26:6-13). Perhaps Judas thought it was a waste; John's Gospel says it was because he was the group's treasurer and used to help himself to their common purse (Jn. 12:6). According to Matthew, Judas actually asks how much betraying Jesus is worth and he is given thirty pieces of silver (Matt. 26:15). This is quite a lot of money, about four months' wages for a labourer, but it has other resonances too. If your ox killed someone's slave, it was the amount of compensation to be paid for the slave's life (Ex. 21:32). When God tells the prophet Zechariah to work as a shepherd for a flock which is being killed, he too is paid thirty silver shekels, 'this lordly price at which I was valued by them' (Zech. 11:12-13).

Thus perhaps, like Michael Eddington, Judas thought he was going to help the cause of liberation by his betrayal, or perhaps, like Cypher, he was just tired of the struggle and wanted the material and financial comforts he was offered to betray Jesus. Jesus, however, is aware of what is going on, and warns the rest of the disciples at the last supper that 'one of you will betray me' (Matt. 26:21). Not surprisingly, they are 'greatly distressed' about this and wonder who it is (26:22). All Jesus will say is that it is one who has shared their meals together (26:23). What makes the betrayal of the Potters by Black or Pettigrew so awful is that they were all such close and trusted friends, 'inseparable' (*Prisoner of Azkaban*, pp. 152, 259). Furthermore, while Jesus accepts that he must face his destiny 'as it is written', it would have been better for the betrayer 'not to have been born'. There has been much debate about the meaning of Cypher's name in *The Matrix*, but it does stand for 'zero' in most codes, or a figure of no account — like one 'not born'.

Whatever Judas' motives may have been, things do not seem to have turned out as he expected. Like Harry Potter's parents' friends, he knows where Jesus is hiding and brings the soldiers there to arrest him in the Garden of Gethsemane, where he betrays Jesus with a kiss (Matt. 26:48-49). But Matthew also goes on to recount Judas' change of heart: 'When Judas, his betrayer, saw that Jesus was condemned, he repented and brought back the thirty pieces of silver to the chief priests' (Matt. 27:3). Now that he has done his job and they have Jesus, the priests are not interested in Judas' remorse, so he throws the silver into the temple, which is exactly what Zechariah had done with his thirty shekels (Matt. 27:5; Zech. 11:13). Because it is 'blood money' the priests cannot put it into the temple treasury, so after Judas has hanged himself, they use it to buy a field for burials (Matt. 27:5-10).

It is so easy to make Judas into the villain of the piece, and yet our stories have all suggested that being betrayed by friends is all too common in our experience. C. S. Lewis also suggests this in the way that Edmund betrays his brother and sisters to the wicked witch in Narnia to get some more of her 'Turkish Delight' (*Lion, Witch and Wardrobe,* pp. 35-43). And yet this becomes the reason why Aslan sacrifices himself at the Stone Table (pp. 128-141). Similarly, Cypher's betrayal is the catalyst which inspires Neo to go back into the Matrix, rescue Morpheus and have the final showdown with the Agents. So too, Judas' betrayal, whatever his motives, is taken up by God as the next step in the drama of our salvation. For the Jesus whom Judas betrays is the one who will not fight and kill to bring liberation, but the one who will lay down his life for his friends, including Judas himself, that we may all be forgiven by his heavenly Father.

For Prayer and Meditation

Lord God, have mercy on all your disciples
who are tired of the struggle,
or tempted to betray themselves and you;
keep us faithful in our resolve
and when we fall, restore us.

43

Greater Love

The chief priests and the Pharisees called a meeting of the council, and said, 'What are we to do? This man is performing many signs. If we let him go on like this, everyone will believe in him, and the Romans will come and destroy both our holy place and our nation.' But one of them, Caiaphas, who was high priest that year, said to them, 'You know nothing at all! You do not understand that it is better for you to have one man die for the people than to have the whole nation destroyed.' He did not say this on his own, but being high priest that year he prophesied that Jesus was about to die for the nation, and not for the nation only, but to gather into one the dispersed children of God. So from that day on they planned to put him to death. . . .

Jesus said: 'This is my commandment, that you love one another as I have loved you. No one has greater love than this, to lay down one's life for one's friends. You are my friends if you do what I command you. I do not call you servants any longer, because the servant does not know what the master is doing; but I have called you friends.'

JOHN 11:47-53; 15:12-15

It was common in many episodes of the original series of *Star Trek* that the crew have only a few seconds to get the engines working again or to stop the warp core blowing them up, or some such last-minute race against the odds. Usually it is 'Scotty' the engineer who manages to save the day, even if he 'canna change the laws of physics'. However, at the end of the second movie, *Star Trek II: The Wrath of Khan,* even he cannot save the *Enterprise* from the Genesis shock wave which is rapidly advancing upon them. Mr Spock quietly slips away from the bridge, goes down to Engineering and enters the radiation chamber itself. He lifts off the reactor cover, exposing himself to the lethal radiation, and puts his hands inside to fix it, allowing the engines to fire into life and take the ship to safety at the last possible moment. Captain Kirk rushes to Engineering to see his lifelong colleague blinded and horribly burned, dying from radiation poisoning. Kirk assures him that the ship is safe and Spock replies, 'Don't grieve. It is logical. The needs of the many outweigh the needs of the few or the one.'

Obi-Wan Kenobi makes a similar choice in the original *Star Wars* film. They are in the Death Star, where Obi-Wan has turned off the tractor beam to allow Han Solo's ship, the *Millennium Falcon,* to escape with Luke and Princess Leia aboard. To gain them more time, Obi-Wan starts a lightsabre duel with Darth Vader which concludes as he allows Vader to strike him down, saying that if he dies, 'I will grow more powerful than you can possibly imagine'. This theme of sacrificing oneself for others recurs with the death of Qui-Gon Jinn fighting the evil Darth Maul in *The Phantom Menace,* as well as the sacrifice of all the anonymous fighter pilots in the various space battles in the *Star Wars* films. In a similar vein, when the earth is threatened by a large asteroid on a collision course in the film *Armageddon,* Harry Stamper, played by Bruce Willis, chooses to stay behind on the asteroid and detonate by hand the nuclear explosion which splits it apart, and thereby saves Harry's daughter, and the rest of the human race!

Caiaphas the High Priest agrees with Mr Spock's logic. After Jesus' arrival in Jerusalem, his clearing out of the temple and his teaching there, things were getting increasingly dangerous. The two main power groups, the chief priests (responsible for the temple) and the Pharisees (particularly concerned for the law), did not always have much time for each other. But here they can recognize that Jesus is dangerous to both of them, so they convene a meeting of the council, the Sanhedrin (Jn. 11:47). The concerns of both groups are seen in their anxiety that 'everyone will believe in him' and that 'the Romans will destroy our holy place' (11:48). Caiaphas was actually High Priest from AD 18 to 36, and he has learned the logic of power and government. 'It is better for you to have one man die for the people than to have the whole nation destroyed' (11:50).

At one level, this is the same equation as Spock's 'the needs of the many outweigh the needs of the few or the one'. And yet, John looks beyond the cynicism of this political calculation and sees it as a true prophecy (11:51). It was a Jewish belief that the High Priest could prophesy — and it did not necessarily have to be conscious. Here then Caiaphas speaks more truly than he could possibly have imagined. Jesus is going to die 'for the nation', not because of a cynical calculation but because of his willing self-sacrifice. Furthermore, he will die not just for the Jewish nation, but for all the 'dispersed children of God' (11:52). Like Harry Stamper, he will save the whole human race!

Spock's sacrifice, however, is motivated by more than mere logic, for all his calculations about the many and the one. For his last words are 'I have been — and always will be — your friend' as he sinks down the glass panel separating him from the now sobbing Kirk. It was because of his love for his friends with whom he has travelled for so many years that he went into the radiation chamber, so that, even if he dies, they will be safe. Equally Obi-Wan Kenobi's self-sacrifice is not just that of one man letting several escape, but because he loves Luke and Leia. In *3001: Final Odyssey,* Frank Poole contacts his old friend and former crewmate Dave Bowman, who now exists with HAL as programs inside the monolith, which is about to destroy the human race; in the penultimate chapter — significantly headed 'Deicide' — Dave and HAL let a computer virus loose which will disable this almost omnipotent machine, even though it is extremely likely that the virus will damage them too. When it turns out that they are also infected, Poole buries a memory tablet containing his 'sleeping friends' in a vault on the moon: 'Good-bye, old friends. You've done well' (pp. 239-246).

Jesus, too, is aware that his coming death is not simply a result of the scheming calculations of a High Priest determined to hold on to power — but because of his own free and willing choice for his friends. Earlier in John's Gospel, he described himself as the 'good shepherd' who 'lays down his life for the sheep' — and he stressed that he would do this not under compulsion but 'of my own accord' (Jn. 10:11, 18). Now at the last supper he is trying to comfort and reassure his disciples in advance of his coming death. Usually disciples saw themselves as 'servants' of their Rabbi or master (15:15). They would follow him, look after him and care for him — but as so often with Jesus, here everything is the other way round. He has already been their servant, washing their feet at the start of the meal (13:1-16). Now he calls them his 'friends' — and the word means 'beloved'. He loves them with the ultimate expression of love — to lay down his life for them (15:13). Therefore, he wants them also to 'love one another as I have loved you' (15:12).

We have all been exposed to the lethal poisoning which radiates from sin and we have been trapped by the forces of evil. But Jesus comes into our situation and takes upon himself the certain death facing us. He does this not out of calculating logic or political expediency, but simply because he loves us — and not just us, but the whole human race, all 'the dispersed children of God'. He has been — and always will be — our friend, and in response he wants us to love one another.

For Prayer and Meditation

Lord Jesus,
thank you for your love for us and all God's children,
and for taking your love to the ultimate sacrifice;
inspire us so to love one another
that we may be willing to lay down our lives for our friends.

44

The Agony

He came out and went, as was his custom, to the Mount of Olives; and the disciples followed him. When he reached the place, he said to them, 'Pray that you may not come into the time of trial.' Then he withdrew from them about a stone's throw, knelt down, and prayed, 'Father, if you are willing, remove this cup from me; yet, not my will but yours be done.' Then an angel from heaven appeared to him and gave him strength. In his anguish he prayed more earnestly, and his sweat became like great drops of blood falling down on the ground. When he got up from prayer, he came to the disciples and found them sleeping because of grief, and he said to them, 'Why are you sleeping? Get up and pray that you may not come into the time of trial.'

LUKE 22:39-46

When we first meet Dr Heywood Floyd in *2001: A Space Odyssey* en route to investigate the monolith on the moon, we discover that his wife died in an aeroplane crash ten years previously (*2001*, p. 49). He then sends Bowman and Poole in *Discovery* out to Jupiter, where they all seem to be lost. By 2010, Floyd has married again and has a two-year-old son, Christopher. However, he still feels responsible for those lost on the first flight, and when he is asked by the President to go to Jupiter on *Leonov* he has an agonizing decision to make, whether to leave his wife and young son behind for two and a half years — especially since he will be in hibernation for most of it (*2010*, pp. 31, 40). He decides to go and discovers the birth of a whole new world out there, but at the cost of losing his family as his wife decides not to wait for him to return (p. 191). In 2061, he is dealing with the consequences of that fateful decision as he tries to build a relationship with his grandson — but still feels 'he had no real choice in the matter' (*2061*, p. 26).

Frodo also has some hard decisions to take. When Gandalf tells him that the Ring can only be destroyed in the fires of the Cracks of Doom, Frodo complains, 'I am not made for perilous quests. Why did it come to me? Why was I chosen?' But Gandalf is clear: 'The decision lies with you.' Frodo takes it to Rivendell where Elrond convenes his Council and decides that the Ring must go south to Mount Doom — but who will take it? Frodo struggles between 'a great dread' and 'an overwhelming longing to rest and remain at peace by Bilbo's side in Rivendell' — but eventually announces, 'I will take the Ring, though I do not know the way' (*Lord of the Rings,* pp. 74-75, 288).

On Venus, Dr Elwin Ransom struggles to counter the arguments of the evil force controlling his former colleague Weston as it tries to persuade the newly created Woman to go against Maleldil's wishes. Ransom is getting very tired, and wonders why Maleldil has not done anything to prevent it — when suddenly he realizes that his presence there is what Maleldil has done. All night long he struggles with himself, trying to find a way through or out of the situation; but eventually he accepts that he — and he alone — must fight the evil monster. He moves from Frodo's question 'Why me?' to 'Lord, why not me?' — and the answer comes from the darkness: 'It is not for nothing that you are named Ransom' (*Voyage to Venus,* pp. 128-137).

In each case, our hero faces an agonizing decision, not so much about which action to choose, as in coming to accept willingly the way which is obviously right, but even more obviously so difficult and painful in the sacrifice it will demand of them. For Jesus in the Garden of Gethsemane, the right decision may be similarly obvious, but the cost and sacrifice entailed makes him want to draw back. In Luke's Gospel, he has been heading towards this moment all his ministry, from when he first 'set his face to go to Jerusalem' (9:51). Furthermore, he has always known what the likely outcome there will be: 'I must be on my way, because it is impossible for a prophet to be killed outside of Jerusalem' (13:33). John's Gospel does not include the story of Gethsemane, but gives us an earlier insight into Jesus' internal dialogue which is not unlike those of our heroes: 'Now my soul is troubled. And what should I say — "Father, save me from this hour"? No, it is for this reason that I have come to this hour. Father, glorify your name' (Jn. 12:27-28). But it is one thing to have been heading in a certain direction all your life — and quite another when the actual crucial moment arrives.

After the fuss caused by the crowd at his entry into Jerusalem and the incident in the temple, Jesus would not have needed divine insight to realize that things were approaching a climax. Being questioned about his identity and authority by chief priests and scribes also indicated their growing concern — and now Judas had slipped early out of his last supper with them all! But Jesus still goes, as usual, to the groves on the slopes of the Mount of Olives to pray (Lk. 22:39; see also 21:37). After all, it was on his route anyway; like most pilgrims, Jesus and his disciples would have had to have found lodging outside the city during the Passover. It would seem that they were staying over the east side of the Mount of Olives on the road to Jericho, perhaps near Bethany (see Lk. 19:28-29). To be safe, all he needed to do was to get out of the city as quickly as possible, up through the olive groves and down into the quiet, anonymous villages and valleys beyond. The temptation to keep going must have been very strong, yet he stops to pray in one of the groves, which Mark and Matthew call 'Gethsemane', the Aramaic for 'oil-press', where the olives would have been pressed for their oil (Mk. 14:32; Matt. 26:36). The fact that this was a place where he prayed regularly, 'as was his custom', just made it all the more dangerous, and likely that Judas would know where to bring the temple police to find him — so why not just keep going?

But here in this olive grove with an oil-press, Jesus' faith is put under more pressure than any olive ever was. He tells the disciples to 'pray that you may not come into the time of trial'. The word *peirasmos* means a time of testing, which may include 'temptation', the traditional translation, but which is also used for the ultimate test of tribulation and persecution. He has already taught the disciples to pray to 'our Father' to 'lead us not into *peirasmos*' (Lk. 11:4). So now he tells them to pray this again — and again when he finds them asleep (22:40, 46).

While they doze, Jesus faces his own trial and testing — to get up and walk over the hill to safety, or to stay here and wait for the police to find him, arrest him and take him off to a prophet's death in Jerusalem. Jesus would not have been incarnate as fully human if this prospect did not horrify him. Therefore his first prayer is that God might not ask this sacrifice of him. Throughout Luke's Gospel in particular, Jesus is constantly shown at prayer at every important juncture in his ministry, from his baptism to his transfiguration, with nights in prayer before making a decision like calling his disciples (3:21; 6:12-13; 9:29). So now, he prays, 'Father, if you are willing, remove this cup from me' (22:42). The metaphor of 'cup' is regularly used in the Hebrew prophets for the wrath of God, death or judgment (see Is. 51:17, 22; Jer. 25:15). Like Frodo or

Ransom, Jesus would really rather prefer it if God could find somebody else or some other way: 'Why me?'

And yet, that is only half of his prayer. Equally like Frodo and Ransom, Jesus comes to accept 'Why not me?', that this is the way he has to go. Like Floyd, he has 'no real choice in the matter' if he wants to do his father's will: 'Yet, not my will, but yours be done' (Lk. 22:42). There is much debate about verses 43-44, describing Jesus' agony and anguish, sweating blood as he tries to accept God's will and being strengthened by an angel. Some of the early manuscripts have these verses and some do not, just as some modern translations include them, while others place them in a footnote. Whether they are part of Luke's original text or an early Christian explanation of what Jesus must have gone through does not really matter here. However you describe it, it would have been an agonizing decision, costing Jesus 'blood, sweat and tears', to face the 'time of trial' while so close to safety, and not run away. And yet, it is the only way. As Frodo and Ransom both realize that the only hope in defeating evil depends upon their decision to pay whatever sacrifice the next day might bring, so Jesus gets up from his knees to face the torchlight of Judas and the arresting party. Only in this way can he show the 'greater love', to lay down his life for his friends, to face the extremes of evil and death — and to overcome them with love.

For Prayer and Meditation

Father, not my will but yours be done.

45

Death or Victory?

Then he handed him over to them to be crucified. So they took Jesus; and carrying the cross by himself, he went out to what is called The Place of the Skull, which in Hebrew is called Golgotha. There they crucified him, and with him two others, one on either side, with Jesus between them. . . . Meanwhile, standing near the cross of Jesus were his mother, and his mother's sister, Mary the wife of Clopas, and Mary Magdalene. When Jesus saw his mother and the disciple whom he loved standing beside her, he said to his mother, 'Woman, here is your son.' Then he said to the disciple, 'Here is your mother.' And from that hour the disciple took her into his own home. After this, when Jesus knew that all was now finished, he said (in order to fulfil the scripture), 'I am thirsty.' A jar full of sour wine was standing there. So they put a sponge full of the wine on a branch of hyssop and held it to his mouth. When Jesus had received the wine, he said, 'It is finished.' Then he bowed his head and gave up his spirit.

JOHN 19:16-18, 25-30

Nearly every one of the stories we have taken with us on our journey climaxes with the self-sacrifice of a leading character. This can show their love, saving their friends from some terrible disaster by paying the ultimate price, as with Spock's sacrifice of himself so that the rest of the crew of the *Enterprise* might escape as we saw on Wednesday. However, more often the hero sacrifices himself out of love for others in the battle against evil.

Thus in *Star Wars* Obi-Wan Kenobi sacrifices himself out of his love for Luke and Leia as he dies fighting Darth Vader. Obi-Wan's death allows his friends to escape, but it also makes him 'more powerful than you can possibly imagine', and he continues to guide Luke against the evil Empire, showing him the right place to attack the Death Star and directing him to his Jedi Master, Yoda, for training. In the climactic final battle in *The Return of the Jedi,* Luke realizes that he cannot fight evil with anger and hatred, for that would turn him to the dark side. So he refuses to fight the Emperor, appealing to what good there is still left in his father, Darth Vader. Vader hurls himself upon the Emperor, absorbing the evil energy to save Luke, but at the cost of his own life. He dies in Luke's arms, knowing that evil has been destroyed.

Gandalf's self-sacrifice in the Mines of Moria is motivated by love but it happens as he battles to save his friends from the evil Balrog, a huge, seething mass of fire, created by the special effects department in the film. As the Balrog leaps onto the narrow bridge, Gandalf smashes it with his staff so that the Balrog falls into the dark chasm below — but unfortunately it takes Gandalf with him (*Lord of the Rings,* pp. 348-350). The rest of the Company are saved, and evil defeated — but at what a cost: Frodo says, 'Gandalf was our guide and he led us through Moria; and when our escape seemed beyond hope, he saved us, and he fell' (p. 375).

Something very similar happens with Captain Sisko on *Deep Space Nine.* He has travelled a long way over seven years since Kai Opaka first recognized him as the Emissary, as he has gradually accepted that role. In the seventh and final series, Sisko leads Starfleet's victory over the Dominion, but then has to battle to save Bajor from the evil Pah-wraith spirits led by the resurrected form of his old enemy, Gul Dukat. As the embodiment of evil, Dukat is extremely powerful and forces Sisko onto his knees in the Fire Caves. However, Sisko manages to take Dukat with him, hurling them both down into the raging flames below, as Gandalf fell with the Balrog.

The evil Voldemort killed Harry Potter's father and his mother as she tried to protect the baby Harry, but he could not kill Harry himself then, or subsequently. As Dumbledore, the headmaster of Hogwarts, explains, this is what protects Harry: 'Your mother died to save you. If there is one thing Voldemort cannot understand, it is love. He didn't realize that love as powerful as your mother's for you leaves its own mark' (*Philosopher's Stone,* p. 216). When Harry has his own battles with Voldemort, he too is prepared to sacrifice his life, although he has survived — so far! (e.g. *Chamber of Secrets,* pp. 231-237; *Goblet of Fire,* pp. 552-581).

Finally, when Neo goes back into the world of the Matrix, he does it out of love for Morpheus, telling Trinity, 'I *have* to go'. He finds and saves Morpheus, getting him back out down the phone line to safety in the ship — but this leaves him to face the heavily armed Agent alone. As they battle it out in the subway, Neo ends up letting evil do its worst, filling him with bullets to kill him.

Some people today wonder why Christians should think that the tortured death of one man long ago is so important. After all, what can one man accomplish? On the other hand, many Christians stress that Jesus died on the cross to forgive them their individual sins — and that is an important way of understanding the crucifixion in both the Bible and in Christian thought and theology. But these stories remind us of two other major ways of seeing the cross, again both in the Bible and down the centuries.

The first is that Jesus' death on the cross is the supreme example of God's love. We saw on Wednesday that 'no one has greater love than this — to lay down their life for their friends' (Jn. 15:13). Thus for God, the creator and source of all life, to become human and die for us is the supreme self-sacrifice. This emphasis is seen particularly in Luke's account. On his way to be crucified, Jesus stops to care about the women of Jerusalem, telling them to weep for themselves because of what will happen to them and their children later, probably referring to when the Romans will sack and destroy Jerusalem. Then, as he is nailed to the cross, he prays to his father to forgive the soldiers 'for they do not know what they are doing'. As he spent his life bringing people to God, so now as he is dying, he tells the penitent thief, 'Today you will be with me in Paradise.' Finally, he breathes his last with a simple prayer of quiet trust, committing his spirit to his heavenly father (Lk. 23:28, 34, 43, 46). Thus the cross is ample demonstration, like a grand cosmic visual aid, of the love of God. As the old saying goes, 'I asked God how much he loved me, and he said, "This much" as he spread his arms wide open — and died.'

But our stories also show us that self-sacrifice on its own is not enough, if evil can still triumph after the hero has died. What is powerful is that the hero's primary concern is to destroy evil and save others — and their self-sacrifice happens as they are doing that. Thus Sisko and Gandalf take evil with them as they fall down into the depths, or Darth Vader, Harry's mother and Neo force evil to wreak its destruction upon them rather than the one they love. Mark and Matthew both show Jesus letting evil do its worst, as he falls into the darkness and utter depths of human despair: 'My God, my God, why have you forsaken me?' (Mk. 15:34; Matt. 27:46). It is not enough for God, with all his power and glory, to tell us he loves us or even to show it by his death. He has to enter into our experience of evil and total desolation.

It is in John's Gospel, however, that we find the rest of the story. First, we see Jesus' love, even while he is dying, as he cares for his mother and his closest friend, bringing them together so that 'the disciple took her into his own home' (Jn. 19:26-27). Then, we get a glimpse of the desolation described by Mark and Matthew as Jesus says that he is thirsty — and is only given sour wine to drink. But it is given to him on a 'branch of hyssop' which was also used to put the blood of the sacrificial lamb on the door posts at the Passover; so John points out the deeper significance of Jesus' death (19:28-29; see Ex. 12:22-23). Finally, at one level his last words, 'It is finished' (19:30), look like a final admission of defeat and despair, that it is all over and evil has won — and so it must have seemed as his lifeless body hung there. Yet the word here actually means 'it is fulfilled' or brought to a successful conclusion, 'It is accomplished!' What can a broken man accomplish? But what can a dying mother like Lily Potter, or a single officer like Sisko, accomplish? As they let evil wreak its fury upon them, so they negate its power and take it out of the world with them. Evil is to be defeated not by resisting it with more violence, but by absorbing it and removing it through the power of love.

In Narnia, as Aslan gives himself to the witch to sacrifice on the Stone Table in Edmund's place, so she screams in triumph that now she will have Narnia for ever, and kill all the children — and yet that moment is actually the start of the end of her power. The mystery of the cross is that when it seems 'it is finished' and evil has triumphed in Jesus' death, that is really the moment when God takes upon himself everything we human beings and the cosmos can do to him, absorbs it and takes it with him down into the depths. At the time of their apparent triumph, evil, sin and death are disarmed and the cross becomes the place of victory, where 'it is accomplished'!

For Prayer and Meditation

Lord Jesus Christ, merciful Friend and Redeemer,
thank you for your suffering for us on the cross
and grant that we may share in the triumph of your victory.

46

Good Grief!

And when all the crowds who had gathered there for this spectacle saw what had taken place, they returned home, beating their breasts. But all his acquaintances, including the women who had followed him from Galilee, stood at a distance, watching these things. Now there was a good and righteous man named Joseph, who, though a member of the council, had not agreed to their plan and action. He came from the Jewish town of Arimathea, and he was waiting expectantly for the kingdom of God. This man went to Pilate and asked for the body of Jesus. Then he took it down, wrapped it in a linen cloth, and laid it in a rock-hewn tomb where no one had ever been laid. It was the day of Preparation, and the sabbath was beginning. The women who had come with him from Galilee followed, and they saw the tomb and how his body was laid. Then they returned, and prepared spices and ointments. On the sabbath they rested according to the commandment.

LUKE 23:48-56

There is an eerie silence in Torpedo Bay 2 as the whole crew on the *Enterprise,* in full dress uniform, have gathered to pay their last respects to Spock, who freely gave his life in Engineering's radiation chamber so that they could escape destruction. A Mark VI photon torpedo has been emptied out to contain Spock's body and it is now draped in a flag. Admiral James T. Kirk is on the brink of tears as he speaks about the coolly logical Vulcan who was his friend: 'Of all the souls I have encountered, his was the most human'. Then, as Scotty wheezes through 'Amazing Grace' on his bagpipes, the torpedo capsule slowly moves through the mourners and is launched out into space. Spock died to save them from the bow wave of the Genesis explosion, an experimental project to generate new life by reorganizing matter at the molecular level. It is only appropriate, therefore, that the torpedo containing his body comes to rest amid the lush, green ferns on the previously barren planet regenerated by the explosion.

With that last scene of the film *Star Trek II* in mind, numbed audiences and fans stumbled out of cinemas in grief and shock — could they really have killed off Mr Spock? Rumours were circulating about what may be being planned for the third movie, not due for another two years' time, but for the moment there was nothing to do but go home, and wait. So too 'all the crowds' in Jerusalem who had 'gathered for this spectacle', the entertainment of a public execution, are somehow affected by Jesus' death, and return home mourning (Lk. 23:48). But this was nothing compared to the grief and desolation which would have been felt by all Jesus' 'acquaintances', who had been watching 'at a distance', including 'the women who had followed him from Galilee' (23:49).

Earlier, Luke had described a number of women as being together with 'the twelve' with Jesus. Like the rest of the disciples, they came from a wide range of backgrounds, from 'Mary Magdalene, from whom seven demons had gone out' to 'Joanna, the wife of Herod's steward Chuza', that is, one of his ministers of state! Her importance and wealth, together with those of 'Susanna and many others', are actually what paid for Jesus and his mission, as they 'provided for them out of their resources' (Lk. 8:1-3). It is also Luke who tells us the story of Mary who acted like a man and 'sat at the Lord's feet and listened'; when her sister Martha complained that she should be doing the women's work, Jesus had to calm her down and say that Mary had 'chosen the better part' (10:38-42). It would have been very unusual for a rabbi to include women among his disciples, but they followed Jesus all the way from Galilee — and are now still there to witness his death.

In addition, one member of the council of the Sanhedrin is prepared to stand up for he thinks is right. Joseph of Arimathea has been 'waiting expectantly for the kingdom of God' (23:51). Now that things have not turned out as he 'expected', he is willing to care for Jesus' dead body, to ask for it from Pilate and to wrap and bury it in a newly cut tomb nearby. Meanwhile, the women are still there, watching to see where Jesus' body is laid, and then they go off to get all the 'spices and ointments' ready for when they can do the work of anointing him after the sabbath (23:55-56).

C. S. Lewis depicts this beautifully with the poignant scene in Narnia after the witch has killed Aslan and taken her evil forces off to complete what she thinks is her triumph. Then Susan and Lucy creep out of the bushes where they have been hiding and watching the sacrifice of Aslan. All night they stay huddled to his lifeless body, crying and weeping, trying to wipe away 'the blood and the foam as best they could'. They even manage to remove the muzzle to be able to kiss his cold face, but they cannot untie the knotted cords. The hours go by until, just before dawn, hundreds of little mice come and start to nibble away the ropes (*Lion, Witch and Wardrobe,* pp. 142-145).

We saw yesterday that Jesus' death, when 'It is finished' might have meant that everything was all over and lost, is actually the moment of victory, when 'It is accomplished'. But it would not have felt like it then, and Jesus was still dead. Like the fans who could not accept Spock's death, too many Christians want to go straight from the garden of Gethsemane to the garden of the empty tomb without going via the hill of crucifixion and the stone-cold body. It is too painful to sit in silence, waiting and grieving. And yet nothing of the reality of Christ's victory over evil on the cross, or our faith in the resurrection to come tomorrow, must be allowed to shield us from the awful brute fact that Jesus died. Such is the love of God that he did not just 'splash down', come and enter into our world to show us what he is like (as we saw at the start of our journey), nor did he just spend a few years playing at being human to see what it was like. No, he loved us even 'to the uttermost end'; his prayer in Gethsemane may have been 'Take away this cup', but his resolve was to 'drink the cup that the Father has given' (Jn. 13:1; 18:11). That meant that he had to die a real death — for himself and for us.

Being human means being born to die, and only a God who is willing to share that can actually help us face our own mortality and that of those we love. Death is real and grief hurts — and sometimes we just have to sit in silence and cry and wait. Jews still spend seven days after a funeral 'sitting *shivah*', sitting on low stools at home in quiet. For once it is *not* like one of our stories, where Neo is only dead for a few seconds in *The Matrix* and bursts back to life before Trinity has hardly had a chance to start to grieve! Christian faith is much more honest and realistic than that. Do not rush straight from the events of Good Friday to the Easter garden, but take some space to be quiet. It may be hard work — but it's not only for the women!

For Prayer and Meditation

Spend some time in silence.
Thank God for Jesus' human life and death.
Grieve for him and for all 'those whom we love but see no longer'.
Pray too for our own deaths, still to come in God's good future.

PART 8

TO INFINITY AND BEYOND!

Our journey here may be ending — but the joy of the resurrection and the anticipation of heaven are calling us home.

47

He's Alive!

Early on the first day of the week, while it was still dark, Mary Magdalene came to the tomb and saw that the stone had been removed from the tomb. So she ran and went to Simon Peter and the other disciple, the one whom Jesus loved, and said to them, 'They have taken the Lord out of the tomb, and we do not know where they have laid him.' . . . Mary turned around and saw Jesus standing there, but she did not know that it was Jesus. Jesus said to her, 'Woman, why are you weeping? Whom are you looking for?' Supposing him to be the gardener, she said to him, 'Sir, if you have carried him away, tell me where you have laid him, and I will take him away.' Jesus said to her, 'Mary!' She turned and said to him in Hebrew, 'Rabbouni!' (which means Teacher). Jesus said to her, 'Do not hold on to me, because I have not yet ascended to the Father. But go to my brothers and say to them, "I am ascending to my Father and your Father, to my God and your God."' Mary Magdalene went and announced to the disciples, 'I have seen the Lord'.

JOHN 20:1-2, 14-18

Star Trek III starts where *Star Trek II* finished, with the photon torpedo containing Spock's body lying in the rapidly growing greenery of the Genesis planet. The subtitle of the film makes the theme clear: *The Search for Spock.* For in this lush garden, something is happening as new life springs up all around. Suddenly, Dr David Marcus, Kirk's son and the inventor of the Genesis device, monitoring progress from up in orbit, registers the presence of a life-form on the surface. He and the Vulcan Lt Saavik 'beam down' and find the photon tube empty, except for Spock's discarded burial robe. Where can the body have gone?

John's Gospel notes that 'in the place where he was crucified there was a garden, and in the garden a new tomb' where Jesus was laid to rest (Jn. 19:41-42). We saw yesterday that the women who wanted to anoint Jesus' body had to rest on the sabbath. So now Mary Magdalene comes very early to the tomb and finds it open (20:1). She assumes the worst, that either the authorities have taken the body away or that grave robbers have come in the night, so she rushes off to get Peter and the 'disciple whom Jesus loved'. To have lost Jesus himself was bad enough, but this desecration drives her to pour out her story: 'They have taken the Lord out of the tomb, and we do not know where they have laid him' (20:2). They run back to the garden, go into the tomb and, like David and Saavik, find only the burial robes, 'the linen wrappings lying there and the cloth which had been on Jesus' head' (20:6-7). The disciples too are confused and then, rather strangely, they return home (20:10) — and so miss the fact that 'something wonderful' was about to happen! Mary, however, is so trapped in her grief and pain that she stays weeping at the tomb, pouring out her story about Jesus being taken away, first to two strange figures in white in the tomb, and then to someone standing behind her whom she does not recognize (20:11-14).

After Gandalf 'fell into shadow', the rest of the Company eventually becomes separated into several groups. The unlikeliest combination, Aragorn the man, Legolas the elf and Gimli the dwarf, are following the hobbits' tracks through the ancient forest of Fangorn when they become aware of an old, hooded figure in 'dirty grey rags' approaching them. They are not sure who it is, but assume that it is Saruman 'the White', the wizard who has opposed them and serves the Dark Lord. Their fears are confirmed when he puts a spell on them, and then reveals his white robe under the grey rags — and yet, at that very moment, as he makes a familiar gesture, Legolas realizes it is Gandalf. Gandalf did indeed fall into the utter depths fighting the evil Balrog, and spent a long time under the earth; eventually he was rescued by Gwahair the Windlord of the eagles who took him to Lothlórien where he recovered. Having sacrificed himself for evil, he has also removed the power from Saruman and become Gandalf 'the White' — and now he has returned to help his friends (*Lord of the Rings,* pp. 513-517). Similarly, Luke Skywalker is at first taken aback when he seems to hear the voice of Obi-Wan Kenobi advising him how to attack the Death Star. Later he realizes that Obi-Wan's sacrifice of himself has made him even more powerful and Luke begins to recognize him when he 'appears' to guide Luke.

So too Mary is taken aback by the figures in white she meets in the garden, but she is too absorbed in her own grief to pay much attention to what they say (Jn. 20:12-13). More surprisingly perhaps, she is so locked into her story that, like Aragorn and the others, she does not recognize the very person she longs to see. When he gently asks her why she is weeping and whom she is looking for, she launches on her tale of woe again; mistaking Jesus for the gardener, she asks him, if he has taken the body, to 'tell me where you have laid him, and I will take him away' (20:14-15). It is only when he speaks again, this time gently whispering her name, 'Mary', that she finally turns around and recognizes him — the very one she has been longing to see (20:16).

And yet, we must not be too hard on her. None of us expect to meet someone we have just buried, and there seems to have been something different about Jesus in most of his resurrection appearances. There is the fabulous irony of the two friends on the road to Emmaus explaining all about Jesus' death to someone they do not recognize, or Peter and the others taking instructions from the stranger on the shore of Galilee. It is only when, like Gandalf, he does something familiar, like breaking the bread or inspiring a miraculous catch of fish, that they suddenly realize who he is (Lk. 24:30-31; Jn. 21:6-7). Jesus too has returned different and more powerful from his sacrificial struggle with evil but wants us to look for him and recognize him in the familiar ways.

After Elliot has spent the night on the hillside helping 'ET' to 'phone home', he awakes to find him missing. When they find the extraterrestrial wet and cold in a stream, he is very sick. The attempts by the white-suited authorities to help him only make things worse, and his pulse fails and he dies. His squashed, rubbery body is put into an ice-cold coffin and Elliot is left alone with him. Through the tears of his grief and pain, he sobs, 'ET, I love you' — and suddenly ET's heart starts beating again. He points to the sky and wants to return 'home' to his parents. 'He's alive!' shouts Elliot as ET appears in a white robe with the red beating light of his heart demonstrating his new life through the love of the children. Similarly, when Neo has been shot dead by the Agents in *The Matrix,* Trinity whispers, 'I love you' and kisses him. This causes Neo to revive again and Trinity shouts out, 'Now get up'. This theme of new life and love even comes on the Genesis planet as Saavik has to help Spock's rapidly growing new body through his first experience of *pon farr,* the Vulcan bonding urge.

Jesus is raised to new life by the love of God, but it is right that he appears first to a woman who loved him so much that she was not only one of the very few present when he died, but the first at the tomb that

Sunday morning and who stayed there even when his friends had 'gone home'. There is no mistaking the tenderness of the exchange — 'Mary', 'Master' — as she replies to her name with the Aramaic form denoting a dear attachment, *Rabbouni, 'my* rabbi!' (Jn. 20:16). Similarly, it is to Susan and Lucy, who have waited all night by his body, that Aslan appears in the light of dawn — and they become 'a happy laughing heap of fur and arms and legs . . . such a romp as no one has ever had except in Narnia'. But when it is over, there is 'business' to be done, and the children have to step back as Aslan roars out his challenge, and they go off for the final defeat of the witch (*Lion, Witch and Wardrobe,* pp. 148-149). So too, Mary has to be warned not to 'hold on to me', not to cling on to the old ways they used to have. Like ET, Jesus has to ascend, 'up home', back to his Father, and Mary has a new task — to be the first apostle of the resurrection: 'Go and tell my brothers'. Now with tears of joy replacing her old story of grief, she obeys and 'announces' the good news: 'I have seen the Lord!' (Jn. 20:17-18). And so too for us on each and every Sunday. As we near the end of our journey, the time for grief and sorrow has passed. We must look for Jesus in the unexpected places, but recognize him from his familiar ways of love for us, so that we can also go and shout to the entire cosmos, 'We have seen the Lord!'

For Prayer and Meditation

Risen Lord Jesus,
come to us in the blindness of our grief;
give us eyes to see you, hearts to love you
and lips to tell the world of your victory,
for you are alive for ever and ever, Amen.

48

All Good Things

When it was evening on that day, the first day of the week, and the doors of the house where the disciples had met were locked for fear of the Jews, Jesus came and stood among them and said, 'Peace be with you.' After he said this, he showed them his hands and his side. Then the disciples rejoiced when they saw the Lord. Jesus said to them again, 'Peace be with you. As the Father has sent me, so I send you.' When he had said this, he breathed on them and said to them, 'Receive the Holy Spirit.' . . . A week later his disciples were again in the house, and Thomas was with them. Although the doors were shut, Jesus came and stood among them and said, 'Peace be with you.' Then he said to Thomas, 'Put your finger here and see my hands. Reach out your hand and put it in my side. Do not doubt but believe.' Thomas answered him, 'My Lord and my God!' . . . Jesus came and took the bread and gave it to them, and did the same with the fish. This was now the third time that Jesus appeared to the disciples after he was raised from the dead. When they had finished breakfast, Jesus said to Simon Peter, 'Simon son of John, do you love me more than these?' He said to him, 'Yes, Lord; you know that I love you.' Jesus said to him, 'Feed my lambs.' . . . After this he said to him, 'Follow me.'

JOHN 20:19-22, 26-28; 21:13-15, 19

After Frodo and Sam have finally completed their long journey and the Ring has been destroyed at Mount Doom, they are rescued by the eagles. Then begins a long sequence of celebrations and parties for the Company as the effects of evil are removed and things are put to rights. Aragorn is now revealed as the rightful King and crowned. Then there are the festivities when he marries Arwen Undómiel, and Faramir and Éowyn are also wed. The gradual procession home next stops at Rivendell to celebrate Bilbo's 129th birthday. When the hobbits get home to the Shire, that too has to be cleaned out and properly restored before there finally comes the long summer of 1420 with its parties, weddings and abundant harvest — and all is once again well (*Lord of the Rings*, pp. 984-1062).

The *Star Wars* films also come to a climax with the final party at the end of *The Return of the Jedi*. In cities across the galaxy, huge crowds celebrate the end of the evil Empire, while in the forests of Endor, humans and furry Ewoks dance together around bonfires. As the eating and drinking continues, Luke looks up and sees a vision of Obi-Wan Kenobi, Yoda and his father Anakin together, smiling down at him.

The end of John's Gospel also has a procession of reunions, as Jesus appears first to Mary in the garden, next to the disciples in the upper room without Thomas, then to include Thomas, and finally to have breakfast with them all on the shores of Galilee. Each time, it becomes a bigger event. We saw yesterday how the risen Jesus appeared to Mary in her desperate grief all alone in the garden after Peter and the beloved disciple had 'gone home' (Jn. 20:10-18). That evening, the disciples were meeting behind locked doors, afraid that they might be arrested and executed next. But now that Jesus has conquered sin, death and evil, he cannot be stopped by mere human locks! So he comes and stands among them, and says, 'Peace be with you' (20:19). This 'peace' is God's gift of *shalom*, that perfect wholeness and sense of rightness as we saw in our studies on healing. Jesus promised it to the disciples as a parting gift which he would leave to encourage them when he went away (14:27; 16:33). It is very unusual for a bequest to be delivered in person, but now Jesus brings them peace as his legacy. As Aragorn, the newly crowned King, hands out gifts, so Jesus brings his peace, when and where he wishes. But Thomas is missing, and so the following week Jesus once again appears behind the locked doors. Again he gives them 'peace' — and this time he is concerned especially for Thomas (20:26-28).

Finally, we have the story at the end of John's Gospel, set by the side of the Sea of Galilee. Peter has returned to his old ways — 'I'm off fishing' — but does so all night without any success (21:3). At dawn, the risen Jesus appears on the shore and tells them where to find some fish. When they come ashore, they find that he already has a charcoal fire cooking breakfast for them, but tells them to bring some of their catch. As Peter counts it, he discovers what an enormous haul they have made. So Jesus hands round bread and fish, a veritable feast worthy of any other of our heroes' celebrations (21:13).

It is also at the feast on Endor that Princess Leia reveals to Han Solo that she is Luke's sister, whose identity has been hidden to protect her through the evil years. This resolves the 'love triangle' between Leia, Luke and Han over the three films and puts all the relationships right for the future. This too is an important theme in the various weddings and settlements at the end of *The Lord of the Rings,* particularly as the faithful Sam marries Rosie and they move into Bag End with Frodo and start to have children. Arthur C. Clarke also puts it all right for Dr Heywood Floyd at the end of his *Space Odyssey.* After being a widower and feeling responsible for the loss of the crew of *Discovery* in *2001,* and then losing his new wife and little son, Chris, in *2010,* Floyd is enabled in *2061* to build a relationship with his grandson, also named Chris, through their common experiences of the monolith. Unknown to any of them, Floyd has also been 'echoed' during a dream, copied by David Bowman and HAL into a new program so that he is reunited with them within the monolith itself as a 'Trinity', the title of the final chapter (*2061,* pp. 280-283, 291).

The final series of *The Next Generation* was also preoccupied with the theme of putting the relationships of the *Star Trek* 'family' and friends to rights. The long-running hints of a possible love between Captain Picard and Dr Crusher are finally explored; Counsellor Troi discovers she had a sister who died; Lt Worf is reconciled with his human step-brother; Data discovers his 'mother', the wife of his creator, who then turns out also to be an android; Ro Laren finds a new 'family' by joining the Maquis; and Wesley Crusher sets off to explore the galaxy! The very last episode, 'All Good Things . . .' concludes with Picard leaving the Captain's rooms to join the others in their regular poker game. He looks round at them all with a rueful smile: 'I should have done this a long time ago', and he deals the cards as the *Enterprise* heads off into the galactic nebulae, saying, 'The sky's the limit'.

Similarly, when the risen Jesus appears at the end of John's story, it is also to restore relationships and put things right. We have already noted how Mary was trapped by her grief, repeating her tale of loss about Jesus again and again. When Jesus gently speaks her name, he sets her free, and gives her a new task and identity as the first apostle of the resurrection to go and tell the others, 'I have seen the Lord!' (Jn. 20:11-18). Then the disciples need to be set free from the fear which keeps them behind locked doors, given the gift of peace and a new calling to continue Jesus' mission: 'As the Father sent me, so I send you' (20:21). Thomas, however, was missing that night, perhaps because he had withdrawn into himself in his pain and grief. He was always the pessimist (11:16; 14:5), and now he wants proof — which Jesus provides when he appears to him the following week (20:27-28). According to Christian tradition, Thomas went on to become the apostle who brought the gospel to India, which shows how far you can go when restored to a new task.

Finally, there is the little matter of Peter's denial of Jesus when he was trapped by the 'charcoal fire' in the High Priest's courtyard (18:17-18, 25-27). Now that Jesus has fed him with fish cooked on another 'charcoal fire' (21:9, the only other occurrence in the New Testament), he needs to restore him spiritually as well. As the Healer asks Peter three times if he loves him, once for every denial, so Jesus commissions him to 'feed my lambs' (21:15-17). Peter will become a shepherd instead of a fisherman, caring for 'the flock of God that is in your charge' (1 Peter 5:2). Like the Good Shepherd, he too will lay down his life for God's people in the future (21:18). And Jesus' last words are the same as his first in this Gospel, 'Follow me' (21:19, 22; see 1:42-43).

It is not enough for our heroes just to reach the end of the quest, conquer evil and reappear at the end of our stories. We want there to be a feast, and everything and everyone restored and all put right again. So too the risen Jesus comes back to his friends, cooks them breakfast and restores them individually and as a Company. But like the very best tales, he also gives us a new task and opens another chapter as he calls us to follow him to save the galaxy.

For Prayer and Meditation

Imagine yourself invited to breakfast in Galilee.
Watch Jesus hand out his gifts and instructions to everyone.
Hear the call, 'Follow me.'
What is your response?

49

Lift-Off

Now the eleven disciples went to Galilee, to the mountain to which Jesus had directed them. When they saw him, they worshipped him; but some doubted. And Jesus came and said to them, 'All authority in heaven and on earth has been given to me. Go therefore and make disciples of all nations, baptizing them in the name of the Father and of the Son and of the Holy Spirit, and teaching them to obey everything that I have commanded you. And remember, I am with you always, to the end of the age.'

MATTHEW 28:16-20

After Trinity whispers her love to Neo's dead body and he comes back to life, he totally defeats the evil Agents and destroys them. As he stops their bullets in mid-air, Morpheus cries out, 'He is the One!' Neo is an anagram of 'one', as well as meaning 'new', hinting at both his messianic identity and new life. As the evil Agents are eradicated, Neo picks up a phone to speak to the computer machines: 'I am going to show these people . . . a world without rules and controls, without borders or boundaries, a world where anything is possible.' The computer goes into 'System Failure' as the film soundtrack starts playing a song called 'Wake Up' by the band Rage Against The Machine. Neo, who had been afraid of heights earlier, hangs up the phone, looks around at all the crowds of human beings and takes off, soaring up into the sky.

Similarly, when the grief-stricken Elliot croaks, 'ET — I love you' and closes the lid of his freezer-coffin, ET's heart lights up and he revives. Elliot can hardly believe it and asks if this means that they are coming back for him. A beaming ET just keeps looking up and saying, 'Home — home'. A mad chase ensues as the children hi-jack ET's 'coffin' from the authorities and enlist their friends' help on bicycles. Earlier, Elliot had shown ET how to play with plastic *Star Wars* figures; in another delightful crossover from one of our stories to another, one friend asks, 'Can't he just beam up?' referring to the *Star Trek* method of transportation.

Elliot retorts that 'This is reality, Greg' and they all set off for the prearranged meeting place up on the forest-clad mountain. As the spaceship lands, ET and the children exchange tearful goodbyes. ET touches Elliot tenderly as he says his last words — 'I'll be right here' — and then he shuffles back up the entry ramp. The final shot as the doors close focuses on his still-pulsing red heart, and then the ship lifts off, back up into the clouds, trailing a rainbow in the sky.

Our journey to leave behind the Mess of sin and evil started in Chapter 5 with a 'splashdown'. We noted then that this was the reverse of the usual sequence for astronauts — and this is even more true as we draw to a close with 'lift-off', which is usually how they begin! However, we could only begin our journey because Jesus has entered into our world, and splashed down to be baptized in solidarity with us. Now we have travelled all this way through his ministry, passion and resurrection, it is time for him to 'ascend', to return to his heavenly Father.

Some people find the idea of the ascension of Jesus as funny as some mediaeval pictures of feet sticking out of clouds. But to concentrate on Jesus' 'escape velocity' or primitive conceptions of a three-decker universe with heaven 'up there' is to miss the point. The ancients may have thought that mountains and high places were holy because they were close to the gods, as ET goes up the mountain to 'phone home'. Thus Moses met God and received the law on Mount Sinai, and we have studied Elijah's experiences on mountains. So now Matthew ends his Gospel on a mountain in Galilee. But he keeps his feet firmly on the ground and his focus on Jesus' commission and his promise to the disciples. As ET's last words were 'I'll be right here', so Matthew ends his story with 'I am with you always'. This is a conscious echo of the beginning of the Gospel where he called Jesus Emmanuel, 'God with us' (Matt. 1:23; 28:20). The doctrine of the ascension is about Jesus being reunited with his Father, so that we might always know his presence with us. It is because he is exalted to God 'on high' that we can trust him to bring us all safely 'home'.

But the ascension of Jesus leaves us with a new mission here on earth. In *The Matrix,* before Neo lifts off into the sky, he delivers a speech down the phone reminiscent of Sir Winston Churchill's comment on the 'end of the beginning': 'I didn't come here to tell you how this is going to end. I came to tell you how it's going to begin.' Now that the power of evil has been broken, we have to learn to live in a new world, 'where anything is possible'. ET's final instructions to Elliot's little sister Gertie (played by a very young Drew Barrymore) are briefer, but not dissimilar: 'Be good!'

Jesus also has some news to announce: 'All authority in heaven and on earth has been given to me'. That which the devil falsely offered him at the temptations is now freely given him by God (Matt. 4:8-9; 28:18). But in an example of the topsy-turvy nature of spiritual logic, because *Jesus* has the authority, *we* are to go. His earthly ministry may have finished, but this is not the end but the beginning. Our journey through this book may have ended, but our mission to the universe is only just starting: 'Go therefore and make disciples of all nations' (28:19). Our Christian journey began because somebody came to tell us about Christ; so we now go and tell others what we have learned along the way. We entered upon our pilgrimage when we were baptized; now we are to baptize others 'in the name of the Father and of the Son and of the Holy Spirit'.

The other *Star Trek* series may have finished, with *Voyager* back home and the *Enterprise* all one happy family and Sisko appearing after his death to let his friends know that he has gone up to be with the prophets. However, the first *Enterprise* is now making contact with new peoples across the galaxy, and Neo spoke of a world 'without borders or boundaries'. What we have learned on our journey is too precious to keep to ourselves. We must 'boldly go' and seek out new opportunities to share the good news that we live in a new world 'where anything is possible'. We do not have to live in the Mess where human beings oppress and kill each other. Like Evangelist in *The Pilgrim's Progress,* we are to direct all those who are burdened to the Gateway where our journey started, our response through baptism to the call of God. So we will encourage others to come and join the Company of the church, to share the Conflict with evil and to Find the Way through with us. And Jesus will be with us always, 'even to the end of the age', Feeding and Healing us. As we remember his self-sacrifice for us, so he gives us the new life of his resurrection so that we too may one day be lifted up with him in the presence of God our Father.

For Prayer and Meditation

Lord Jesus Christ, risen, ascended, glorified,
may we know your presence with us always,
even to the end of time;
guide us in our journey and encourage us in our mission
so that we and all the world may come to your heavenly kingdom.

50

The Celestial City

Then I saw a new heaven and a new earth; for the first heaven and the first earth had passed away, and the sea was no more. And I saw the holy city, the new Jerusalem, coming down out of heaven from God, prepared as a bride adorned for her husband. And I heard a loud voice from the throne saying, 'See, the home of God is among mortals. He will dwell with them as their God; they will be his peoples, and God himself will be with them; he will wipe every tear from their eyes. Death will be no more; mourning and crying and pain will be no more, for the first things have passed away.' And the one who was seated on the throne said, 'See, I am making all things new.' . . . Then the angel showed me the river of the water of life, bright as crystal, flowing from the throne of God and of the Lamb through the middle of the street of the city. On either side of the river is the tree of life with its twelve kinds of fruit, producing its fruit each month; and the leaves of the tree are for the healing of the nations.

REVELATION 21:1-5; 22:1-2

We began our Faith Odyssey in the African valleys with the early man-apes of *2001: A Space Odyssey. 2001* ends as David Bowman's space-pod rests 'on the polished floor of an elegant, anonymous hotel suite that might have been in any large city on Earth' (p. 241). Here he becomes the Star-Child. After Heywood Floyd has joined Bowman and HAL as the 'Trinity' within the monolith, *2061: Odyssey Three* ends by the UN building in central Manhattan. *3001: The Final Odyssey* closes with Bowman's crewmate, Frank Poole, returning to his suite in Africa Tower, a 36,000-km-high building stretching from the Equator up to geo-stationary orbit. But the Epilogue is chillingly fascinating: 'Their little universe is very young, and its god is still a child. But it is too soon to judge them; when We return in the Last Days, We will consider what should be saved' (p. 249). Even Sir Arthur C. Clarke, when I asked him about it, pointed out that he does not identify who says it — but it is a suitably apocalyptic finale for his grand vision.

As *Space Odyssey* began in the valleys and ends in huge cities, so the Bible (and our *Faith Odyssey* studies) also moves from the first people in the garden of Eden to St John the Divine's grand vision of the heavenly city. It is even a new universe, replacing 'the first heaven and the first earth', when 'the holy city, new Jerusalem' descends from God (Rev. 21:1-2), like the vast mother-ship at the end of *Close Encounters of the Third Kind.*

When George Lucas produced the new editions of his first three *Star Wars* films, he added new special effects with his increased technology (and budget!). He gave the grand finale of *The Return of the Jedi* a vast cityscape with huge buildings towering into the sky and enormous crowds spilling out into plazas to celebrate the overthrow of the evil empire. Similarly, in *Dune* the victory of Paul Atreides brings a new order not just to the sand planet Arrakis, which will now be watered by a new climate, but to all the universe as the religion of Muad'Dib, the Dune Messiah, is spread by his Fremen. Last, we noted yesterday the new world order brought by Neo in *The Matrix,* as he flies above the city's high-rise buildings.

John's vision uses all the technicolour of apocalyptic literature to describe the heavenly city in such a way that I wonder what he may have done if he had had Lucas' effects at his disposal! The celestial city is 'coming down out of heaven from God' and its glory is like a bride's splendour (Rev. 21:2). An angel gives us a guided tour, revealing the vast size of the city, a cube, one thousand five hundred miles long, wide — and high! It is made of 'pure gold, clear as glass' with a wall over seventy metres high of jasper, with twelve gates of pearl, inscribed with the names of the twelve tribes of Israel. There are also twelve foundations made of twelve precious jewels bearing the names of the twelve apostles (21:12-21). Here we find the final destination of our Company, Jewish and Christian, whose travels through the wilderness of Exodus and the early church letters we have followed. We began our journey seven weeks ago, and for the Scriptures seven lots of seven brings the perfect Jubilee when the fiftieth shall be holy and for rest and liberty (Lev. 25:8-12). So now today we come to rest with this fiftieth study on our destination, the heavenly city.

As a child, I loved my grandmother's well-thumbed copy of *The Pilgrim's Progress* with its musty smell and beautiful wood-cut drawings. Best of all was the picture of Christian and Hopeful being welcomed with crowns and trumpets by angels into the Celestial City, paved with gold. Here their journey ends as they are arrayed in white, shining robes. Now we see where John Bunyan (and some of our other stories' authors too?) got it all from — in John's amazing vision. After his sequence of sevens — seven lampstands and seven letters to seven churches (Rev. 1–3), seven seals (6–7), seven trumpets (8–11), seven bowls (15–16) — we come to the final Conflict with evil, ending with the victory of the 'white rider' (17–20). As the stranger Strider becomes Aragorn and joins the Company only finally to be revealed as the true king in *The Lord of the Rings,* so the 'King of kings and Lord of lords' turns out to be our long-suffering Companion, who has been with us every step of the journey and who eventually sacrificed himself for us on the cross (19:11-16).

As the hobbits attend Aragorn's wedding to the 'evening star', Arwen Undómiel (p. 1009), so the angel says, 'Blessed are those who are invited to the marriage supper of the Lamb'. We must be transformed ourselves, and, like the hobbits, put on new robes and fine linen (Rev. 19:9). Then we discover the real marvel — that we are to be 'the bride, the wife of the lamb' as the Company of all God's faithful people are united with him for ever, and God makes his home with us (21:2-3, 9). We can finally rest from all the Conflict and from the struggle of Finding the Way through our journey, as death and mourning, crying and pain have all passed away and all is made new (21:4). Here is our final Healing by the waterside. As Muad'Dib brought water to Dune, so now 'the river of the water of life' flows through this Celestial City, lined by the tree of life from the garden of Eden producing 'twelve kinds of fruit', whose leaves are 'for the healing of the nations' (22:2). Like the cosmic vision at the end of our stories, so now all the nations are embraced, welcomed and restored.

Of course, somebody will always ask whether playing a harp for all eternity is a bit boring: what happens next? Let us return one final time to Narnia to see if C. S. Lewis' fertile imagination can help us understand. *The Last Battle* is like Revelation as it starts with a Talking Beast, an Ape, who is the mouthpiece of a false Aslan, who is actually a donkey dressed in a lion's skin. This deception misleads the Narnians, and their enemies begin to enslave the animals and chop down the forests. Jill and Eustace, who had freed Prince Rilian, are called back to assist Tirian, last King of Narnia, in his final stand by the donkey's stable, thought to contain the foul fiend, Tash. To Tirian's horror he sees both the children and his faithful animals killed or pushed into the stable until finally he is forced to the door himself. In a final sacrifice, like Gandalf or Sisko, he grabs his enemy and takes him with himself into the gloom (pp. 118-120). Except that, to his surprise, he finds that he is in bright light, facing Kings and Queens. Two are Jill and Eustace, who introduce him to the High King Peter and the other children, together with Lord Digory and Lady Polly who were there at the beginning when Aslan called Narnia into being. They are all arrayed in fine clothes, as Tirian discovers that he is too. Yet the stable door is still there, and the firelight beyond; and the dwarves think they are still in darkness and make a mess of a beautiful meal set before them (pp. 128-135). Then Aslan appears, like Arthur C. Clarke's mysterious Epilogue, to judge Narnia on its 'Last Days', and shut the door (pp. 138-143).

But instead of the end, as in *The Matrix,* it is only the beginning as Aslan calls them 'farther up and farther in' and bounds off into the distance (p. 144). Then begins the most glorious headlong dash through fields, valleys and rivers, which are new and yet strangely familiar, until Jewel the Unicorn realizes, 'I have come home at last! This is my real country! I belong here. This is the land I have been looking for all my life, though I never knew it till now' (p. 155). They are in Aslan's country, where all that was good about Narnia and England and everywhere is yet more real and beautiful, and everyone they have ever loved is present. At last, they can all be with Aslan for ever: 'The dream is ended: this is the morning'. Lewis notes that 'for us this is the end of all the stories' (p. 165).

So too, after all our travels and struggles, joys and sorrows, we have reached the Celestial City, the end of our journey and of this book. And yet, as Lewis concludes, 'it was only the beginning of the real story'. Everything before, 'all their life in this world and all their adventures in Narnia had only been the cover and the title page: now at last they were beginning Chapter One of the Great Story which no one on earth has read: which goes on for ever: in which every chapter is better than the one before' (p. 165). In that spirit, therefore, it is time for us to make a Beginning.

For Prayer and Meditation

Lord Jesus Christ, Alpha and Omega,
the beginning and the end,
we thank you that you have been our Companion along the way;
grant that we may so walk with you that, at the last,
you will call us to be with you for ever and ever, Amen.

APPENDIX 1

Material for Group Study

Use of this book by groups can vary enormously, depending on the size and membership. Some churches or chaplaincies in universities or colleges have organized formal groups each week during Lent, or other times, to use this material and the issues raised to help people grow in faith. This can also be a way of involving those who do not normally go to such groups or even to church, but who are interested in these books and films. On the other hand, a group might be little more than a few friends meeting for a chat about the book over a drink or a meal. One possibility is to watch one of the films or TV episodes together and then discuss it. Some groups have found it helpful to watch short extracts from the films or programmes at various intervals through the discussion. This helps to stimulate imagination and debate. Borrow videos or DVDs from friends, libraries or local video hire shops!

Whatever your format, it might be helpful to begin by inviting group members to reflect further on the biblical passages and the films, episodes or stories. Do they see the connections being suggested? Are there other connections they wish to make? Encourage group members to discuss their own stories and experiences of the general topic for each week. How do these experiences relate to the biblical passages or to the stories and films? Are there other books or films which group members think are relevant? Depending on your context, it might be appropriate to end each meeting with an opportunity for silent reflection and prayer together. This could be based upon the suggestions in the book, or use liturgical forms of worship, or free and open prayers as best suits the group — but try to include some silence!

For other suggestions, visit the Faith Odyssey website, http://www.faithodyssey.net.

Part 1 — The Mess

What are your experiences of this world? Is it a Mess? Are we stardust — or ashes? Why and how do we turn people who are brothers and sisters into the 'Others'? Where are the areas of oppression in our world — and in our own lives? Do we feel alienated — lost and in a strange land? When and why? Does anybody know the way home?

Part 2 — The Way In

Encourage group members to share their own stories of finding the way in through baptism or conversion. What difference does it make that Jesus has entered into our world of human experience and been baptized like us? How can Jesus be both the door and the way? Do group members have any experiences of escaping from enemies or waking up from a dream-world, like Neo? How do we hear the call of God today? Can we relate to the experiences of the prophets, or people like Sisko or C. S. Lewis? How do we respond to the invitation to turn around and become truly human?

Part 3 — The Company

What are group members' feelings about and experiences of the church? What does it mean to travel along with others in the Company? What are the barriers today which need to be broken down in church and between Christians — and others? How do we deal with other members whom we find difficult? How should we handle disagreements and splits in churches? What are our gifts and how can we use them to build up others? How can we promote church growth, both in numbers and in maturity?

Part 4 — The Conflict

Encourage group members to discuss their experiences of spiritual conflict and struggle. What do you believe about evil, the devil and ideas of spiritual warfare? Is there a Cosmic Conflict — and what form does it take? Is it like the 'dark side of the force' or more personal, like Gul Dukat? What all-demanding idols are we tempted to worship instead of God? Share your stories and experiences of the Holy Spirit. How can you encourage one another to use the armour of God and to grow in the fruit of the Spirit? What do people think about our place in the cosmic scheme of things? Do we feel that we are sons and daughters of God?

Part 5 — Finding the Way

What have been the ups and downs for group members in their spiritual journey? Who have been the masters or the guides like Yoda or Paul? Share your experiences of spiritual direction in its many different forms. Discuss the different ways each of you pray. Is silent prayer difficult for some — and can others help? How do members read the Bible? Is it like a 'guidebook' — and, if so, how? Share ideas and resources which you have found helpful. What do you think about dreams and visions? Share some of them. How can we interpret them today and what are the dangers to avoid? Does God speak to us through them?

Part 6 — Healing and Feeding

Where have been the oases for group members? What about going away together for a day or two? What do group members believe about healing — physical, mental and spiritual — today? Does anyone have experience of being healed which they would like to share? What areas of our lives need to receive Christ's healing touch? How can we 'regenerate' like Seven and Odo, or find refreshment, as the hobbits did, on our journey? Are we thirsty or hungry? Ask God to help. What does the holy communion mean to group members? Visit a church from a different tradition and share in their communion service.

Part 7 — Greater Love

How do group members mark Jesus' passion and death? Share different experiences and ways of keeping periods like Holy Week. How can we welcome Jesus into our lives — and into our city? What needs a good clear-out? Will we let him? Discuss the ways in which we are tempted to betray or deny our faith in Jesus. Like Floyd, Frodo or Ransom, are there hard and agonizing decisions we have to take? How can we follow Jesus' example and let God's will be done in our lives? Discuss your different understandings of the cross. What did Jesus achieve through his death? How do the different accounts in the Gospels help us here? Look at some hymns or songs about the cross — what understanding of the crucifixion do they contain? What are our experiences of grief? Can we sit and wait, mourning for Jesus?

Chapter 8 — To Infinity and Beyond!

Discuss members' understandings of the resurrection. What does it mean to say 'Jesus is alive'? What evidence is there for this claim? As Jesus came to his followers in specific needs, what might the risen Jesus say to each of us today? What needs to be put right or restored in our lives? What does the idea of the ascension mean to us? Where or to whom should we be taking the good news? Do you think about heaven? Are you looking forward to the Celestial City? How can we follow Aslan 'farther up and farther in'?

APPENDIX 2

Books, TV, Films and Resources

Arthur C. Clarke's *Space Odyssey* novels:
2001: A Space Odyssey, Arrow, Hutchinson & Co., 1968
2010: Odyssey Two, Granada, 1982
2061: Odyssey Three, Grafton, Collins, 1988
3001: The Final Odyssey, Voyager, HarperCollins, 1997

Films:
2001: A Space Odyssey, Stanley Kubrick, MGM, 1968
2010, Arthur C. Clarke & Peter Hyams, MGM, 1984

J. R. R. Tolkien's Lord of the Rings books:
The Hobbit, George Allen & Unwin, 1966
The Lord of the Rings, George Allen & Unwin, 1968

Films:
The Fellowship of the Ring, Peter Jackson, 2001
The Two Towers, Peter Jackson, 2002
The Return of the King, Peter Jackson, 2003

C. S. Lewis' Narnia stories:
The Magician's Nephew, Puffin, Penguin, 1955
The Lion, the Witch and the Wardrobe, Puffin, Penguin, 1950
The Horse and His Boy, Puffin, Penguin, 1954
Prince Caspian, Puffin, Penguin, 1951

The Voyage of the 'Dawn Treader', Puffin, Penguin, 1952
The Silver Chair, Puffin, Penguin, 1953
The Last Battle, Puffin, Penguin, 1956

C. S. Lewis' science fiction trilogy:
Out of the Silent Planet, Pan, 1952
Voyage to Venus (Perelandra), Pan, 1953
That Hideous Strength, Pan, 1955

Frank Herbert's *Dune* books:
Dune, New English Library, 1968
Dune Messiah, New English Library, 1972
Children of Dune, New English Library, 1977

Film:
Dune, Universal Pictures, 1984

Douglas Adams' *Hitchhiker* Trilogy:
Hitchhiker's Guide to the Galaxy, Pan, 1979
The Restaurant at the End of the Galaxy, Pan, 1980
Life, the Universe and Everything, Pan, 1982
So Long, and Thanks for All the Fish, Pan, 1984
(Also BBC Radio series, 1978 and 1980; BBC TV series, 1981)

J. K. Rowling's *Harry Potter* books:
Harry Potter and the Philosopher's Stone, Bloomsbury, 1997
Harry Potter and the Chamber of Secrets, Bloomsbury, 1998
Harry Potter and the Prisoner of Azkaban, Bloomsbury, 1999
Harry Potter and the Goblet of Fire, Bloomsbury, 2000

Films:
Harry Potter and the Philosopher's Stone, Chris Columbus, Warner Brothers, 2001
Harry Potter and the Chamber of Secrets, Chris Columbus, Warner Brothers, 2002
Harry Potter and the Prisoner of Azkaban, Alfonso Cuaron, Warner Brothers, 2004

Books:

Terry Pratchett, *Small Gods,* Corgi, 1993
(The rest of the *Discworld* novels are equally well worth reading.)
Carl Sagan, *Contact,* Arrow books, 1988

Film:

Contact, Warner Brothers, 1997

George Lucas' *Star Wars* films:

Star Wars: Episode I The Phantom Menace, 1999
Star Wars: Episode II Attack of the Clones, 2002
Star Wars: Episode IV A New Hope, 1977
Star Wars: Episode V The Empire Strikes Back, 1980
Star Wars: Episode VI The Return of the Jedi, 1983

Other films and TV series mentioned:

Armageddon, Michael Bay, Touchstone Pictures, 1998
Close Encounters of the Third Kind, Steven Spielberg, 1977
ET: The Extra-Terrestrial, Steven Spielberg, 1982; special edition, 2002
Galaxy Quest, Dean Parisot, Dream Works, 1999
Stargate, Roland Emmerich, MGM, 1994
The Matrix, Larry and Andy Wachowski, Warner Brothers, 1999
Tron, Steven Lisberger, Walt Disney 1982
The X-Files, Chris Carter, Twentieth Century Fox, TV series, 1993-

Film:

The X-Files Movie, Chris Carter and Rob Bowman, Twentieth Century Fox, 1998

***Star Trek* TV series:**

Star Trek, the original series conceived and produced by Eugene Wesley Roddenberry, 1966-1969
The Next Generation, produced by Gene Roddenberry and Rick Berman, 1987-1994
Deep Space Nine, created by Rick Berman and Michael Piller, 1993-1999
Voyager, created by Rick Berman and Michael Piller and Jeri Taylor, 1995-2001
Enterprise, created by Rick Berman and Brannon Braga, 2001-

Star Trek movies mentioned:

Star Trek II: The Wrath of Khan, Paramount Pictures, 1982
Star Trek III: The Search for Spock, Paramount Pictures, 1984
(The rest of the movies are equally well worth seeing.)

For full coverage and good discussion of _Star Trek_, see

Larry Nemecek, *The Star Trek: The Next Generation Companion*, revised edition, Pocket Books, 1995

Judith & Garfield Reeves-Stevens, *The Making of Star Trek Deep Space Nine*, Pocket Books, 1994

Terry J. Erdman, *Star Trek Deep Space Nine Companion*, Pocket Books, 2000

The Official Star Trek Fact Files, Fabbri Publishing, London

For further reading:

Mike Alsford, *What If? Religious Themes in Science Fiction*, DLT, 2000

Francis Bridger, *A Charmed Life: The Spirituality of Potterworld*, DLT, 2001

Stephen May, *Stardust and Ashes: Science Fiction in Christian Perspective*, SPCK, 1998

Jennifer E. Porter and Darcee L. McLaren, *Star Trek and Sacred Ground: Explorations of Star Trek, Religion and American Culture*, State University of New York Press, 1999

David Wilkinson, *Alone in the Universe? The X-Files, Aliens and God*, Monarch Books, 1997

David Wilkinson, *The Power of the Force: The Spirituality of the Star Wars Films*, Lion, 2000

Homer's *Odyssey* and John Bunyan's *The Pilgrim's Progress* are also essential reading!

APPENDIX 3

Index of Bible Passages

Genesis 4:1-12 6
Genesis 12:1-4a; 15:1, 5-6 37
Exodus 1:8-14 10
Exodus 14:10, 21-29 29
Exodus 17:1-7 157
Deuteronomy 8:2-6; 9:6-7 55
1 Kings 19:1-4, 8-10 111
Job 42:6 3
Psalm 23 141
Psalm 51:1-3, 9-11 3
Psalm 137:1-6 14
Proverbs 8:1, 10-13, 20-22, 32-36 119
Isaiah 40:27–41:1 127
Jeremiah 1:1, 4-7 41
Jonah 1:1-3, 10 41
Matthew 3:13-17 21
Matthew 4:1-11 85
Matthew 11:28-30 149
Matthew 26:14-16, 21-25 179
Matthew 28:16-20 209
Mark 1:23-28 153
Mark 1:29-34 145
Mark 11:15-18 175
Luke 6:12-16 51
Luke 22:39-46 187
Luke 23:48-56 195
John 6:4-14 161
John 6:60, 66-71 67
John 10:1-3, 7-10 25
John 11:47-53 183
John 12:12-16 171
John 14:16-18, 26-27 93
John 15:12-15 183
John 16:7-8 93
John 19:16-18, 25-30 191
John 20:1-2, 14-18 201
John 20:19-22, 26-28; 21:13-15, 19 205
Acts 2:14-18 135
Acts 2:42-47 59
Acts 15:36-41 67
Acts 26:9, 12-18 45
Romans 1:18-25 89
Romans 8:9, 14-17, 21-23, 37-39 105
1 Corinthians 11:23-26 165
1 Corinthians 12:4-13 71
Galatians 5:16-25 101
Ephesians 2:12-19 63
Ephesians 4:11-16 75
Ephesians 6:10-18 97
Philippians 4:4-8 123
Colossians 2:12; 3:5-14 33
2 Timothy 1:1-7 115
2 Timothy 3:14-17 131
Hebrews 4:4, 9-11 149
Revelation 12:7-9, 13, 17 81
Revelation 21:1-5; 22:1-2 213